the Ma
Wi
buff's
Road
Trip

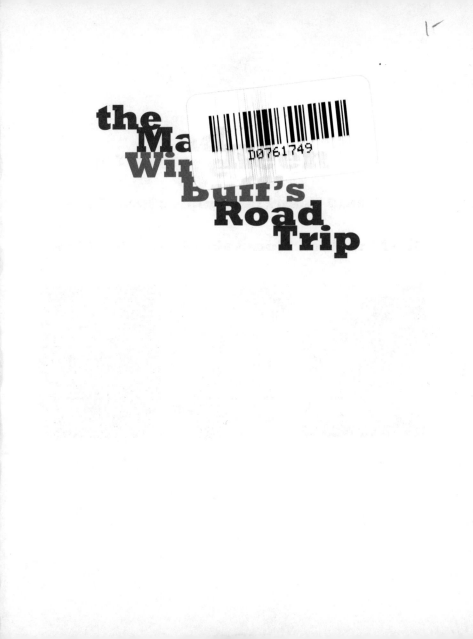

Other titles in this series

the Mad Keen Golfer's Road Trip

the Mad Keen Fisherman's Road Trip

the Mad Keen Mountain Biker's Road Trip

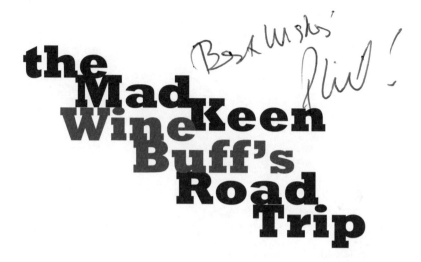

the Mad Keen Wine Buff's Road Trip

Phil Parker

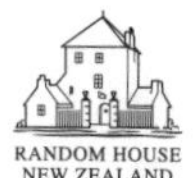

A RANDOM HOUSE BOOK published by Random House New Zealand, 18 Poland Road, Glenfield, Auckland, New Zealand

For more information about our titles go to www.randomhouse.co.nz

A catalogue record for this book is available from the National Library of New Zealand

Random House International, Random House, 20 Vauxhall Bridge Road, London, SW1V 2SA, United Kingdom; **Random House Australia Pty Ltd**, Level 3, 100 Pacific Highway, North Sydney 2060, Australia; **Random House South Africa Pty Ltd**, Isle of Houghton, Corner Boundary Road and Carse O'Gowrie, Houghton 2198, South Africa; **Random House Publishers India Private Ltd**, 301 World Trade Tower, Hotel Intercontinental Grand Complex, Barakhamba Lane, New Delhi 110 001, India

First published 2008

ISBN 978 1 86941 955 4

Cover illustration: Getty Images
Cover and text design: Nick Turzinsky
Maps: Debbie Hinde
Printed by Everbest Printing Co Ltd., China

Contents

Introduction

This book is a handy insider's guide for anyone keen to jump in the car, get out of the city and explore the variety, flavour and colour of our unique heartland wine regions. Each of the regions from north to south has its own distinctive scenery — from snow-capped mountains and rolling green countryside, to pohutukawa-studded, golden beaches. Any time of the year is a good time to visit — a sunny outdoor tasting overlooking neat rows of green vines in summer, or sampling in a cosy cellar door with a blazing log fire in winter.

In order to facilitate the mad keen wine buff's smoothest road trip, the book has been divided into separate regions and sub-regions, each containing a number of two-day weekend packages. Detailed, up-to-date information is provided on wineries, wine styles, hours of operation, vineyard cafés or restaurants, and pricing. We've also included suggestions for all budgets on other places to eat, local attractions, artisan foods and accommodation. Pricing included is correct at the time of writing, but please note this will vary.

So often I hear the refrain: 'But I'm no wine expert . . .'

Do you like wine?

Yes.

Okay. That's where we all start.

Relax. Nobody is an expert. After eight years in the industry as a wine tour operator and wine writer, and having gone through countless wine tastings and courses, I'm still discovering new wine knowledge almost daily. There are always new wineries, vintages and obscure wine varieties to discover, both here and in the classic wine regions of the world. That is the joy of being involved in an industry populated by genuine enthusiasts who share a passion and commitment to making excellent wine.

So, you don't have to be an expert to use this book, but I have assumed the reader has a basic knowledge of the New Zealand wine varieties and enjoys drinking at least one of them.

We can be rightly proud of our wines, now ranked alongside the world's best. Our sauvignon blancs are internationally famous, pinot noir is gaining a solid reputation in America and Britain, and we even beat the South Africans and Australians in 2006 with a Hawke's Bay shiraz (Trinity Hill Syrah).

This book allows for a leisurely pace — usually no more than four winery visits in a day, allowing time for a relaxed lunch and the exploration of local attractions. Of course, for those with more than a weekend to spend, the guide will be useful in coordinating more extensive exploration of the regions.

Winery visits

At the time of writing, hours of operation of cellar door tasting rooms are up-to-date. For some of the smaller wineries, it does pay to phone in advance especially in the off-season when many have reduced hours or may choose not to open. Also the wine industry is a very, er, fluid business: wineries may change ownership, close down, open cafés and change hours of operation — all without much warning.

Tasting fees

Some wineries charge a fee for tasting (which is often deducted from any wine purchases). I don't think anyone should have a problem with this — wineries go through hundreds, if not thousands of dollars worth of wine in tasting rooms each week. Many smaller wineries simply can't afford to do it for free, especially with their more expensive wines.

Drink driving

This is a self-drive guide, but assumes that the designated driver will behave responsibly. It makes sense to use the tip bucket to spit or tip out wine when you are sampling at a number of wineries and also driving. Drink plenty of water, don't necessarily sample every wine on offer, and take time for a good relaxed lunch. Two winery visits before lunch and two after is ideal. Apart from the added benefit of having food to aid alcohol absorption, a lunch stop gives your palate a rest and enables you to start afresh afterward.

Winery etiquette

Luckily, this industry is full of knowledgeable and hospitable cellar door staff, who are more than keen to answer questions and guide you through tastings. There is no pressure to buy wine, but if at all possible you should take advantage of the keener pricing compared with city retail. Many wineries will ship free or for minimal freight charges within New Zealand if you buy a case and don't want to struggle with it on your holiday. If you can't buy, then be courteous and thank them for the tasting.

Our wine history

Some of the first wines made in New Zealand hail from the far North and West Auckland. In 1819 Anglican Missionary the Reverend Samuel Marsden planted the very first vines in the rich soils of Kerikeri, and in the late 1830s, official British resident James Busby produced the first recorded example of wine made in New Zealand. It was a sparkling white wine and adjudged 'very drinkable' by a passing French official.

Then, at the turn of the nineteenth century, a trickle of immigrants from what was Yugoslavia began to arrive in search of a better life — an escape from poverty and political instability in Europe. Into the 1920s and 1930s more immigrants arrived from the Adriatic coastal region of Dalmatia. They worked hard, literally scratching a living, digging up kauri gum (resin) from ancient forests north of Auckland. And it was bloody hard yakka. Iron spears blindly located the buried treasure, and then it was manually dug out of the heavy yellow clay. At the time, there was a thriving trade in kauri gum for making varnishes and glues.

Gradually, these gumdiggers saved up enough money to buy land. Some of them settled in the north around Dargaville, Whangarei and Kaitaia, and a few intermarried with local Ngapuhi Maori. The majority settled in northwest Auckland's Oratia, Henderson valley and Kumeu regions, where they grew fruit and vegetables alongside their family vineyard, growing grapes to make their own wine for daily consumption, as they had done in the old country. These were the humble beginnings of some of our prominent wine labels: Kumeu River, Babich, Matua, Corbans and Delegats.

Around the same time, some smaller Auckland labels were making a start, such as West Brook, Soljans, Mazurans, Collards and Selaks. 1961 was a particularly good year for New Zealand wine — George Fistonich started Villa Maria wines in Mangere, the same year that Frank and Maté Yukich began Montana in Titirangi.

Today, the Big Three — Montana, Nobilo and Villa Maria — are all Auckland-based and export huge volumes of wine overseas to the thirsty markets of Australia, the Pacific, North America and Britain.

Aside from attempts at grape growing by French settlers in Akaroa, and German settlers in Motueka, Hawke's Bay represents the other major component in New Zealand's wine history. Thanks to the Catholic church's Marist Order, the Mission Vineyard was primarily established to produce sacramental wines. Mission Vineyard was therefore one of our earliest commercial vineyards with first sales recorded in 1895. Now, Hawke's Bay has grown to become our second largest wine region with almost one fifth of New Zealand's vineyards.

Into the 1950s and 1960s there was still very little demand for table wines. The majority of wines sold in New Zealand in those days were ports and sherries (sweet wines fortified with grape spirit). Beer had been the national beverage for decades, but slowly, over the years and into the 1970s, the Kiwi palate became a bit more sophisticated.

Wine producers rose to the challenge and produced easy-drinking sweet wines like 'sauternes' and 'Rhine rieslings' from bulk-produced white grapes. Even in the mid 1970s, there was the notorious sparkling, sweet red wine from Montana — Cold Duck. Over the next ten years, easy drinking, sweet-to-medium white wines like riesling, gewürztraminer and muller thürgau dominated the market. Awful bag-in-box wines were very popular, some not even technically wine. I recall a brand named Brother Dominic 'White' which was allegedly largely made from ethyl alcohol, flavourings and chemicals. Some of my worst hangovers and more regrettable incidents are related to this beverage.

Due to over-planting, by the mid 1980s, the government was actually paying growers to pull out their vines, in the hope that they would return vineyards to pasture land. In the event they did rip out the old ones, but many growers replaced inferior vines with improved varietal clones of the classical grape varieties we see now.

By happy coincidence, Marlborough's sauvignon blanc output was gaining international acclaim and planting of chardonnay, riesling, merlot and many other varieties was encouraged.

The industry has since grown exponentially, with what seems every part of the country exploring grape growing. Wine is now second only to agriculture as New Zealand's largest export product, with sauvignon blanc still leading, but pinot noir gaining more recognition to the extent that it is our second largest grape variety.

At last count, there were 572 wineries in New Zealand, and new ones are regularly popping up as the industry expands. Now, all yours to enjoy . . .

Cheers.

New Zealand's main wine varieties

New Zealand's temperate climate favours white grape varieties (accounting for 90 per cent of plantings). The remaining grapes are mainly early ripening, cool climate reds like pinot noir and merlot.

White wines

Sauvignon blanc

Sauvignon blanc is our most planted grape variety and our largest export wine which allegedly 'put us on the map' internationally. (Personally I tend to attribute that to seismic activity, and the hand of the Almighty.) Nevertheless, the majority of our sauvignon vines are in Marlborough, but some are grown in Nelson, Central Otago, Waipara, Martinborough and Hawke's Bay. The character that typifies the Marlborough and some Nelson sauvignon blancs, is the acidic, intensely grassy, green bell pepper and gooseberry quality of the aroma and flavour. Hawke's Bay sauvignons, on the other hand, because of the warmer climate, have a less crisp profile and can have some tropical flavours like melon and pineapple. Some winemakers take the option of allowing the wine to ferment and/or age for a short period in oak barrels. This has the effect of softening and rounding out the wine, normally without any detectable oak flavour. As they age, after about three years, sauvignon blancs take on vegetable characters' like tinned peas and asparagus.

Chardonnay

New Zealand's chardonnays, our third most planted variety, are famous for their intensity of fruit and concentrated aromas. Winemakers have a multitude of options available to them which influence the flavour of the wine, including varying periods of grape skin contact, different yeasts and types of oak, adopting barrel toasting and the length of oak maturation, and Malolactic fermentation (a secondary bacterial fermentation that removes acidic flavours and gives a smooth buttery character). Oak ageing for 12 months or more imparts complexity, tannins and some oxidation, which softens the more assertive acids. Flame-seasoned barrel treatment can add toasty characters. Many regions grow chardonnay successfully, however Gisborne has earned the title 'Chardonnay Capital of New Zealand' and rightly so for its full-bodied lush and fruity wines that typically show tropical and stone fruit characters.

Hawke's Bay chardonnays tend to taste more of citrus with some tropical flavours. Chardonnay from Marlborough tends more to a mineral and citrus flavour profile. Almost every region has a crack at this variety, with Auckland's Kumeu River being acknowledged as one of the world's best.

Riesling

Riesling is the classic white wine of Germany. The grapes are low-cropping, ripen late in the season, and flourish in colder climates where intensity of fruit flavour develops. Our rieslings are mainly dry or 'off-dry' — a little sweet. More than 80 per cent of plantings are in the South Island — Marlborough, Canterbury, Waipara, Nelson and Central Otago. These cool-climate areas help to create wines with crisp acidity, enabling some of the best to age for up to 15 years. Typical aromas and flavours can include citrus, floral (honeysuckle, orange blossom) and dried fruit (raisins, muscatel). As rieslings age, they can take on honey, apricots, and dare I say it, kerosene/petrol characters.

Pinot gris

This is the same grape as Italian pinot grigio (a distant cousin of pinot noir). An increasingly trendy wine, it can be a tad hard to nail flavour-wise, but is commonly described as tasting like pear juice, with musky and spicy flavours — somewhere between a riesling and a gewürztraminer. Plantings are widespread in New Zealand, from Central Otago to North Auckland. The cooler regions in the south tend to produce crisper, light-bodied wines, whereas the riper grapes from the north can lead to some high-alcohol, lush and full-bodied wines.

Gewürztraminer

Okay — many people don't buy it because they can't pronounce it. Get over it. 'Gah-Vertz-Tra-Meaner.' This is a variety best known in Alsace, the French wine region on the Rhine bordering Germany. In New Zealand it has generally been under-appreciated, despite it having gorgeous spicy ginger, cinnamon and Turkish Delight/rosewater and lychee flavours. Gisborne, Marlborough and Hawke's Bay are the main regions, with the majority coming from Gisborne.

Cooler regions produce more mineral-flavoured wines. It's a fantastic match with spicy (not chilli-hot) foods such as Thai and Japanese.

Viognier

Pronounced 'Vee-Yon-Yay', this is a French Rhône grape variety with delicate, light apricot flavours, and constitutes about 0.05 per cent of New Zealand's grape harvest. Viognier grapes ripen early, often with high sugar levels, and can result in wines that are quite high in alcohol. Viognier has become the über-groovy white wine, now that the novelty of pinot gris is on the wane. Classic flavours are apricot and peach.

Arneis

Pronounced 'Are-Nace', this North Italian grape can be produce wine very high in alcohol, with restrained spice and stone fruit flavours. Only two wineries here produce it — Clevedon Hills and Coopers Creek.

Red wines

Pinot noir

Pinot noir is our second most widely planted grape variety. The famous velvety wine of Burgundy is produced in Marlborough, Canterbury, Waipara, Central Otago and the Wairarapa — with the latter two being our premium pinot regions. Pinot noir thrives in cool climates, giving the wine a complexity of scents and flavours.

It is not an easy grape to grow. In fact, pinot noir is notoriously difficult. Tight bunches of small, thin-skinned grapes are prone to rot late in the season. Even when the grapes are crushed, it takes a skilled winemaker to turn it into a successful wine. Domestically, a large proportion of our pinot noir grapes go into champagne-style sparkling wines like Lindauer, usually combined with chardonnay. Clear pinot juice is fermented without any contact with the skins, hence a white wine results.

Young medium-bodied pinot noir tastes of strawberries and raspberries. In the prime pinot regions of Central Otago and the Wairarapa, the wines can be rich, silky and full-bodied with black cherry and black fruit flavours. Some wine critics describe a classic pinot noir aroma as 'barnyardy' — slightly pooey.

Merlot

Our second most popular red grape is merlot. Until recently its role was in blending with cabernet sauvignon, but now 100 per cent merlot is gaining popularity. Merlot can be deceptively soft, smoky, fruity and silky, and low in tannins — like a more powerful version of pinot noir. Aromas and flavours are similar to cabernet sauvignon but more rounded and reminiscent of tobacco, chocolate and leather. Around three-quarters of New Zealand's merlot is grown in Hawke's Bay, with the remainder from Gisborne and Marlborough. The North Island merlots are generally riper, softer and higher in alcohol than the South Island variety.

Cabernet sauvignon

This red wine of Bordeaux is based on a red grape more suited to hotter climates and is 'A tough nut to crack in New Zealand,' according to wine expert Michael Cooper. Still, a good vintage from Hawke's Bay or Waiheke Island can stack up against some of the world's best reds.

It is often blended with the other Bordeaux varieties — merlot, malbec, and cabernet franc. Newly fermented or under-ripe cabernet sauvignon can have a stemmy, herbal-minty character. High tannins mean that this wine will cellar well, giving it time to mellow. Typical flavours from oak give cigar box characters. Fruit characters are typically blackcurrant, cherry, berry fruits and plums.

Syrah

Syrah is exactly the same grape as shiraz. Unlike the big tannic knock-down-drag-out Aussie wine, our syrahs are soft, ripe and medium-to-full-bodied, with earthy flavours of liquorice, spice, black pepper and cherries. Increasing popularity makes syrah our fourth most planted red, with acreage increasing fourfold in the last eight years. Hawke's Bay has become 'Syrah Central', with Trinity Hill's Syrah winning the 2006 Tri-Nations Wine Challenge.

Other reds

Malbec

Fruity, earthy, spicy blackcurrant flavours, with high tannins.

Pinotage

A hybrid of pinot noir and 'hermitage' (cinsault) developed in South Africa. Typically it has smoky aromas and red, plummy fruit flavours.

Sangiovese

Italian red chianti grape. Grown in very small amounts in New Zealand. Earthy warm, spicy and savoury.

Sparkling wines

The vast majority of our sparkling méthode traditionelle is made from Marlborough chardonnay and pinot noir. It used to be also called méthode champenoise before the French got all protective about the name. The traditional method uses a secondary fermentation in the bottle — by adding more yeast and sugar after the first fermentation is finished — to produce characteristic CO^2 bubbles. New Zealand sparkling wine has been a huge success in Britain where over 250,000 cases found their way in 2007, with Pernod Ricard's Lindauer leading the pack. Small wineries find traditional sparklers very labour intensive and too expensive to produce, yet there are some boutique-style examples like Quartz Reef, Nautilus, No.1 Family Estate, Morton and Amisfield. Simple, cheap and often sweet, sparklers are made by injecting CO^2 into still wine before bottling.

Sweet wines

Dessert wines, aka 'stickies', are unfortunately rejected by a lot of wine drinkers just because they are sweet. That's a pity, as suitably aged dessert wines can be the perfect partner to a citrus pudding, liver pâté, or strong cheeses like cheddars and blues.

The most famous dessert wines in France come from Sauternes (a geographical region), but in New Zealand most stickies are made from riesling, sémillon or sauvignon blanc. They fall into three categories: botrytised or noble wines, late harvest wines and ice wines. In botrytised or noble wines a mould called botrytis (noble rot) has affected the grapes, and natural sugars are intensified by the action of tiny mould organism filaments which suck out water content.

In late harvest wines the grapes are left on the vine for an extended period where they ripen even further and start to shrivel like sultanas.

The grapes for ice wines — most notably from Germany, Oregon and Canada — are harvested in the early hours of the morning while they are still frozen; crushing them straight away leaves the ice content behind and produces a sugar rich juice. In New Zealand we give Mother Nature a hand and tank-freeze the fresh juice, filtering off the sweet content and leaving the ice crystals behind.

Because of the preservative quality of high sugar levels in the wine, and despite low alcohol, these dessert wines (other than our ice wines) reward cellaring for ten years or longer.

Storing your wine — drink now or later?

A question I am often asked is: 'How long should I keep this wine?' A very good question to which there is no simple answer. Statistically, around 90 per cent of wines in New Zealand are consumed within about two hours of purchase, so the truthful answer would be 'About 120 minutes'.

At the other end of the scale, it can be a mistake to keep a wine too long. And it is a myth that the older a wine is, the better it will be. Every wine has a specific lifespan and will hit a peak, beyond which it will deteriorate.

Most New Zealanders do drink their wines very young. Sauvignon blanc, for example, is a wine whose appeal is largely attributed to its youth — a zingy fruit-bomb, like a smack in the mouth with a gooseberry-flavoured lemon. Other stainless steel tank-fermented wines like riesling, pinot gris, gewürztraminer, viognier and unoaked chardonnay are also very attractive when consumed as young, fresh wines. Many of these are released onto the shelves a mere five months from harvest.

If you like clean, concentrated fruit flavours then these white wine varieties are best consumed within 18 months. After that, they lose fruit intensity, but in the longer term can also mellow out and develop more complicated flavours and aromas, which can be more appealing to different palates. For example, put away a Marlborough sauvignon blanc for two to five years and it will develop totally different characters of canned peas, asparagus and roasted bell pepper, with a complex integrated profile totally different to an acidic young, just-released sauvignon.

New Zealand red wines and chardonnays are generally designed to last at least two to five years because most have been aged in oak barrels. Tannins extracted from red grape skins during fermentation also act as a preservative, giving full-bodied reds their longer life expectancy. Our top New Zealand reds can take at least five years before they reach their peak — often more.

Two other factors that make wine last longer are (a) high alcohol and (b) sugar content. Wines such as 'late harvest' or 'noble' sweet dessert wines often have low alcohol content, but will have very high natural grape sugar levels which act as a preservative, meaning these can be put away for ten years or more. Conversely, a big tannic Hawke's Bay cabernet sauvignon clocking in at 15.5 per cent alcohol is going to last a lot longer than a light rosé at ten per cent. For the best of both worlds, a fortified sweet wine, like a quality vintage port (around 18 per cent alcohol), will keep for decades.

Price is often a factor. Realistically, your $7.99 supermarket bargain bin merlot is not likely to be one to put away until 2020. On the other hand, if you're forking out $150 for a Stonyridge Larose Cabernet, then expect it to be one to cellar. If you are into buying wine at that price then the retailer should be expected to give you informed cellaring advice. If they can't do that, then I strongly suggest you buy your wine elsewhere.

What about that bottle of champagne, put away for a celebration? If it is a 'vintage' champagne (it has a date on the label) it's a keeper. If not, drink it now — non-vintage (NV) champagnes are blended from various vintages and designed to be drunk on release.

So, if you have decided to put a few wines away, where is the best place? Ideally your cellar should have a constant temperature of about 10 to 15°C. Any warmer and your wines will mature quicker, and will thus need to be drunk earlier. Sunlight is also bad for wine, so I'm afraid the old wine rack, slap bang up against the stove in the sunny cottage kitchen, is not a good idea. The best place is a central point in your house where there is little temperature variation. In my old Auckland bungalow I use a dingy cupboard backing onto the bathroom in the centre of the house. The temperature varies from about 12°C in winter to 18°C in summer — not ideal, but okay for my modest bottle collection.

Northland

The area from the Bombay Hills, just south of Auckland, to the tip of Cape Reinga grows around just three per cent of New Zealand's grapes. Yet the greater Auckland region encompasses most of our major exporters and has around 40 per cent of New Zealand's wineries.

North of Auckland City there are a few wineries sprinkled from Mangawhai Heads and Whangarei to Russell and Kaitaia. Northland is still a marginal wine region because sub-tropical summer temperatures and humidity make it difficult to grow many varieties. However, the few who soldier on are getting surprisingly good results, and sometimes making top-level wines.

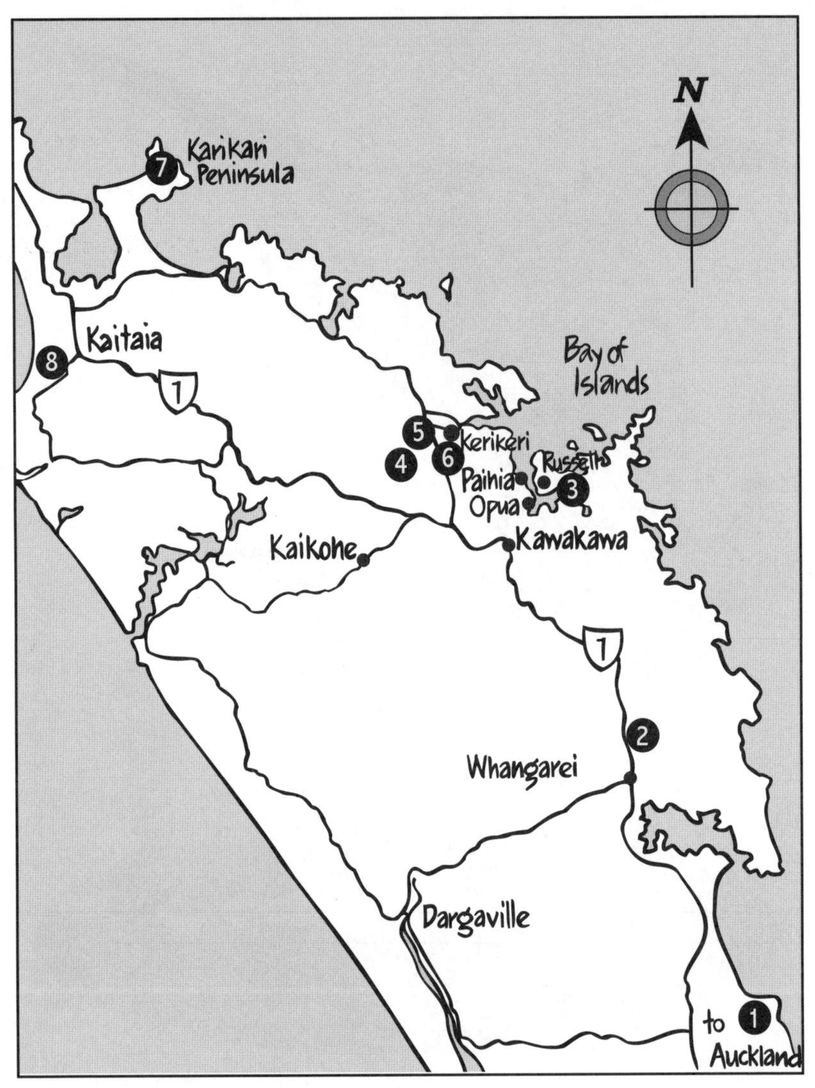
N
Karikari Peninsula
Kaitaia
Bay of Islands
Kerikeri
Russell
Paihia
Opua
Kawakawa
Kaikohe
Whangarei
Dargaville
to Auckland

Saturday
Okay — head off north on State Highway One . . .

Lochiel Estate B&B and Winery

60 Brook Lane
Mangawhai Heads
09 431 4554   021 488 842   www.lochielestate.co.nz
Open daily 10.00 am–4.00 pm except Saturday morning, pays to phone ahead

The first of the Northland wineries, Lochiel Estate B&B and Winery is located close to Mangawhai Heads. Winemakers Gary Cameron and his son Rob started in 2000 with a four-hectare (10-acre) vineyard growing chardonnay, pinot gris, merlot, malbec and syrah. They have a fully equipped winery onsite, complete with a temperature-controlled barrel hall. Chardonnay and a port-style sweet fortified malbec have been released so far. Pinot gris and syrah await release soon.

Notable wines

Chardonnay ($25).

Accommodation

The large homestead has a guest wing with three bedrooms, all with ensuite. There are two rooms with Queen-size beds and a twin room with two King single beds. French doors in each room open out to the patio and views of the vineyard and hills beyond. Tariff: $140 to $160 per room including breakfast. Dinner by prior arrangement.

Longview Estate

State Highway One (two hours north of Auckland on State Highway One)
Whangarei
09 438 7227 www.longviewwines.co.nz
Open summer 8.30 am–6.00 pm, winter 8.30 am–5.00 pm, closed Sundays all year round

Mario Vuletich's Croatian forebears pioneered commercial winemaking in the Far North in 1969, establishing Northland's oldest winery. Mario and his wife Barbara now have seven hectares (17 acres) planted in chardonnay, gewürztraminer, cabernet sauvignon, merlot, cabernet franc, malbec and syrah. The vineyard overlooks Whangarei Harbour and Bream Head. Near vintage time, inflatable life-size dolls in teeny weeny bikinis are used to scare birds — and disturb passing motorists.

Notable wines

Gumdiggers Reserve Cabernet Sauvignon/Cabernet Franc/Merlot ($22), Mario's Merlot ($15).

Food

N/A

Now, bypass Whangarei town and head up to Paihia. After a suitable stop to catch your breath, take the ferry across to Russell.

Omata Estate

Aucks Road, RD1
Russell
09 403 8007 www.omata.co.nz
Open for lunch 12.00 noon–3.00 pm and dinner from 6.30 pm, restaurant and cellar door hours are the same

As well as its own wines, Omata Estate offers high-end dining and boutique luxury accommodation overlooking the sea at Pipiroa Bay on the Russell Peninsula. A little hard to find, the winery restaurant and accommodation are in a secluded cove, down a private driveway, on the left, about five minutes' drive from the Opua/Russell car ferry. Chardonnay, merlot and syrah are grown on the property, with winemaking done by Rod McIvor of Marsden Estate.

Notable wines

Omata Estate Reserve Syrah ($55).

Food

The Omata Estate Vineyard Restaurant offers a gourmet à la carte menu. The wine lists are exclusively top New Zealand wines (including Stonyridge Larose 1998 at $280 a bottle). Lunch dishes can vary wildly in cost — a platter of select meats and local seafood for two is $100, where a simple tempura fish & chips is $25. Dinner entrées are around $20, mains $35, sides $7 and desserts around $16. A new venture is The Chef's Bench — an al fresco, six-course, interactive degustation menu (food and wine match) prepared by chef Kim Steevens.

Accommodation

Two choices for those with a friendly bank manager:

- The Loft — one bedroom suite within a short stroll of the beach. Tariff: $400 high season, $350 low season.
- The Boathouse — private one-bedroom suite, right on the beachfront. Tariff: $520 high season, $480 low season.

Take the ferry back to Opua and drive north to Kerikeri

Marsden Estate

Wiroa Road
Kerikeri
09 407 9398 www.marsdenestate.co.nz
Open seven days August–May 10.00 am–5.00 pm, June–July 10.00 am–4.00 pm

Marsden Estate's vineyards, with 3.5 hectares (9 acres) of vines, were planted in 1993 and comprise pinot gris, chardonnay, merlot, malbec, pinotage, cabernet sauvignon and chambourcin (a French/American hybrid red). Six other small vineyards in the area also supply fruit to the winery, helping complement their range with syrah and cabernet franc. Annual production is around 4000 cases.

Notable wines

Black Rocks Chardonnay ($35), Pinot Gris ($26), Syrah ($30).

Food

The restaurant serves bistro-style food and is open as above, plus dinner Friday and Saturday nights all year round.

Ake Ake Vineyard

165 Waimate North Road
Kerikeri
09 407 8230 www.akeakevineyard.co.nz
Open Wednesday–Sunday 10.00 am–5.00 pm, winter closedown late June–late July (phone if in doubt)

John Quenault, formerly from the island of Jersey, was lured to the Bay of Islands by local girl Aynsley. They quickly produced award-winning wines and a son, Jaluka. On the small four-hectare (10-acre) site they grow chardonnay, syrah, tempranillo and chambourcin.

Notable wines

Chambourcin ($29), Syrah ($20).

Food

Restaurant chef Paul Jacks produces simple, tasty vegetarian and seafood dishes from fresh local produce, served in their stylish restaurant. In the evening from Thursday to Sunday, candles adorn the tables as you watch the sunset from the deck, or you can sit in front of the wood fire when it's colder.

Vineyard dog

Pip — a perennially hungry fox terrier.

Cottle Hill Winery

State Highway Ten (corner of State Highway Ten and Cottle Hill Road just south of Kerikeri, 20 minutes drive from Paihia)
Kerikeri
09 407 5203 www.cottlehill.co.nz
Open seven days November 1–March 31 10.00 am–5.30 pm, open five days April–October 31 10.00 am–5.00 pm (closed Mondays and Tuesdays)

Californians Michael and Barbara Webb, sailed from San Diego to New Zealand aboard their 10-metre yacht, and fell in love with the Kerikeri region. They decided to stay on, and established Cottle Hill Winery in 1996. On their home vineyard they grow pinot noir, pinotage and syrah. Gisborne and Hawke's Bay contract growers supply other grapes. The cellar door offers spectacular views from the highest peak in Kerikeri.

Notable wines

Chardonnay ($19), Sauvignon Blanc ($19), Syrah ($24).

Food

N/A

Karikari Estate

Maitai Bay Road
Karikari Peninsula
RD3 Kaitaia
09 408 7222 www.karikariestate.co.nz
Open November–April 11.00 am–5.00 pm May–October by appointment

No small-time operator, Karikari Estate has 41 hectares (100 acres) of chardonnay, viognier, syrah, merlot, cabernet sauvignon, cabernet franc, malbec, pinotage and montepulciano. The first vines were planted in 1998 and production began with the first vintage in 2003. Karikari is part of the 1200-hectare (3000-acre) Carrington Resort comprising luxury accommodation, a championship 18-hole golf course designed by American designer Matt Dye, an Olympic skeet shooting range, and a Black Angus beef farm.

Notable wines

Chardonnay ($29), Cabernet Sauvignon/Merlot/Cabernet Franc ($27), Merlot/Cabernet Sauvignon/Malbec ($27).

Vineyard dog

'KC' — hyperactive dalmatian.

Food

Carrington's dining room — open 11.30 am–3.30 pm — provides fine dining at prices to match. Open to house guests for breakfast and dinner every day of the year and luncheon is served at the winery. Non-resident diners are welcome but reservations are essential. Executive Chef Scott Fraser and his team create menus daily with a focus on food grown on the estate (Angus beef, native eel, honey, vegetables and fresh herbs) as well as showcasing the abundance of local seafood and cheeses. Open for dinner from Labour Weekend through Easter, seven nights a week from 6.00 pm.

Accommodation

- Lodge: ten large, air-conditioned bedrooms with ensuite and King-sized beds. Each room opens on to a wide veranda with views to the ocean and native bush. Tariff: $495 November to the end April, rest of year, $395.
- Villas: two-storey self-contained villas. Ground floor has a wood burning fireplace and veranda overlooking the golf course and Pacific Ocean. The second floor has two double bedrooms with ensuite plus a small studio (ideal for a child or young adult). Tariff: about $500 for one to two guests, about $600 for two to four guests.

Okahu Estate

520 Okahu Road (3.5 kilometres from Kaitaia on Awarora Road on the way to Ahipara, at the southern end of Ninety Mile Beach, the estate vineyard is on the corner of Awarora Road and Okahu Road, with the winery frontage off Okahu Road)
Okahu
09 408 2066 0800 806 806 www.okahuestate.co.nz
Open seven days December–February 10.00 am–5.00 pm, rest of the year Monday–Friday 10.00 am–5.00 pm

Local identity Monty Knight is another wine pioneer — starting in 1984 and going on to win New Zealand's first Gold and Trophy (Gold medal award, and trophy for best syrah) in the 1996 Royal Easter Show. On the three hectare (7.5-acre) vineyard he also grows pinotage, malbec, cabernet franc, merlot and chambourcin. Okahu has also done well with chardonnay, and viognier is the latest variety planted. The elevated vineyard site slopes west-nor-west, with impressive rural views out to the sand hills of Ninety Mile Beach and Shipwreck Bay. The cellar door offers free tastings of their wines, plus a range of local sauces, olive oil, honey, chutneys, nuts, cheese, jellies and jams. There are three tiers of wine: start with Shipwreck Bay, then premium Okahu, and finally the flagship Kaz Shiraz.

Notable wines

Chardonnay ($25), Merlot ($29), Syrah ($29) Kaz Shiraz ($50) — formerly 100 per cent syrah but now a blend and very hard to get hold of.

Places to eat

Kamakura Restaurant

29 The Strand
Russell
09 403 7771 www.kamakura.co.nz
Brunch/lunch 11.00 am–3.00 pm, dinner 6.00 pm onwards

Superb waterfront location. Pacific Rim cuisine, from seafood laksa to Dijon lamb rack. Entrées about $18. Mains around $33. Excellent New Zealand wine list.

Waterfront Café

23 The Strand
Russell
09 403 7589
Open seven days 8.00 am–4.00 pm

Hearty breakfast and lunch options like porridge, pancakes, the large breakfast special, nachos and the super panini. Good coffee.

Gannets Restaurant
Corner York and Chapel Streets
Russell
09 403 7990   www.gannets.co.nz
Open for dinner from 6.00 pm, closed Mondays

Varied Pacific Rim-influenced menu, with the emphasis on seafood. Starter or mains option on all items. About $20 and $30 respectively.

Duke of Marlborough Hotel
35 The Strand Russsell
09 403 7829   www.theduke.co.nz

Restored, gracious old hotel which has been there for more than 160 years. Bistro menu with mains around $15, kids' menu $9.50. Restaurant menu — usual suspects: venison, lamb, seafood about $30.

Things to do

Northland has long been a haven for beach-goers, boaties, big game fishers and scuba divers, and is hugely popular in summer months. There is no end of eco-tours, scuba tours, dolphin excursions and fishing charters for those so inclined.

Aside from that, Northland has history in abundance, native forests, and breathtaking coastal scenery.

Russell

Once known as 'the hell hole of the Pacific' when it was the 'shore leave' destination for sailors, whalers, sealers and traders during the early nineteenth century, Russell is now a tranquil, quaint spot and a favoured part of the Bay of Islands for boaties seeking safe anchorage. Historic buildings to visit include the rammed-earth Pompallier Catholic mission house, and Christ Church, which still carries musket holes from the early wars.

Kerikeri

Historical highlights are the Kerikeri Mission House, the country's oldest standing European building, built by one John Butler in 1821, and the Mission's Stone Store dating from 1832 — New Zealand's oldest stone building.

Paihia

Paihia is in the heart of the Bay of Islands, and very busy in tourist season, but stunningly beautiful nonetheless. Cafés, restaurants, hotels and accommodation abound.

Waitangi

One of New Zealand's most historic sites, this is the place where both Maori and European joined in signing the Treaty of Waitangi in 1840. The Treaty House is located amongst a vast, rolling green estate which looks out into the Bay of Islands. Don't miss the meeting house, one of the largest Maori war canoes and the visitor centre and gallery.

Cape Reinga

The northern-most tip of New Zealand (chronically mispronounced by your average Kiwi as Cape Rianga for no apparent reason). See the Tasman Sea and the Pacific Ocean clashing together. The name of the cape comes from the Maori word 'reinga', meaning 'the Underworld'. Another Maori name is 'Te Rerenga Wairua', meaning the leaping-off place of spirits. Both refer to the Maori belief that the cape is the point where the spirits of the dead travel to their spiritual afterlife in Hawaiki.

Events

Bay of Islands Country Music Festival

(www.country-rock.co.nz)
Multiple venues attract around 3000 visitors and over 60 acts to this annual event. It is generally held around May. Artists attend from New Zealand, Australia and America.

Bay of Islands Jazz and Blues Festival

(www.jazz-blues.co.nz)
Held around May, this is a three-day weekend, with live music on the streets of Paihia and Russell. More than 35 acts attend and a free shuttle bus takes fans around the venues.

Places to stay

Kauri Cliffs Lodge and Golf Course

Matauri Bay Road
Matauri Bay
Northland
09 407 0010 www.kauricliffs.com

Kauri Cliffs is an exclusive all-out-luxury retreat for the well-heeled, and on a par with Blanket Bay and Huka Lodge. Set on 2430 hectares (6000 acres) near Matauri Bay, the lodge has spectacular 180-degree views of the Pacific Ocean, Cape Brett and the Cavalli Islands. It consists of eleven separate guest cottages, each with two guest suites. On offer: in-house spa treatments, fine dining, barbecues, fishing, sea kayaking, boar and possum hunting, swimming pool, tennis, mountain biking, and basketball.

Tariff: suite around $700, deluxe suite around $900, owner's cottage around $6000. Alternatively, you could just buy the best tent you can get and camp at the gate (with spare change).

Kauri Cliffs golf course was designed and built by David Harman of Orlando, Florida. The par-72 championship golf course measures 7119 yards (6510 metres).

The Boathouse

Beechy Street
Opua
0800 683 722 www.theboathouseopua.com

The Boathouse consists of two, self-contained luxury apartments with a nautical theme, located entirely over the water. Both apartments offer sweeping views over the Bay of Islands. Tariff: rates vary depending on the number of nights and season — around $300 to $500.

Wharepuke Subtropical Garden and Cottages

190 Kerikeri Road
Kerikeri
09 407 8933

Robin Booths has a Diploma in Horticulture and has a two-hectare (five-acre) subtropical garden lifetime collection of rare and unusual plants. His garden was awarded Garden of Regional Significance in 2006.

Nestled in the garden are self-contained 'eco cottages'. Garden tours and visits to a print artist's gallery are also available. Tariff: around $160.

Saltwater Lodge

14 Kings Road
Paihia
09 402 7075 0800 002 26 www.saltwaterlodge.co.nz

Setting the standard for backpacker accommodation by gaining a Qualmark 5-star rating; ultra modern (or is that post-modern) design. Walking distance to the beach. An ideal choice for groups or families. Tariff: A six-bedroom unit including ensuite is $25 per person, private double rooms for couples available at $110 (not available Christmas to February).

Matakana

Northeast Auckland's Matakana is a groovy, up-and-coming winemaking region with most wineries established less than ten years. A 50-minute drive from Auckland City, its sunny north-facing hillsides produce ripe red wines from varieties such as sangiovese and pinotage. The white grapes — chardonnay, viognier and pinot gris — are also doing extremely well. Some vineyards bring in a small amount of grapes from Hawke's Bay and Marlborough, but most grow the vast majority onsite.

Located on the Pohutukawa Coast, with stunning views out to the Hauraki Gulf and beyond, this picturesque region offers a wide range of activities all year round, from fishing and diving, a thermal aquatic park, swimming, golf and horse riding, to nature walks. Almost every winery has food available, and the whole area has many upmarket B&Bs, cafés and restaurants, plus a honey centre and one of the most distinctive potteries in the region.

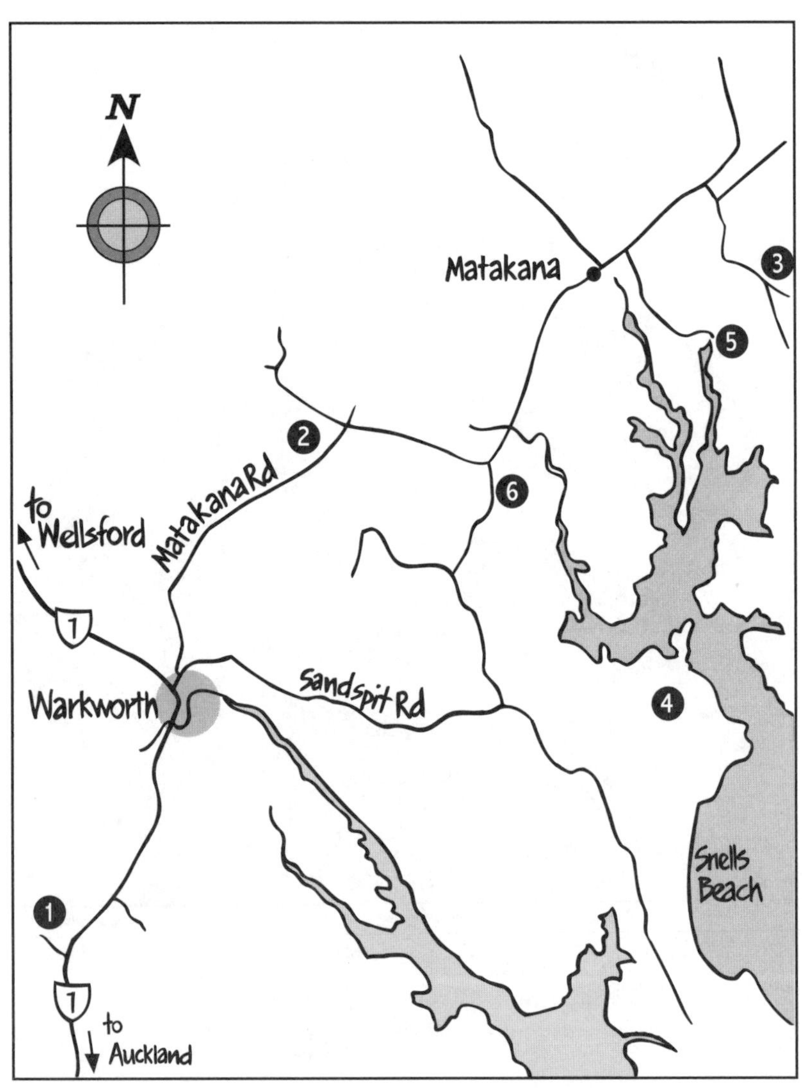
N
Matakana
3
5
2
Matakana Rd
6
to Wellsford
1
Warkworth
Sandspit Rd
4
Snells Beach
1
to Auckland
1

Ransom Wines

46 Valerie Close
Warkworth
09 425 8862   www.ransomwines.co.nz
Open 10.00 am–5.00 pm, closed Mondays

This is the first winery on the Matakana Wine Trail as you approach from the south, about three kilometres out from Wellsford. Stylish winery architecture and pretty vineyard views impress. The place is owned by a couple curiously named Robin and Marion. The first vintage was 1993, and on their six hectares (15 acres) they have merlot, cabernet sauvignon, malbec, cabernet franc, chardonnay and pinot gris. There is also a new discovery — thought to be cabernet franc, but which in fact is carmenère — an extinct French Bordeaux variety thought to be unknown outside Chile. It is a stunning wine with sweet savoury, earthy characters.

Notable wines

Pinot Gris ($23), Dark Summit Cabernet Sauvignon/Carmenère/Cabernet Franc/Malbec ($35).

Food

Platters from $12 to $18 per person, selection from: tapas, cheese, nibbles, dips. Wines by the glass at about $7. Also available: espresso coffee and biscotti.

Warkworth

Just before you head out to the wineries, on Matakana Road, hang a right into the thriving township of Warkworth — another historic riverside town, featuring Victorian-era wooden buildings from the 1860s. For local information, your best bet is the Warkworth Information Centre at 1 Baxter Street. There is plenty of information on local activities, historic sites, vineyards and accommodation. Also drop in to Taste Matakana at 2 Neville Street. They have cookware, speciality foods, and local wines. Ginger Café is also worth a visit for baked-on-the-premises artisan breads and pastries.

Matakana Farmers' Market

Okay, back at the traffic lights take Matakana Road and follow the signs to Matakana Village. A local farmers market has been operating for about two years now, and features up to 31 local growers and food producers selling organic fresh fruit and vegetables, plus Swiss organic chocolate specialities, eggs, jellies and preserves, chutneys and pickles, olive oils, breads, speciality meats, honey and flowers. Eat a hearty brunch, accompanied by espresso coffee or squeezed fruit juice. Wander by the river while musicians perform. In summer the market is held on Saturday 8.00 am–1.00 pm, in winter Saturday 9.00 am–1.00 pm.

Ascension Vineyard and Restaurant

480 Matakana Road
Matakana
09 422 9601 www.ascensionvineyard.co.nz
Wine tasting seven days 10.00 am–5.00 pm

Established in 1994 by Darryl and Bridget Soljan. Darryl is part of the West Auckland Soljan winemaking dynasty. Just 4.6 hectares (11.5 acres) of grapes and a top-class restaurant in a stunning rural setting. Neat rows of vines climb a north-facing hill beside Tuscan-styled winery buildings. Only around 5000 cases are produced per year. Almost all sales are from the cellar door or to a mailing list. A $6 tasting fee allows you to sample at least six wines.

Notable wines

Pretty well every one of the 12 or so wines available for tasting is a prime example of the variety and most have won awards (priced from mid $20 to mid $30). Only three of their varietals are not grown on the estate — sauvignon blanc, riesling and gewürztraminer. They also do a lovely Old Tawny fortified port-style wine.

Food

If you haven't had lunch yet, this restaurant is hugely popular as a lunch stop, especially in summer and over public holidays. A new venture at Ascension, The Oak Grill has a seasonal menu featuring lots of fresh local produce. The Oak Grill menu is inclusive of veggies and wedges at about $37. Wines by the glass or bottle.The restaurant serves lunch seven days from 11.00 am and dinner every Thursday, Friday and Saturday from 6.30 pm. It pays to book in advance.

Matakana weekend — Sunday

Omaha Bay Vineyards

189 Takatu Road (opposite Whitmore Road)
Matakana
09 423 0022 www.omahabay.co.nz
Open in summer seven days 10.30 am–5.00 pm, in winter Wednesday–Sunday 10.30 am–4.00 pm

Hegman and Bev Foster opened their vineyard for tasting in May 2007. They have three estate-grown wines: flora, pinot gris and the Italian variety montepulciano.

They also stock wines made from Marlborough, Hawke's Bay and West Auckland grapes. As you drive through the vineyard to arrive at the tasting room and wine cave, there are breathtaking views of Omaha Bay and Little Barrier Island from the elevated cellar door.

Notable wines

Pinot Gris ($30), Hawke's Bay Merlot and, my pick, full-bodied Montepulciano ($35). Tasting fees: whole range $10, three wines $5.

Food

All day menu of gourmet platters.

Vineyard dog

Kate — black lab.

Brick Bay Wines

Arabella Lane
Snells Beach
09 425 4690 www.brickbay.co.nz
Open seven days from 10.00 am–5.00 pm

As one of the youngest wineries in Matakana — the first wines were released in 1998 — Brick Bay Wines has been open for tasting since January 2007. It is owned by the Didsbury family who were instigators of the Matakana Farmers' Market and Matakana Cinema Complex. Production is very small — about 1000 cases per year from the tiny five-hectare (12-acre) vineyard.

With very stylish architecture by Noel Lane, Brick Bay Wines has an airy 'glasshouse' tasting facility, cafe and offices cantilevered over a large mirrored pond.

Sculpture trail

At $10 per head including a map and catalogue, it takes approximately an hour to walk the trail through the undulating farm and vineyard grounds. Large outdoor works by leading New Zealand artists are featured and are also for sale.

Notable wines

Just four wines, all grown on the property, with winemaking by award-winning Anthony Ivicevich of Kumeu's West Brook Winery — a pinot gris, two blended Bordeaux-styled reds and montepulciano. Tasting fee of $5, refunded on purchase.

Food

A variety of platters. Good coffee and fine teas are also available.

Vineyard dog

Jazz — Hungarian vizsla (loves the pond).

Hyperion Wines

188 Tongue Farm Road
Matakana
09 422 9375 www.hyperion-wines.co.nz
Open seven days January 10.00 am–5.00 pm, February–December open, Saturday, Sunday and Public Holidays 10.00 am–5.00 pm

John and Jill Crone are the owners and John describes himself as a computer geek turned winemaker. Only around 1200 cases of wine are produced per year. The tiny tasting room and winery building was once a cowshed. A good range of wines for such a small facility. Many have been awarded trophies in New Zealand wine competitions.

Notable wines

Helios Chardonnay — whole-bunch pressed and barrique fermented. Kronos Cabernet Sauvignon/Merlot/Malbec — medium to light style with cherry and plum flavours.

Food

N/A

Heron's Flight Vineyard and Café

49 Sharp Road
Matakana
09 422 7915 www.heronsflight.co.nz
Open for lunch seven days from 11.00 am, dinner is served on Thursday, Friday and Saturday nights

David Hoskins (ex Philadelphian) and his partner Mary Evans started off in 1988 with plantings of chardonnay, cabernet and merlot. Then in 1994 David's infatuation with Italian wines led him to plant the chianti variety sangiovese. Since then, all the other vines have been pulled out and replaced with either sangiovese or the northern Italian grape dolcetto. They now boast a brand new handsome cellar door and restaurant — built on sustainable eco principles and using recycled materials wherever possible.

Notable Wines

A $10 tasting fee gives you a tutored tasting of the full range.

Dolcetto ($33) ripe fruity mid palate, with a dry finish.

Sangiovese ($50) Heron's Flight's premium red wine — full bodied and soft, and made only from the ripest fruit.

Il Rosso ($22) a light style food wine, vinted from the same sangiovese grapes. Rich but sharp flavours of cranberry and raspberry.

Sangiovese juice ($4.00) unfermented pure grape juice, bursting with flavour and natural sweetness.

Food

Fresh local and organic food features on their Tuscan-inspired menu.

Things to do

With so many options for local activities and accommodation on the Matakana Coast, probably the best place to start is the brand new Matakana Information Centre located in the foyer of the Matakana Cinema Complex, just by the roundabout at the Matakana Valley Road/ Leigh Road intersection. Here's a small sample.

Puhoi

As you head north on State Highway One, the turnoff to the quaint township of Puhoi is about ten minutes past Orewa Beach. Puhoi region is an historic area, first settled by immigrants from Bohemia in 1863 — a German-speaking part of the new Czech Republic and about 60 kilometres from Prague. Many locals are direct descendents of the immigrants and there is a strong local culture of celebrating festivals associated with the old homeland. Today Puhoi is most famous for Puhoi Valley cheese.

Art of Cheese Café and Shop

275 Ahuroa Road
Puhoi
09 422 0670 www.artofcheese.co.nz
Open seven days from 9.00 am–5.00 pm

Turn left at Puhoi turnoff, follow the main road through the village and keep going, and going, and going, on the winding road (about three kilometres). Art of Cheese Café is settled next to green sweeping lawns, a children's play area and duck pond with fountain. The main factory is discreetly tucked away. Puhoi's speciality cheeses are available for tasting: edam, gruyére and the renowned double cream blue brie. Café fare features cheese-based dishes, plus tasting platters, muffins, good coffee, and teas. You can see into the blue brie cheesery area and watch cheese being made.

Puhoi pub

The Seymour family has been running the pub for more than 40 years. Once a notorious bikers' pub, the interior is studded with cigarette-stained memorabilia from its colourful past: agricultural tools, old yellowed banknotes, dishonoured cheques, business cards and so on. There is a bra collection behind the door. Feel free to contribute.

Puhoi Museum

Historical items from the 1800s. www.puhoihistoricalsociety.org.nz

Puhoi River Canoe Hire

Paddle your own canoe, or share a tandem. Open depending on tides.
09 422 0891 www.puhoirivercanoes.co.nz

Mustardmakers

An artisan business producing gourmet mustards, condiments, chutneys and luxury jams and marmalades. www.mustardmakers.co.nz

Other Stuff Antiques

Devonshire teas and a classic rural general store selling local Lothlorien fruit wines.

Zealandia Sculpture Gardens

138 Mahurangi West Road (about halfway between Puhoi and Warkworth, on the right, heading north)
Warkworth
09 422 0099 www.zealandiasculpturegarden.co.nz

Terry Stringer is a leading New Zealand sculptor and a key figure in the history of art in New Zealand. In 2003 he received the country's most prestigious national honour, the ONZM (Officer of the New Zealand Order of Merit). The garden consists of large indoor and outdoor works. Open every weekend from November–end of March by appointment. Open every day in January 10.00 am–4.00 pm. Guided tours at 1.00 pm and 2.00 pm. Admission charges apply.

Charlie's Gelato Garden

17 Sharp Road (on the left after you turn right off the Leigh–Matakana Road into Sharp Road)
Matakana
www.charliesgelato.co.nz

Inspired by a trip to Italy, Charlie Wrigglesworth and Heather King decided to launch their own gelataria, using fresh fruit including local seasonal strawberries, grapes and raspberries. Both gelato and sorbetto (dairy-free) available.

Matakana Patisserie

70 Matakana Valley Road
Matakana Village
www.matakanapatisserie.co.nz

New Zealand Bakery of the Year 2007. Award winning European breads and pastries, bagels, quiche, cakes, filled rolls and Gugelhopf.

Brookview Tea House

1335 Leigh Road
Matakana Village (right opposite the roundabout)
Open 9.00 am–4.00 pm; Closed Tuesdays.
09 423 0390 www.brookviewteahouse.co.nz

Lunches and morning and afternoon teas use fresh seasonal organic produce. Located in a restored 1920s bungalow, the Brookview Tea House offers a selection of fine teas, freshly baked goods, traditional cream teas with tiered cake stands and a glass of bubbly. Fully licensed.

Tawharanui Regional Park

Takatu Road
Matakana

This park is the northern-most Auckland Regional Park and lies astride the Takatu Peninsula, which juts out into the Hauraki Gulf. Pastures fall away to rugged reefs, shingled bays and white sand beaches. Farm trails and an especially signposted ecology trail guide your walk on the coastline and in forest.

Matakana Cinemas

2 Matakana Valley Road
Matakana Village
09 422 9833   www.matakanacinemas.co.nz

A three-cinema movie theatre featuring current releases. And while you're there . . .

The Vintry Wine Cellar

Located at the end of the cinema foyer, the cellar features wine tasting and sales of local wines at winery prices (many of which don't have a cellar door). Tastings ($10) are done in 'flights' of five glasses, e.g. five local pinot gris — all served 'blind' with the big reveal at the end as to which is which.

Morris & James Ceramics and Pottery

Tongue Farm Road
Matakana
09 422 7116   www.morrisandjames.co.nz

Anthony Morris kicked things off in 1977 and in the early days, the company struggled through fires, receivership and other disasters. Now they are one of New Zealand's most distinctive and successful ceramics producers. A strong native design element is dominant in their handcrafted pottery made from Matakana terracotta clay (excavated right on the property). Check out the seconds department for bargains.

Glass Bottom Boat

Operates from Goat Island Marine Reserve
09 422 6334   025 979 764   www.glassbottomboat.co.nz

See our dazzling coastal marine life up close, with informative commentary. Most popular trip is the 45-minute Round-the-Island trip, which takes you to the big caves of Goat Island.

Kawau Kat Cruises

Sandspit Wharf
Sandspit
09 425 8006   0800 888 006   www.watertaxi.co.nz

Join the Royal Mail Run Cruise departing at 10.30 am from Sandspit Wharf to Kawau Island. It includes a cruise around all the bays and inlets on Kawau Island, commentary and morning tea and a BBQ lunch onboard. Cruises allow time at Mansion House, former home of Governor Sir George Grey.

Pakiri Beach Horse Riding

Taurere Park, Rahuikiri Road
Pakiri Beach
09 422 6275   www.horseride-nz.co.nz

Ride on wild Pakiri Beach on a horse to suit your riding ability on any day of the year: one or two hours, half or a whole day, or three-, five- or seven-day treks.

Omaha Beach Golf Club

Omaha Drive
Omaha
09 422 7551   www.nzgolfcourses.co.nz/omaha/

Omaha Beach Golf Club is built on undulating sand dunes taking advantage of natural features such as the kahikatea forest and wetlands area. Stunning views out across the beach to Little and Great Barrier islands on the new John Darby-designed Back Nine, and across the Whangateau Harbour on the Front Nine.

Places to stay

Quest Matakana

170 Green Road
Matakana
0800 423 0353 www.questmatakana.co.nz

New luxury villas each with their own kitchen and laundry, and BBQ on the north-facing decks. Each sleeps up to a total of six guests. Tariff: from $350 (1–2 guests) to $450 (5–6 guests).

Rosemount Homestead B&B

25 Rosemount Road
Warkworth
09 422 2580 0274 966 654 www.rosemount.co.nz

Built in 1900, Rosemount Homestead was constructed from a twin-trunk kauri felled on the property by an early settler. Three ensuite guestrooms. Set on six hectares (15 acres), Rosemount provides extensive rural views. Tariff: $225 per night double room, $195 per night single room.

The Saltings Estate

1210 Sandspit Road
Sandspit
09 425 9670 021 625 948 www.saltings.co.nz

Luxury vineyard accommodation where they grow syrah and Bordeaux reds using biodynamic principles. Tariff: around $300 per night double room.

Takatu Lodge and Vineyard

518 Whitmore Road
Matakana
09 423 0299 021 825 285 www.takatulodge.co.nz

Very upmarket, Qualmark 5-star. Includes breakfast and a tasting of their wines with antipasti. Tariff: $490 per night for a double room.

Warkworth Lodge Motel
Corner Falls and Bank Streets
Warkworth
09 4222 500   027 4422 513   www.wwlodge.co.nz

Centrally located in Warkworth township, the lodge features heated pool, spa and BBQ area. Tariff: self-contained units from $180 per night, room with ensuite $140 per night.

Walton Park Motor Lodge
2 Walton Ave
Warkworth
09 425 8149   www.waltonpark.co.nz

Affordable accommodation in Warkworth, the 25 recently refurbished units are suitable for individuals to large family groups. Tariff: from $85 per room per night. Breakfast available.

Henderson

Even though the Henderson/Kumeu region was pretty well the birthplace of our wine industry thanks to Croatian immigrants, Henderson itself has been sadly neglected by successive city councils that have allowed rampant industrial and residential development.

Once a rural region that offered vineyards, orchards, market gardens and about 50 wineries, it is now very built-up with none of the countryside charm of other wine regions. Many of the old family wineries and vineyards have been sold to developers, or moved elsewhere. Today only about eight winemakers struggle on in the busy urban sprawl, but there are still a few interesting wineries worth hunting out . . .

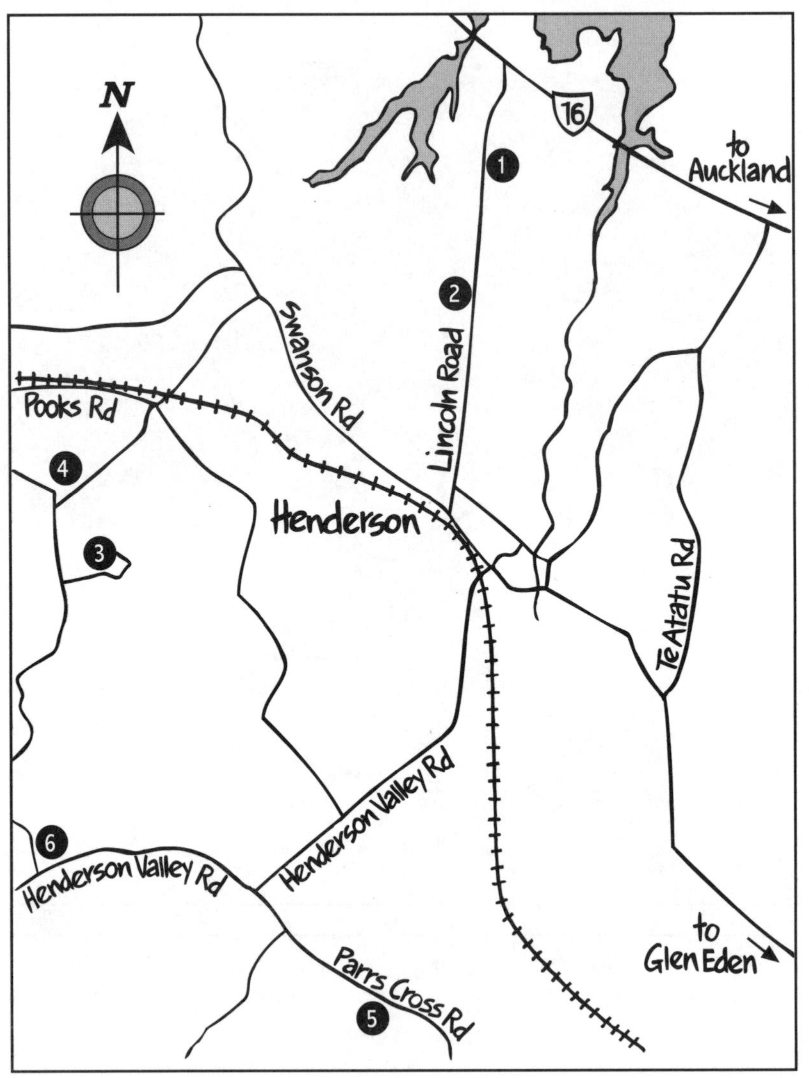

N
16
to Auckland
1
2
Lincoln Road
Swanson Rd
Pooks Rd
4
3
Henderson
Te Atatu Rd
Henderson Valley Rd
6
Henderson Valley Rd
to Glen Eden
Parrs Cross Rd
5

Henderson — Saturday (could be combined with Kumeu or Waimauku weekends)

First off, head up Lincoln Road, left of State Highway 16 heading away from the city.

Mazuran's Vineyards

255 Lincoln Road
Henderson
09 838 6945 www.mazurans.co.nz
Open Monday–Saturday 9.00 am-6.00 pm, Sunday 9.00 am–5.00 pm

On your left as you head up Lincoln Road from the State Highway16 turnoff. Mazuran's is one of our oldest and most distinguished producers of fortified wines. George Mazuran arrived in New Zealand from Croatia in 1926. Eventually he bought a block of land on Lincoln Road in 1938 where his first vintage was harvested four years later. The small cellar door facility built in the 1940s has hardly changed since then. Historic photographs, accolades and barrels celebrate each of the vintages. Limited quantities are available of special releases dating back to 1942. Their sherries and ports have won many international awards over the years.

Notable wines

Their amazing range of recent and vintage ports and sherries, plus a cabernet/merlot blend.

Food

N/A

Note: If you are planning to start with Mazuran's, then stop for a coffee before your next winery. Otherwise your palate will find dry wines very unappealing after sweet ports and sherries. Alternatively, make Mazuran's your last stop.

Lincoln Wines

130 Lincoln Road
Henderson
09 838 6944 www.lincolnwines.co.nz
Open Monday–Friday 9.00 am–5.30 pm, Saturday 10.00 am–5.00 pm, Sunday 12.00 pm–4.00 pm

The Fredatovich family has been in business since 1937 when founder Petar Fredatovich developed the winery in Henderson. They no longer grow any grapes there, but source fruit from Gisborne, Hawke's Bay and Marlborough. Petar's grandson Peter now runs the winery. Wine quality has gone from strength to strength in the last five years and winemaking is done by Andy Nicole, who has made wines in France, America, Italy and Australia. The Heritage range is about $17 a bottle, the Reserve range about $27 a bottle.

Notable wines

Reserve Gisborne Chardonnay, Reserve Hawke's Bay Merlot, Premium Reserve Ice Wine (Gewürztraminer/Semillon).

Food

N/A

Now off into the more rural bits of Henderson and Oratia.

3

Babich Wines

Babich Road
Henderson
09 833 7859 www.babichwines.co.nz
Open Monday–Friday 9.00 am–5.00 pm, Saturday 10.00 am–5.00 pm, closed Sundays

Still family-owned and one of New Zealand's largest wineries, Babich Wines is located in the Henderson Valley, where lush green vineyards climb the rolling slopes, and housing estates push against the boundaries. Babich also source grapes from Marlborough and were one of the first wineries to establish vineyards in the red metal soils of Hawke's Bay's Gimblett Gravels region. Founder Josip Babich was a Dalmatian gumdigger who emigrated from Croatia in 1914. His sons Peter and Joe carry on the tradition in the Henderson Valley, and grandson David is now general manager.

Notable wines

Irongate Chardonnay ($35), Winemakers Reserve Sauvignon Blanc ($25), Winemakers Reserve Pinot Noir ($30) Winemakers Reserve Syrah, The Patriarch (cabernet sauvignon and merlot 60/40 blend) ($60).

Food

N/A

St Jerome

219 Metcalfe Road
Henderson
09 833 6205 www.stjerome.co.nz
Open Monday–Saturday 9.00 am–6.00 pm

Brothers Miro and Davorin Ozich own a family vineyard and winery named after a Croatian saint. Their cellar door is a tiny room, which can fit only a few people at a time. The brothers make chardonnay, gewürztraminer, riesling and sauvignon blanc from contract growers down country, but their flagship wines are uncompromisingly tannic Bordeaux-style reds. The top tier is Matuka, named in honour of their father.

Notable wines

Matuka (cabernet sauvignon and merlot 60/40 blend) ($43).

Food

N/A

Then, off to Oratia and beyond . . .

5

Artisan Wines

99 Parrs Cross Road
Oratia
09 838 7979 www.artisanwines.co.nz
Open seven days from 11.00 am–5.00 pm with extended hours in summer

Local viticulturalist Rex Sunde and his wife Maria front the operation. Rex's family has historic West Auckland roots, and they have grown grapes on the Oratia Valley for over 100 years. The stylish, brand new tasting facility is in the rural backblocks of Henderson Valley, and features a café. Grapes come from far and wide — four small local vineyards, Hawke's Bay, Tolaga Bay and Marlborough. A $5 tasting fee gives you a choice of four wines to sample. They share a driveway with the weekly Sunday Farmers Market, a café and a curio shop.

Notable wines

Eight Rows Gewürztraminer ($22), Kauri Ridge Chardonnay ($24.50), Ridge Cabernet Merlot. Michael Cooper gives their Fantail Island Syrah five stars ($48.50).

Food

Café open 11.30 am–3.00 pm. Platters available Monday–Wednesday, à la carte menu Friday–Sunday.

The Packing Shed Café and Gallery

Displays the work of West Auckland artists. Has a wide range of artwork from photographs and paintings to pottery, woodwork, glassware, sculptures and jewellery. Opening hours Monday to Sunday 9.00 am–4.00 pm.

Just Plane Interesting
Curio and antique shop.

Oratia Sunday Farmers' Market
9.00 am–12.00 pm
Undercover stalls. Olives, handmade chocolates, chilli sauce, free-range eggs, local cheeses, flowers, plants, honey, olive oil, muffins and pastries.

Pleasant Valley Wines

322 Henderson Valley Road
Henderson
09 838 8857
Open Monday–Friday 10.00 am–5.00 pm, Saturday–Sunday 12.00 pm–4.00 pm

Pretentious, it ain't. Pleasant Valley is a blast from the past — an extremely basic winery and tasting facility. Having said that, they lay claim to being the oldest family winery in New Zealand — founded in 1895 by Stipan Jelich (later Anglicised to Stephen Yelas). They still have a vineyard in Henderson which produces pinotage, cabernet sauvignon and merlot; and they use contract growers in Marlborough for their white wines.

Notable wines

My pick — the Auckland Yelas Pinotage — ripe, fruity and smoky. Also a range of fortified port and sherry wines.

Food

N/A

Places to eat

Henderson is a sprawling industrial and residential zone, so there is not much in the way of choice for food. However, highly recommended is:

The Falls Restaurant

Corner of Alderman Drive and Edmonton Road
Henderson
09 835 0070 www.thefalls.co.nz
Open seven days from from 9.00 am

With its award-winning beef and lamb dishes and an extensive wine list, this is probably the best fine dining in the Henderson region. The Falls Hotel is a two-storey kauri building, built in 1854 by 'Long John' McLeod, a mill manager for Thomas Henderson (the founder of Henderson). It was constructed to provide accommodation for the workers at Henderson Timber Mill.

Sample menu: South Island salmon wrapped in maple cured bacon, pan seared, with palm sugar and banana relish. Or, how about cinnamon rubbed roast duck on creamed leeks with oven dried cherry tomatoes. Mmmm — cherry tomatoes.

Things to do

Titirangi Village

This lively village has a bustling café and restaurant scene and Lopdell House Gallery — Waitakere City's regional art gallery — which hosts regular exhibitions.

Arataki Visitors Centre
Waitakere Ranges (drive through Titirangi Village and at the roundabout, take Scenic Drive, the visitor centre is on the left five kilometres along Scenic Drive)
Open winter 10.00 am–4.00 pm, summer 9.00 am–5.00 pm

Information centre, bush walks (see mature kauri trees), wildlife displays, souvenirs. An 11-metre high pou (guardian post) at the entrance, represents ancestors of local Maori (Te Kawerau a Maki) and is one of the largest of its kind in New Zealand. Inside are five other ancestral guardian carvings. See both harbours from the viewing deck. There are maps available of bush tracks which you can navigate. A moderate fitness level is required, all tracks are well-maintained.

Places to stay

The Kumeu region is close by, so there is the option of basing yourself there. Alternatively, Titirangi, a little further west, has some very good accommodation options.

Waitakere Estate
573 Scenic Drive
Waiatarua
09 814 9622 www.waitakereestate.co.nz

A substantial, boutique hotel complex comprising 14 hotel rooms and three Garden suites, a fine dining restaurant and hotel bar. Located deep in the Waitakere native forest. There is an enormous fireplace in the guest lounge. Tariff: $170–$245

Rangiwai Lodge B&B
29 Rangiwai Road
Titirangi
09 817 8990

Surrounded by native trees and with sweeping elevated views to the Manukau Harbour, the lodge is a few minutes' stroll to Titirangi Village's vibrant café and art attractions. All guest rooms feature French doors that open on to individual private decks and have their own bathroom with designer bathrobes and quality toiletries. Also indoor heated pool with a view. Tariff: around $250 a night. For a family suite (two bedrooms, two bathrooms) around $470.

The Ferns
B&B and self-catering
81 Park Road
Titirangi
09 817 1956   0274 979 262   www.theferns.co.nz

Peaceful hideaway with luxury appointments. B&B in the main house or cater for yourself in the separate chalet, which is nestled in ponga fern trees. Just a stroll from Titirangi Village. Tariff: about $200 a night.

Bethell's Beach Cottages
Bethell's Beach
Auckland
09 810 9581   www.bethellsbeach.com

Situated on a rise with spectacular views of Auckland's west coast and the Tasman Sea, this is the ultimate hideaway retreat. Choice of two cottages or an apartment. Extra treats include seaweed body wraps, massages and Tai Chi tutoring. Tariff: around $300 per night for a minimum two-night stay. There is a 15 per cent surcharge for single night bookings.

Northwest Auckland

This region takes in Kumeu, Huapai and Waimauku, and is easily reached in a 30-minute drive down State Highway16 from Auckland City. Just go right to the end of the motorway, hang a left at the (big, ugly, can't miss it) retail park, hurry on past the fast food joints and take the right fork at the roundabout.

Once past the roundabout, it's instant countryside with race horses grazing in green pastures, strawberry fields, apple and kiwifruit orchards, sheep, cows, fruit and veggie shops and, of course, vineyards.

A little further west is Muriwai's black volcanic sand surf beach and the Takapu gannet colony. A tad slow and conservative in the past to click on to wine tourism, the region gets better and better, with numerous cafés, B&Bs and restaurants popping up to cater for wine fans.

As a rule, with northwest and Henderson wineries, the majority of grapes are not estate-grown. Heavy clay loam soils and a humid late summer are not ideal for most varieties. Pinot gris, chardonnay, pinot noir and merlot do okay, but for the most part, the whites are brought up as chilled grape juice, mostly from Marlborough, but some also from Gisborne and Hawke's Bay. Whole red grapes are delivered from Hawke's Bay and Marlborough. They have to arrive as grapes in order to extract colour and tannins from the skins during the crushing and fermentation process.

With the exception of Kumeu River and Kerr Farm, most of the west Auckland wineries grow a very small amount of their own vines on the property.

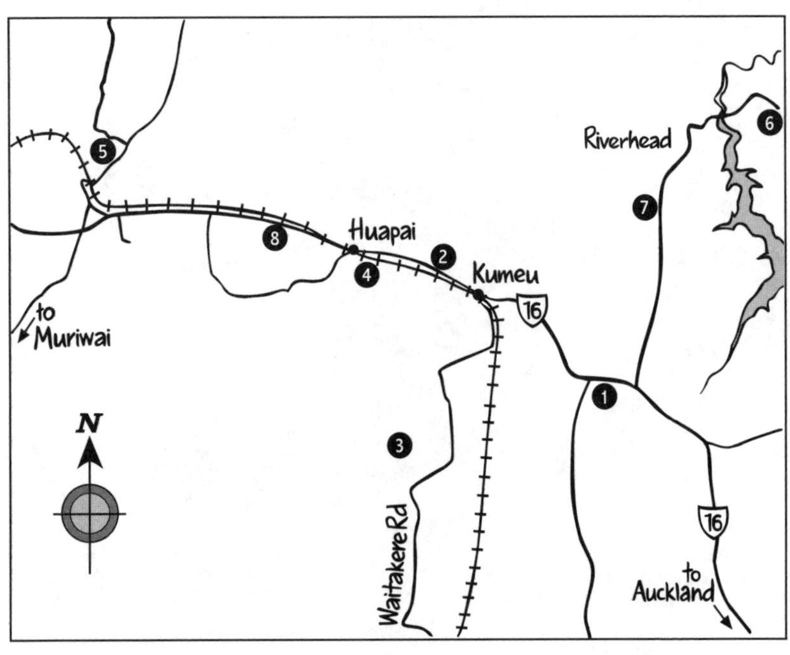

5
6
Riverhead
7
8
Huapai
2
4
Kumeu
16
to
Muriwai
1
N
3
16
Waitakere Rd
to
Auckland

Soljans Estate Winery

366 State Highway 16
Kumeu
09 412 5858 www.soljans.co.nz
Open seven days from 9.00 am–5.30 pm

Soljans is the very first Kumeu winery you come to from the city. The perpetually jovial Tony Soljan is the owner. His grandfather Bartul Soljan planted their first vines in Henderson in 1932, making Soljans one of the first Henderson wineries. The handsome new Hinueva Stone winery and restaurant complex opened in 2001. In a spacious and well-presented cellar door facility, an extensive range of light to medium bodied wines around the $20 mark are available for tasting.

Notable wines

My pick is Legacy, a very good méthode traditionelle sparkling wine, which is usually available for tasting on weekends. Pinotage, a full-bodied style with characteristic smoky aromas and ripe black fruit flavours. Founders Tawny Port from grapes grown on the original property.

Food

Why not stay for lunch? Soljans Café has an interesting and reasonably priced lunch menu that changes seasonally, but my favourite is the smoked salmon hashcake with salad garnish. Soljans wines are available by the glass, and they also do a good espresso. It pays to book ahead on weekends, and also in the summer holiday season. 09 412 2680.

Kumeu River Wines

550 State Highway 16
Kumeu
09 412 8415 www.kumeuriver.co.nz
Open Monday–Friday 9.00 am–5.30 pm, Saturday 11.00 am–5.00 pm, closed Sundays

About seven minutes up the road and on the left is Kumeu River Wines. An iconic chardonnay producer, the winery was established in 1944 by the late Maté Brajkovich. Kumeu River Chardonnay is usually listed in the Top 100 by influential American magazine *Wine Spectator*. Maté's widow, the dynamic Melba, heads this family winery. Eldest son Michael is winemaker. Sons Milan and Paul are in charge of viticulture and sales and marketing respectively, and sole daughter Marijana has recently joined the company.

White wines are the mainstay. All grapes are grown onsite (except for a sauvignon blanc, which is made from Marlborough juice). The top tier Maté's Vineyard Chardonnay (only 1000 cases per year) comes from Maté's original vineyard site, directly over the road from the winery and recently renovated tasting room.

Notable wines

Three levels of chardonnay — from the affordable Village label ($18), to flagship Kumeu River, to the Maté's Vineyard ($47). Pinot gris, rich and mouth filling.Melba, merlot/malbec. Melba is the name given to the wine — full, rich and smooth, a Bordeaux-style red.

Food

N/A

Kerr Farm Vineyard

48 Dysart Lane
Kumeu
09 412 7575 www.kerrfarmwine.co.nz
Open Saturday–Sunday 11.00 am–6.00 pm

Jaison and Wendy Kerr own this tiny 9.3-hectare (23-acre) vineyard which produces about 2500 cases each year. The youngest of the Kumeu wineries, Kerr Farm started making wines in 1995, five years after the Kerrs bought up an old vineyard that was planted mainly in high-cropping hybrids. These were replaced by cabernet sauvignon, merlot, pinotage, sauvignon blanc and chardonnay. The original sémillon vines were left, and are possibly some of the oldest of this variety in New Zealand.

Tasting and sales are located in a lovely old homestead building, which was moved on to the site in 1995. Jaison and Wendy personally run the tastings, with their guests seated around an old farmhouse table.

Notable wines

The sauvignon blanc is pretty interesting, and probably the only savvie grown north of Hawke's Bay. Nothing like a Marlborough sauvignon, but in a good year quite tropical and rich. The pinotage is spicy and full-bodied, and a good example of the former mainstay of West Auckland's reds.

Food

N/A

Nobilo Wine Group

45 Station Road
Huapai
09 412 6666   www.nobilo.co.nz
Open Monday–Friday 9.00 am–5.00 pm, Saturday and Sunday 10.00 am–4.00 pm

Through Kumeu Village and just over the bridge, on the left, is Nobilo, our second largest winemaker, with exports of over a million cases of wine per year (i.e. 12 million bottles). If all those bottles were laid end-to-end, which is highly unlikely, then they'd probably reach quite a long, long way, to some arbitrary point in space.

Nobilo incorporates Selaks and is now part of monster Constellation Brands of America which also owns Hardys (Australia). Grape growing is done in the main wine regions, as is winemaking. All blending and bottling is done in the Huapai facility. Retail manager Irene Morel and her friendly team have excellent knowledge and a passion for wines. A welcoming tasting facility displays a bewildering array of labels: Monkey Bay, White Cloud, Selaks, Rose Tree Cottage, House of Nobilo, Founders Reserve, Drylands, Icon, and others. There is also an Australian section consisting of Hardys and Taylors. Prices vary from $18 to around $35.

Notable Wines

Nobilo Icon series — Sauvignon Blanc, Pinot Gris, Gewürztraminer, Chardonnay, Merlot, Pinot Noir. Founders Reserve series — Chardonnay, Pinot Noir, Merlot Cabernet Franc, Syrah. Selaks Ice Wine — fresh dessert style, made from a freeze-concentrated blend of riesling and gewürztraminer.

Places to eat

Carriages Café

State Highway 16
Kumeu
09 412 9250 www.carriagescafe.co.nz

At this fully licensed cafe you can dine in one of two restored New Zealand Railways carriages, or on the deck overlooking the duck pond. Good coffee and tempting lunch/brunch menu.

Sangam Indian Restaurant

64 Main Road
Kumeu
09 412 6030

Open for lunch: Friday, Saturday, Sunday 12.00 pm–3.00 pm, open for dinner seven days from 5.00 pm–late. Fully licensed and BYO (wine only).

Golden Silk Thai Restaurant

2A/88 Main Road
Kumeu
09 412 2454

Open seven days from 6.00 pm–late. Good-value, standard Thai cuisine and takeaways. Fully licensed.

BeesOnline Honey Centre and Cafe
791 State Highway 16
Waimauku
09 411 7953 www.beesonline.com

Carry on along State Highway 16 past Coopers Creek winery, and about five minutes away is BeesOnline. Speciality honeys, cosmetics and honey products, (organic, GE Free) plus a café which features ethnic New Zealand Maori-influenced dishes with native spices and herbs. Problem is you can't book, so getting a table can be a gamble on weekends.

Things to do

Muriwai Beach Golf Club
09 411 8454 www.muriwai.nzgolf.net

Said to be one of the best links courses in New Zealand. Green fees are $30.

Muriwai Beach Farmstay and Horse Riding
John and Freya Lucas
781 Muriwai Road
Muriwai Beach
09 411 7111 Email: wairimu1@ihug.co.nz

One- or two-hour horse treks through forest, dunes and on the beach from $70 per hour. Also has farmstay at $70 a night per person, including two-course cooked breakfast. Full accommodation, all meals etc. around $125 per person.

Muriwai Beach
Follow the signs to spectacular Muriwai Beach — a popular west coast surfing spot. The beach is 48 kilometres long and is a popular swimming beach, but has a dangerous undertow. Rock fishing is an option most of the year. The wild mood of beaches on the west coast has meant that they have become favoured sites for film-making.

The black sand (iron sand) was eroded from ancient Mt Taranaki volcanic ash, and washed northwards up the coast. A gannet refuge is located at the southern end of the beach and is a protected breeding area. About 1200 pairs of adult gannets nest here each summer, dotted evenly on the flat cliff tops. They can be viewed from an easily accessible lookout between August and March.

Places to stay

Only Fools and Horses

376 Oaia Road
Muriwai Beach
09 411 9342   www.fools.co.nz

B&B, homestay, backpackers and horsestay (bring your own horse). Tariff: from bunkrooms at $30 a night to the villa B&B for $100. There is also have a cosy bach overlooking Muriwai Beach at $180 a night for up to six guests.

Malolo House

110 Commercial Road
Helensville
09 420 7262   Email: malolo@xtra.co.nz

About 20 minutes north of Kumeu this highly rated B&B has great food. Tariff: from $65 for a room with shared facilities, to a villa room with ensuite $110.

Matua Valley Wines

Waikoukou Valley Road
Waimauku
09 411 8301 www.matua.co.nz
Open seven days Monday–Friday 9.30 am–5.30 pm, Saturday and Sunday 10.30 am–5.30 pm

Travel as if you were going to Muriwai, then follow the signs on the right to Matua Valley Wines. Croatian descendents, brothers Bill and Ross Spence, kicked things off in 1973 in a legendary tin shed in Swanson, West Auckland. Matua is now owned by American/Australian company Beringer Blass/ Fosters with large volume exports.

Meanwhile, in the shop there are labels everywhere. The range confuses even top wine critics. No less than eight labels cover 23 wines, from the basic Settlers range at about $11 a bottle through to Ararimu at about $40 a bottle. Generally about ten wines are on offer for tasting, across the board. A children's playground is a welcome diversion for the kids.

Notable Wines

Shingle Peak Pinot Gris and Pinot Noir, Matheson Chardonnay and Syrah, Judd Estate Chardonnay and Gewürztraminer, Ararimu Chardonnay.

Food

The Hunting Lodge Restaurant is open Wednesday–Sunday from 11.30 am onwards. Superb food, great service. Definitely book ahead 09 411 8259.

West Brook Winery

215 Ararimu Valley Road
Kumeu
09 411 9924 www.westbrook.co.nz
Open Monday–Friday 9.00 am–5.00 pm, Saturday 10.00 am–5.00 pm, Sunday 11.00 am–5.00 pm

About ten minutes away, just before Riverhead Forest, is the turnoff to West Brook. West Brook's new winery complex has landscaped manicured lawns leading down to a duck pond with rows of vines beyond.

Third generation Croatian winemaker Anthony Ivicevich and his charming wife Susan own the operation, which produces about 40,000 cases per year. The original family vineyard was planted in Henderson in 1937, but in 1998 they relocated to the new site. Every Labour Weekend, they host a food, wine and jazz festival, with hearty food, wines by the glass and swing jazz to relax to. Last year, a young woman, egged on by mates and (ahem) a 'happy' crowd, swam across the duck pond for $500.

Notable wines

West Brook Riesling, Blue Ridge Sauvignon Blanc, Blue Ridge Chardonnay, Blue Ridge Pinot Noir.

Vineyard dogs

Jessie and occasional vineyard dog Tessa.

Food

Small selection of snacks, cheeses, and deli goods from the cooler. Picnickers welcome: tables, petanque and stunning views await you.

Hallertau Brew Bar and Restaurant

1171 Coatesville–Riverhead Highway (drive through the forest and on to State Highway 28)
09 412 5555 www.hallertau.co.nz
Open Tuesday–Sunday 11.00 am–late

Okay it's not strictly a wine tasting, but you can sample beers and fruit wines. Hallertau is a microbrewery producing naturally brewed German-style hop beers, and a line of fruit wines. You can do a tasting 'paddle' — a wooden paddle with five beers ($8), or four fruit wines (nashi, kiwifruit, boysenberry, feijoa) ($6). Good lively restaurant with varied menu made from local and seasonal produce.

Waimauku/ Huapai weekend — Sunday

Coopers Creek

601 State Highway 16 (just north of Kumeu)
Huapai
09 412 8560 www.cooperscreek.co.nz
Open Monday–Friday 9.30 am–5.30 pm, Saturday and Sunday 10.30 am–5.30 pm

Established in 1980. Andrew Hendry and his wife Cindy are majority shareholders in this company, a medium-sized operation making about 150,000 cases of wine per year. Simon Nunns is winemaker. Over 60 per cent is exported to America, Canada and Europe. Grapes grown on the property are malbec, merlot and pinot gris. Others are sourced mainly from Hawke's Bay and Marlborough.

Fermentation tanks, grape press and other hardware are in full view, under a large tin roof. The cellar door facility has a relaxed rustic-style interior. A warm open fire welcomes guests in winter.

In February, they have live jazz on Sundays from 12.00 noon by the picnic tables, gardens, pond and sculpture works.

Notable Wines

Reserve label (about $25): look out for Sauvignon Blanc, Pinot Noir, and estate-grown flagship Merlot 'The Gardener'. Select Vineyard Viognier and Hawke's Bay Cabernet Sauvignon/Cabernet Franc. And — I have to mention it — Cat's Pee on a Gooseberry Bush, actually a very drinkable Marlborough savvy but a lot of people buy it just for the label.

Vineyard dog

Crocus — standard poodle.

Food

Cheese platters and wines by the glass.

Then lunch at . . .

Blossoms Espresso Café

Corner State Highway 16 and Riverhead-Coatesville State Highway 28
Kumeu
09 412 6071
Closed Mondays

Nestled next to a Braeburn apple orchard, Blossoms provides generous café lunch fare, freshly made on the premises plus excellent espresso and a cake display to die for. Try the raspberry meringue slice or the macadamia and toffee nut cake. Fully licensed and BYO.

And after lunch . . .

Prenzel Kumeu
325 State Highway 16
Huapai (opposite Autoclean car wash)
09 4127550

Award-winning products containing no artificial additives or flavours. Schnapps, pure fruit brandies, liqueurs and ice cream toppings, plus relishes, vinaigrettes, infused olive oils, rice bran oils and goodies. All available for free tasting. You are likely to be offered a Rigid Richard as you walk in the door. Relax — it's a butterscotch Schnapps and butterscotch cream shooter.

Places to eat

Jaffa Café
3 Matua Road
Huapai
09 412 7127
Open Monday–Thursday 8.00 am–4.00 pm, dinner available Friday–Sunday

Bright, new and spacious. Offers good standard café brunch and lunch food at around $16 a meal. Also fully licensed with a great wine list, tapas nibbles are available after 5.00 pm.

Gracehill Vineyard Restaurant
34 Pomona Road
Kumeu
09 412 8622 www.gracehill.co.nz

Fine dining — on a par with Matua Valley's Hunting Lodge. Gracehill Vineyard Restaurant is a functions specialist mainly catering for group bookings, however they do open on special days like Valentines Day, Mother's Day and Father's Day, plus they run a regular Italian 'long table' food and wine night.

Things to do

Spa Di Vine
12 Taylor Road
Waimauku
09 411 5290   www.spadivine.co.nz

They specialise in 'grape-inspired treatments', using beneficial antioxidants and polyphenol products from grape seeds, skins and juice. Indulge and relax after all that strenuous grape-inspired drinking and food sampling. Facials, massage, body wraps etc.

Places to stay

Calico Lodge B&B
250 Matua Road
Kumeu
09 412 8167   www.calicolodge.co.nz

From $140 to $195 for a double/twin room. Lovely rural setting. Sparkling clean with 4-star Qualmark rating.

Vineyard Cottages Luxury B&B
1011 Old North Road
Waimauku
0800 846 800   www.vineyardcottages.co.nz

Individual rustic cottages nestled in the countryside near Matua winery. King-size beds, luxury appointments and superb room service menu, or wander over to five-star fine dining at the Hunting Lodge. $255 a night.

Greater Auckland

Like its close relatives, Kumeu and Henderson, Greater Auckland tends to get overlooked as a wine-growing region. Yet it can claim New Zealand's third largest producer, Villa Maria, and a number of very successful boutique wineries.

Around 125 centimetres of rain per year ensures plenty of natural irrigation and the rolling rural pasturelands are lush green all year round. Long established as a fertile market garden area, Greater Auckland's heavy clay soils and summer humidity, paradoxically, present challenges to wine growers. Grape vines perform much better when stressed by stony soils and hot dry weather. However, careful site selection and vineyard management can still produce some superb wines.

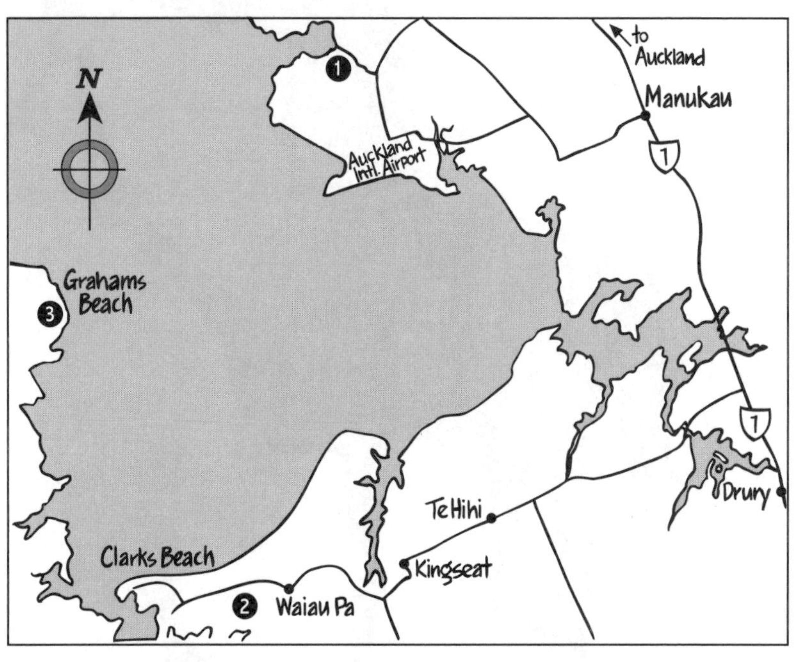

N
to Auckland
Manukau
1
Auckland Intl. Airport
1
Grahams Beach
3
1
Te Hihi
Drury
Kingseat
Clarks Beach
2
Waiau Pa

Villa Maria Estate

118 Montgomerie Road (heading toward Auckland Airport, turn right off George Bolt Memorial Drive, straight ahead through the next two roundabouts and on your left)
Mangere
09 2550666 www.villamaria.co.nz
Open Monday–Friday 9.00 am–6.00 pm, weekends 10.00 am–5.00 pm, winery tours by appointment

Villa Maria is New Zealand's second largest wine producer, established in 1961, owned and managed by industry legend George Fistonich. Villa Maria has been a top producer for many years, with hundreds of awards and accolades both here and overseas. Under the company mantle are brands starting with Riverstone (around $12), Private Bin (around $18), Cellar Selection (around $25), Reserve ($30–$60) and the top end Single Vineyard ($35–$70). Esk Valley and Vidal are separate labels also owned by the company (see the Hawke's Bay section of this book). The Mangere winery is a new state-of–the-art facility with bottling hall, administration, concert venue and large function facilities.

Notable wines

They are all very good. And, you do get what you pay for — the premium wines are superb but more expensive. There is a charge for tasting, depending on your preferences.

Food

Platters are available: bread and dips ($15), cheese and fruit ($30), meat platter ($45).

Karaka Point Vineyard

35C Wallace Drive
Waiau Pa
Clarks Beach
Franklin
09 232 0025 www.karakapointvineyard.co.nz
Open Wednesday–Sunday 12.00 noon–5.00 pm, other days by appointment

Karaka Point Vineyard and Lodge is located on the Karaka Peninsula in southwest Auckland. Established in 1994 by the late Mik Martin, his wife Anne and their three daughters, the location was chosen for its gentle maritime climate and free-draining soils. Anne's labour of love — the estate gardens and lakes — provide an ideal area for visitors to picnic and wander.

Notable wine

Chardonnay ($20).

Food

Platters by arrangement. They also do a 'De Vine Tasting and Picnic' package at $45 per person which includes a personalised wine tasting and picnic hamper. For groups of ten or more, by arrangement, there is a tasting and garden tour with a souvenir wine glass ($10 per head).

Accommodation

Luxurious master suite in the lodge with antiques, fine linens and designer ensuite. Incorporates a French, antique-style living area for dining and relaxing by the fire with a movie, or just lounging back with a glass of good wine. Breakfast included plus access to indoor heated pool.

Awhitu Wines

31 Greenock Drive
Graham's Beach
Waiuku
09 235 1465 www.awhituwines.co.nz
Open weekends and occasionally weekdays, best to phone ahead

Wendy and Dave Hendl grow solely chardonnay and syrah in their boutique vineyard on the Awhitu Peninsula, with winemaking by busy local freelancer Shayne Cox. The vineyard sits on the eastern side of the peninsula, near Graham's Beach.

Notable wines

Chardonnay ($25), Syrah ($30). Both wines very highly rated by Michael Cooper.

Food

N/A

Places to eat

Bracu Restaurant
Simunovich Estate
49 Main Road
Bombay
09 236 1030 www.simuolive.co.nz
Open Wednesday–Sunday 10.30 am–late, dinner from 6.00 pm onwards

Situated in a historic kauri villa on the Simunovich olive oil estate, Bracu offers high-end dining featuring the best of New Zealand seafood and meats. Entrées about $18, mains around $38.

Palazzo Roma
31 Creek Street
Drury
Papakura District
09 294 9004
Open Wednesday–Saturday for lunch and dinner, on Sundays lunch only

French and Italian-style restaurant on the site of Phoenix Italia with outdoor ceramics statues, fountains and bird baths.

Places to stay

No. 40 Carlton Gardens

40 Carlton Road
Pukekohe
09 239 0048 www.no40.co.nz

No. 40 is a spacious and comfortable home in an award-winning private garden setting that looks out on to a mature New Zealand native bush reserve. Two suite options and two room options. Qualmark 4-star. Tariff around $150 a night. Special package deals available.

Brookfield Lodge B&B

2114 State Highway 1
Bombay
09 236 0775 027 292 1422

Twenty-five minutes from Auckland Airport, Brookfield Lodge is set in two hectares (five acres) with established trees, lawns and gardens. Sunny patios surround the house. Spoil yourself with fresh flowers, bathrobes, hairdryers, complimentary tea, good coffee and home baking. Tariff: $130.

Touchwood Motor Lodge

146 Edinburgh Street
Pukekohe
0800 258 348 www.motorlodge.co.nz

Affordable motel option within walking distance of Pukekohe shopping centre. Ten studios, plus one- and two-bedroom units. All rooms have access to wireless internet with the first two hours/200 mb free of charge. Tariff: studio $105, one-bed $130, two-bed $140, spa unit $145.

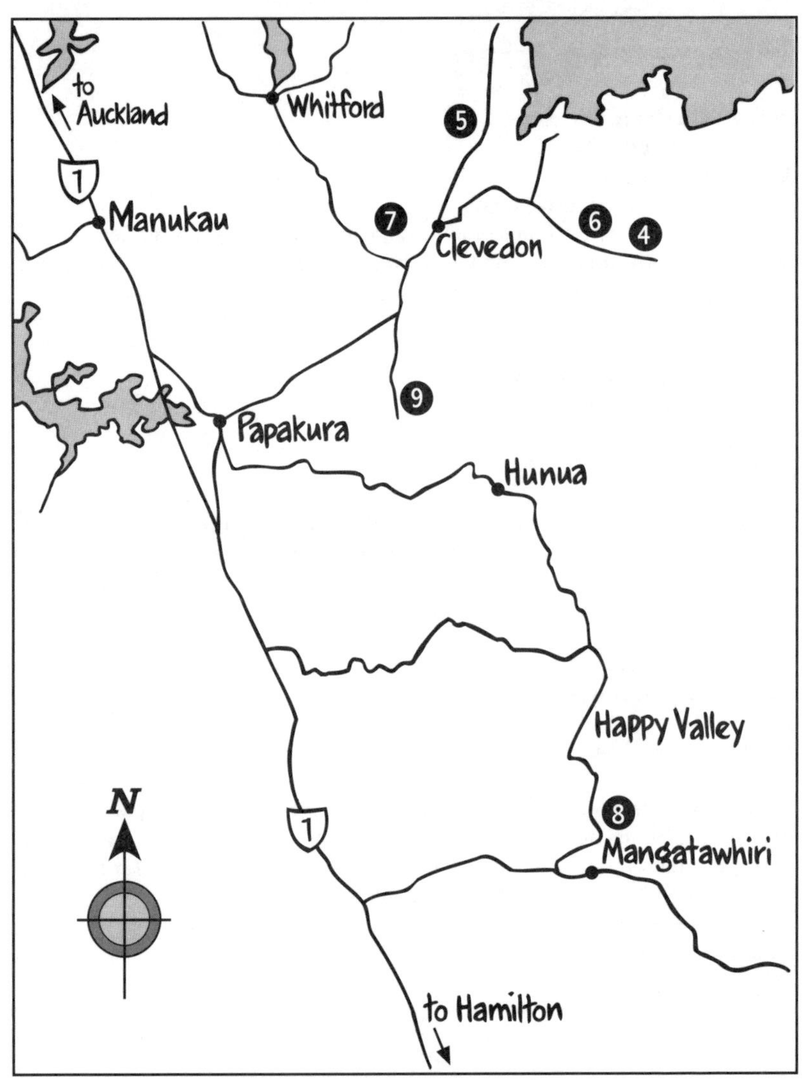
to
Auckland
Whitford
5
1
Manukau
7
Clevedon
6
4
9
Papakura
Hunua
Happy Valley
N
8
1
Mangatawhiri
to Hamilton

Clevedon

Just a 40-minute drive south of Auckland City and Auckland International Airport, Clevedon is a good choice for an afternoon drive or a weekend retreat. Again, a very minor player in terms of New Zealand wine production, but there are some very good wines being grown in the local microclimate terroir.

Speciality grape varieties grown in the region include sangiovese, dolcetto, barbera and montepulciano. For local information, stop at the Clevedon Information Centre, which is located inside the Clevedon Gallery near the roundabout on the main road. Here you can pick up a map of the area with all the local attractions — vineyards, bush walks, cafés, shops and much more.

South Auckland weekend — Sunday

Inverness Estate

Ness Valley Road
Clevedon
09 292 8710 www.inverness.co.nz
Open weekends 10.00 am–4.00 pm

John and Yo Robinson run an upmarket colonial-style B&B and small wine estate in the Ness Valley about ten kilometres from Clevedon. Plantings consist of chardonnay, sémillon and cabernet franc. Their first vintage was in 1999.

Notable wines

Chardonnay ($20), Cabernet Franc ($20).

Accommodation

Inverness Lodge is modelled on the classical colonial country home and offers four luxury suites with ensuite — three doubles (two Super-King and one Queen) and one Super-King twin. Tariff: double or twin $421 per person, single occupancy $478.

Puriri Hills Vineyard and Lodge

398 North Road
Clevedon
Papakura
09 292 9264 www.puririhills.co.nz
Open weekends 11.00 am–4.00 pm

Look out for the green sign at the gate on North Road. In 1997 Judy and Paul Fowler planted the first 1.5 hectares (4 acres) of their estate in merlot and cabernet franc. The following years saw planting of malbec, cabernet sauvignon and further cabernet franc. The total vineyard area is now about 2.25 hectares (6 acres). Their northeast sloping vineyard faces Waiheke Island. The aim is to produce complex, restrained wines in the style of the St Emilion Bordeaux reds. Wine critics Michael Cooper and Bob Campbell are huge fans.

Notable wines

Puriri Hills Estate ($35), Puriri Hills Reserve ($60), Puriri Hills Pope ($120).

Accommodation

Upmarket luxury B&B with dinner available. Self-contained in one wing of the main house, the suite has its own entrance, a living room, a dining room and kitchen facilities, two bedrooms and a bathroom looking into a private walled fern garden. Tariff: $663. A Queen-size room with ensuite in the main house includes a private terrace with rural views. Tariff: $282, with each additional person at $113.

Dinners feature the best of New Zealand's produce: lamb, venison, local fish and oysters, handmade cheeses and, naturally, the wines of Clevedon.

Rannach Vineyard

308 Ness Valley Road
Clevedon
09 292 8828 021 905 754 www.rannach.co.nz
Open weekends 10.00 am–5.00 pm

Tony and Christine Morgan just do one thing — merlot. A rosé style and three vintages of their 100 per cent merlot are on offer at their tasting room in the Ness Valley, near Clevedon.

Notable wines

Rannach Reserve ($30) and Rannach 2005 Merlot ($30), Merlot 2003 and 2004 ($20), Rosé 2006 ($18).

Food

N/A

Twilight Vineyards

105 Twilight Road
Clevedon
09 292 9502 027 212 4583 www.twilightvineyards.com
Open seven days January–February 11.00 am–4.00 pm, November–March Thursday–Sunday, April–October weekends and Public Holidays

Established in 1996 by Bruce and Joy Peart on eight hectares (20 acres) in the Clevedon Valley, just one kilometre from Clevedon Village. With additional fruit from their own vineyard in Gisborne's Ormond region, they produce around 4000 cases a year.

Notable wines

Gisborne Chardonnay ($19), Clevedon Pinot Gris ($19), Clevedon Chenin Blanc $20, Diamonds and Pearls Sparkling Muscat ($17).

Firstland Wines

500 Lyons Road
Heritage Hotel and Spa du Vin
Mangatawhiri
09 233 6304 www.firstland.co.nz
Open seven days from 9.30 am–5.00 pm

One of those wine labels that have had an identity crisis over the years. Formerly de Redcliffe, then Châteaux de Redcliffe, now Firstland. New American owners Edward and Barbara Aster have taken over the boutique luxury hotel and spa complex, which is now part of the Heritage hotel chain. Two ranges of wines — Firstland Range around $25 and the Leeward Landing range at about $10 a bottle.

Notable wines

Reserve Marlborough Chardonnay ($25), Hawke's Bay Cabernet Merlot ($25).

Accommodation

Forty-eight private chalets set in lush gardens with spacious bathrooms, towelling robes and subtle furnishings all provide a private getaway.

Food

The Vineyard Restaurant is open from 7.00 am weekdays, and 8.00 am on weekends for breakfast, lunch and dinner. Dine indoors or outside on the terrace. The Vineyard Grill is about $30 with selected quality meats: Scotch fillet, lamb rack, free-range pork chop, with a choice of sauces from red wine jus, Béarnaise to Dianne green peppercorn. The standard menu includes Italian inspired entrées and mains for about $20.

Vin Alto

424 Creightons Road
Clevedon
Papakura
09 292 8845 www.vinalto.com
Open seven days 9.30 am–4.30 pm, phone ahead

Winemakers Enzo Bettio and his wife Margaret have 15 hectares (37 acres) on the northern fringe of the Hunua Ranges, overlooking the Coromandel Peninsula and Waiheke Island. Vin Alto boasts the largest selection of Italian grape varieties in Australasia, with plantings of white varieties — chardonnay, arneis and pinot grigio (pinot gris) — and red variety nebbiolo. The winemaking uses traditional methods as used in Italian amarone and ripasso wines. Grapes are dried on racks, concentrating the sugars and flavours and naturally decreasing acidity. Their first vintage was in 1996. Enzo also imports Italian gourmet deli goods under the well-known Delmaine label, and has a deer farm on the estate.

Notable wines

La Riserva Chardonnay ($25), Pinot Grigio ($22), Retico Amarone style, ($85), Ritorno Ripasso style ($85), Vin Santo dessert ($33). Also a range of liqueurs — Cassis (blackcurrant), Limoncello (lemon), Liqueur di Café (espresso coffee) and Mandarinello (mandarin).

Food

Sunday lunch includes a five-course meal with wines to match at $89 per person. Traditional northern Italian fare includes aperitif, breads, cheeses, main, dessert and coffee. The children's menu is available at $40.

Places to eat

Clevedon Café

1 North Road
Clevedon Village
09 292 8111

Local produce is matched with local wines in this country-style café. Open seven days for lunch and snacks, and dinner Wednesday to Sunday. Dinner reservations are recommended.

Log Cabin Café and Bar

442 North Road
Clevedon
09 292 8895 www.logcabincafe.co.nz

Rustic café in a garden setting with working water wheel and sheltered courtyard. Light snacks and salads through to hearty country fare and desserts are available.

Wairoa Pub

26 Kawakawa Bay Road
Clevedon
09 292 8783

Good pub food, mainly local fresh seafood, produce and wines. Open seven days. Breakfast/lunch from 9.00 am. Dinner from 5.30 pm.

Things to do

Clevedon Village Farmers' Market

Clevedon A&P Showgrounds
Monument Road
Clevedon
021 523 616 www.clevedonfarmersmarket.co.nz
Every Sunday morning 8.30 am–12.00 pm

Buy locally grown and freshly made produce — vegetables, fruit, flowers, herbs, plants, meat, poultry, fish, seedlings, seeds, nuts, cheese, coffee, pickles, preserves, sauces, baking, eggs, bread, confectionary, wine, beer, juice and homemade cordials.

McNicol Homestead and Museum

McNicol Road
Clevedon
09 292 8421
Open Saturday, Sunday and Public Holidays 1.00 pm–5.00 pm

View Clevedon's history, household antiques and farming implements used by the area's early settlers.

Pukerau Four Wheel Drive

50 Townson Road
Clevedon
09 292 2825 www.pukerau.co.nz
Open by arrangement

A comprehensive range of four-wheel-drive trips into the scenic hill tops behind Kawakawa Bay and over into the Orere Valley. You can take the wheel yourself or enjoy the trip as a passenger.

Clevedon Coast Oysters

914 Clevedon Kawakawa Bay Road
09 292 8017 www.clevedonoysters.co.nz
Open Monday–Friday 7.00 am–4.30 pm, Saturday 9.00 am–2.00 pm, Sunday 10.00 am–4.00 pm

Fresh organic export-quality oysters available year round. USFDA certified — gotta be good for you.

Clevedon Chocolate Shop

31 Main Road
Clevedon
09 292 3091 www.clevedonchocolateshop.co.nz
Open seven days from 9.30 am–5.00 pm

Tony and Alison Shrigley retired from the corporate world to follow their dream of working in the Clevedon area. They specialise in handmade chocolates, Turkish delight, sugar-free sweets, coffee, gifts and gift baskets made to order.

The Italian Kitchen Table

9 Main Road
Clevedon
09 292 8897
Open seven days

Extensive range of Italian and local gourmet products. Enjoy a cappuccino, panini or cake and pick up a loaf of fresh-baked bread. Take the time to browse the gifts, kitchenware and cookbooks during your visit.

The Italian Country Market

439 Papakura–Clevedon Road
09 292 9229
Open seven days

Italian speciality store, full of deli goodies, plus premium fruit and vegetables, Italian meats, cheeses, pastas and much more.

Places to stay

Crabtree Farm Vineyard and Lodge

186 Twilight Road
Clevedon
09 292 9186 www.crabtreefarm.co.nz

Crabtree Farm is a retreat, set in a valley of 40 hectares (100 acres), just two kilometres from Clevedon Village and just a short distance from the Pohutukawa Coast beaches. The barn is a renovated woolshed in the style of a New York loft with cast iron bathtub, fine linens, and Super-King bed. Tariff: $250 per night for two people. Includes a farmhouse breakfast. Candlelight suppers and al fresco lunches and activities are available by arrangement.

Fairfield B&B Homestay

Kawakawa Road
Clevedon
09 292 8852
Email: fairfieldretreat@clear.net.nz

Homestay in a peaceful rural setting. Spacious room with ensuite, fridge, coffee and tea-making facilities, private courtyard and your own entrance.

Kitenga Luxury B&B

700 North Road
Clevedon
09 292 8032 021 973 799 www.kitenga.co.nz

Indulge in luxury Qualmark 4-star-plus accommodation in a secluded rural setting with panoramic views of Clevedon Valley and the Hauraki Gulf, just 40-minutes drive from Auckland City. Relax and unwind, or visit Clevedon's attractions. Enjoy a long soak in the hot spa pool in winter, or a refreshing swim in the pool in summer. Tariff: $250 per night or $400 for a weekend.

Waiheke Island

About 30 years ago, Waiheke was seen as a quaint, if backward, rural weekend retreat for Aucklanders with a holiday home. As for the locals, they earned Waiheke the nickname Cadbury Island (full of fruits and nuts). It is true that Waiheke was a haven for artists, old hippies, dope growers, alternative lifestylers — and combinations of all the above.

Now, of course, many Aucklanders are kicking themselves that they didn't invest in land in what is now premium, million dollar-plus real estate, and one of the trendiest boutique wine regions in New Zealand. The Waiheke microclimate, generally a few degrees warmer than Auckland, helps to ripen red grape varieties like cabernet sauvignon, merlot, grenache and mourvèdre. A tourist mecca in summer, Waiheke's wine, food and stunning views of the Hauraki Gulf draw both local and international visitors. Throughout the year it is also a popular venue for VIP and corporate long lunches, where guests are sometimes helicoptered in.

For the motivated independent traveller lacking a helicopter, the trip is a short 35-minute ferry ride from downtown Auckland's Ferry Terminal. At the other end you can hire a car, or catch a taxi or bus. Alternatively, Sealink can take your car (drive-on/drive-off) on their ferry from Half Moon Bay.

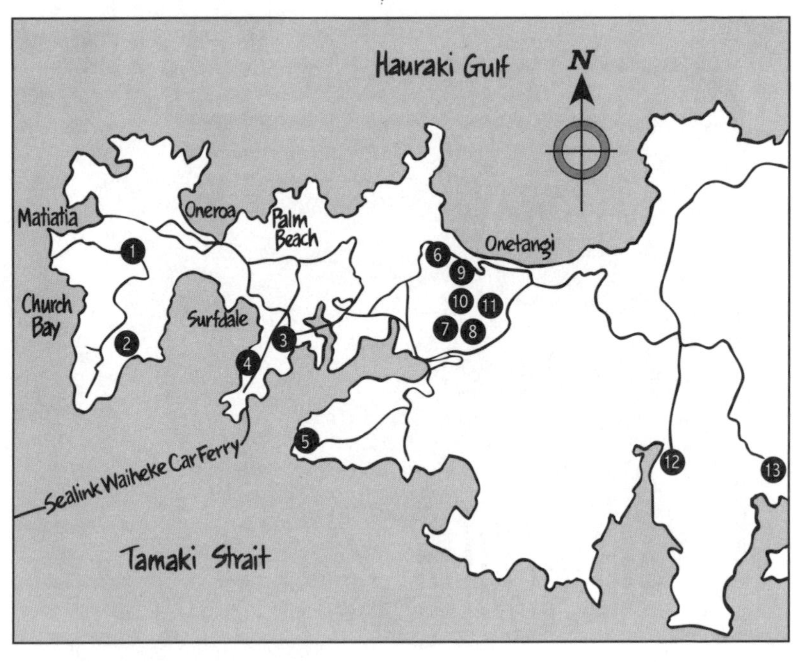
Hauraki Gulf
N
Matiatia
Oneroa
Palm Beach
Onetangi
Church Bay
Surfdale
1
2
3
4
5
6
7
8
9
10
11
12
13
Sealink Waiheke Car Ferry
Tamaki Strait

1

Cable Bay Vineyards

12 Nick Johnstone Drive
Church Bay
Oneroa
09 372 5889 www.cablebayvineyards.co.nz
Open seven days from 11.00 am–5.00 pm

The brand new complex reflects the many different functions of Cable Bay's operations. The main building houses the winery, restaurant, wine bar, tasting room and The Motukaha Room — a private room for meetings. An 'Artspace' in the main building hosts exhibitions, and in the outdoors there are regular sculpture exhibitions — most recently works by one of New Zealand's foremost kinetic sculptors Phil Price. Ownership is by a group of partners, along with winemaker and manager Neil Culley (ex-Babich wines). Total area is around 24 hectares (60 acres) from ten sites around the island. They also own 34 hectares (84 acres) in Marlborough where they source pinot noir and sauvignon blanc. Tastings $5 for six wines.

Notable wines

Waiheke Chardonnay ($34), Five Hills Merlot Malbec Cabernet ($34).

Food

Cable Bay Restaurant serves lunch seven days from midday to 3.00 pm. Dinner is served seven days from 6.00 pm. The restaurant seats 75 inside and 35 in the al fresco courtyard.

Accommodation

Winemakers Loft

Bookings: 09 372 9384 021 510 189
www.winemakersloft.co.nz

Queen-size bedroom with luxury linen, ensuite with shower, basic kitchenette and spectacular sea views back to the lights of Auckland City. Tariff: $220 per night (includes provisions for a self-catered breakfast and a complimentary bottle of Cable Bay wine). Surcharge of $50 for a one-night stay.

2 Mudbrick Vineyard and Restaurant

Church Bay Road
Oneroa
09 372 9050   www.mudbrick.co.nz
Open all year round, but hours are slightly shorter during the colder months, summer season seven days from 10.30 am until approx 5.00 pm

Well-respected wines and a restaurant with a million-dollar hilltop view mark Mudbrick as a must-see winery on Waiheke. Seven hectares (17 acres) are planted in Bordeaux reds, chardonnay and syrah.

Former accountants Robyn and Nicholas Jones purchased bare land on a lifestyle block in 1992 when Nicholas was 28 and Robyn was 27. After many years of hard yakka, disasters and triumphs, their original mud brick barn and vineyards grew to become the hugely successful venture that they still own and operate today. High-end dining and a large wine list add to the prestige of visiting Mudbrick.

Notable wines

Reserve Syrah ($42), Reserve Cabernet Sauvignon ($45), Merlot Cabernet Sauvignon ($30), Shepherd's Point Merlot ($38).

Food

Mudbrick Restaurant

Entrées include seared New Zealand scallops, heirloom radish, garden vegetables, and confit peach vinaigrette ($25). Mains include New Zealand pure black Angus grass-fed eye fillet, with confit shallots, pommes Pont Neuf, and Mudbrick Merlot Cabernet jelly, cooked to your specifications ($40). Sides include mint roasted gourmet and Jersey Benne potatoes ($8). Top it all off with pineapple and lime sorbet 'ravioli', citrus salad, sake vanilla soup ($16). Their cellar door also sells cheese and olive platters for casual picnic-style dining.

Vineyard dogs

Sweep — female fox terrier rabbit hunter. Walter — chihuahua/miniature poodle cross. Very cute, but don't tell Sweep.

Goldwater Estate

18 Causeway Road
Putiki Bay
09 372 7493 www.goldwater.co.nz
Open seven days December–February 12.00 pm–4.00 pm, March–November Wednesday–Friday 12.00 noon–2.00 pm, Saturday and Sunday 12.00 noon–4.00 pm

Kim and Jeanette Goldwater established the island's very first vineyard back in 1978. Since then, they have clocked up numerous awards for their wines, both in New Zealand and overseas. And now they also own vineyards in Marlborough and Hawke's Bay's Gimblett Gravels region. The home vineyard has 14 hectares (35 acres) of clay-based hillside soils, planted with cabernet sauvignon, merlot, cabernet franc and chardonnay.

Notable wines

Boatshed Chardonnay ($20), Zell Chardonnay ($30), Esslin Merlot ($90) with four stars from Michael Cooper, Woods Hill Cabernet/Merlot ($25), Goldie — premium — Cabernet/Merlot ($70) with five stars from Michael Cooper.

Food

Experience the Long Lunch held on the last Friday of every month. Arrive at 12.30 pm. Begin with a glass of Goldwater wine and canapés. Then sit yourself down at long communal tables. Lunch service begins at 1.00 pm with six savoury courses, a cheese course and a sweet course to finish. Cost: $65 a head. Bookings essential. To reserve your place, you can either book online or phone 09 372 7493.

Vineyard dog (part time)

Shanti — lab/border collie/staffy/confused.

Waiheke weekend one — Sunday

Kennedy Point Vineyard

44 Donald Bruce Road
Kennedy Point
09 372 5600 www.kennedypointvineyard.com
Open Tuesday–Friday 10.00 am–2.00 pm, Saturday 12.00 noon–4.00 pm

Hawaiian couple Susan McCarthy and Neil Kunimura fell in love with Waiheke on a visit from home and ended up buying a vineyard. Thirteen years later, they operate onsite accommodation and cellar door, with a reputation for red wines. Established in 1996, Kennedy Point Vineyard is planted on 5.5 hectares (13.5 acres) of steep north-facing slopes, on a warm protected site. Plantings consist of cabernet sauvignon, merlot, malbec, cabernet franc, syrah and viognier. In addition, they have 150 olive trees on the property from which they press their own oil. Wine and olive oil tasting $5 per person.

Notable wines

Waiheke Cabernet Sauvignon ($35), Reserve Cabernet Sauvignon ($45), Syrah ($35), Merlot/Malbec ($25).

Food

Platters available in summer.

Accommodation

Vineyard Guesthouse

Two nights' minimum booking required. Relax, surrounded by one of the oldest and largest stands of pohutukawa on the island. Options include one-bedroom with ensuite, lounge and kitchen/dining area for two people, $200 per night, two-bedroom suite with bathroom, lounge and mini bar for four people, $200 per night (no cooking facility); complete house with three bedrooms, two bathrooms, two lounges, and kitchen/dining area for six people, $375 per night (includes bed and bath linens, TV, stereo and BBQ).

5 Te Whau Vineyard

218 Te Whau Drive
Te Whau Peninsula
09 372 7191 www.tewhau.co.nz
Open six days November–April 11.00 am-5.00 pm (closed Tuesday), Easter–end October Friday, Saturday and Sunday for lunch 11.00 am–4.30 pm, also open for dinners on Saturday nights throughout the year

Another very high-profile winery and restaurant, Te Whau sits atop the Te Whau Peninsula, looking oddly similar to those old abandoned gun emplacements, with expansive views extending from Coromandel to Auckland City and Rangitoto. Winemaking and barrel storage is directly under the restaurant. Just 2.5 hectares (6 acres) is planted in chardonnay, cabernet sauvignon, merlot, cabernet franc and malbec. The vineyard is sited on a steep north-facing, 20-degree slope, just back from the headland.

Owners Tony and Moira Forsyth produced their first wine in 1999 and have gained many accolades and awards for their chardonnay and Bordeaux-style reds.

Notable wines

Chardonnay — five stars from Michael Cooper ($75). The Point — four stars ($60), blended red from their Bordeaux varieties.

Food

Restaurant seats just 60 punters and tends to get booked heavily in summer. *Wine Spectator* magazine describes it as 'One of the best restaurants in the world for wine lovers'. Given that, the prices are pretty reasonable. Entrées about $20 and mains $38. The food is uncomplicated, using fresh local ingredients, and is designed to complement their enormous (600 bottles) wine list. Starter: fresh half dozen tempura Te Matuku Bay oysters with spring onion and Sauce Vincent. Main: twice-cooked duck, vanilla carrots, oyster mushrooms, green apple aioli, duck jus. Sides of veggies or salad around $12. Booking is recommended 09 372 7191.

Vineyard cats

Mr Malbec and Miss Merlot — both Burmese.

Obsidian Vineyard

Te Makiri Road
Onetangi
09 372 6100 027 240 1564 www.obsidian.co.nz
Open seven days Labour weekend–end Easter, 11.00 am–4.00 pm

Nestled in the Onetangi Valley, and first planted in 1993 with a focus on French red varieties, Obsidian has expanded its repertoire to include some Italian grapes. Coopers Creek owner Andrew Hendry is one of a group of investors who took over in 1996. Tasting is done in an unpretentious outdoor venue. Weeping Sands is their second-tier label, taking its name from the English translation of the Maori name 'Onetangi'.

Notable wines

Weeping Sands Cabernet Merlot ($24), Weeping Sands Merlot Cabernet ($25).

Food

N/A — picnickers welcome.

Vineyard dog

Manni, Lowchen (Little Lion Dog), cellar door receptionist. Bad habit — chasing Miss Kitty, the winemaker's cat. Revenge — being chased by Miss Kitty.

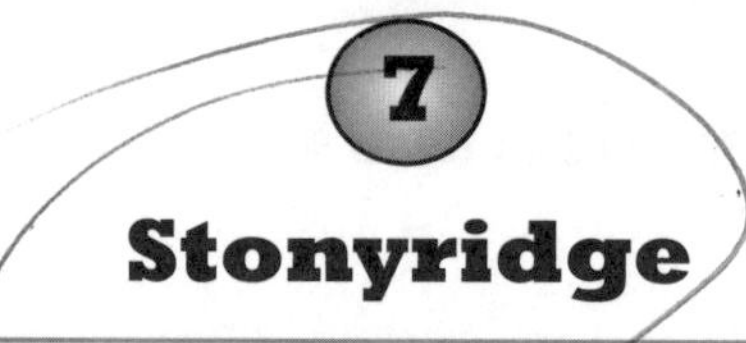

Stonyridge

80 Onetangi Road
09 372 8822 www.stonyridge.co.nz
Open seven days 11.30 am–5.00 pm for lunch and tastings

Iconic is an overused word, but Stonyridge definitely qualifies. The superb blended Bordeaux-style red, Larose Cabernets, is world famous. Michael Cooper lists Larose as his sole 'super classic' New Zealand cabernet dominant blend. I have been lucky enough to get a bottle or two. It is a gorgeous wine — complex, ripe and dense, with black fruit, herbal and spice flavours — best cellared for about ten years. Now the bad news — about $150 a bottle, if you can get hold of it. Most fans buy it 'en primeur', that is they pay for it before it is released at a better price than standard retail. But to do so you need to be on a restricted mailing list, and anyone caught on-selling the individually numbered bottles is kicked out of the club forthwith. Boo hoo. Weep into that cheap Aussie red, loser.

Grape varieties in the Larose are cabernet sauvignon (predominantly), cabernet franc, malbec, and petit verdot. The vineyard also grows other French varieties — syrah, merlot, grenache and mourvèdre. A new-ish entry-level label, Fallen Angel, uses fruit sourced from outside Waiheke and includes a sparkler, pinot noir, viognier and dessert wine. Prices $25–$40.

Owner and winemaker Steve White runs his vineyard on totally organic principles.

Notable wines

Larose Cabernets as above, Airfield Cabernet Sauvignon, Merlot and Cabernet Franc blend ($50), Pilgrim Syrah, Merlot, Grenache and Mourvèdre ($90), Luna Negra Malbec ($70).

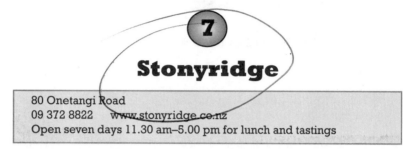

Food

Veranda Café

Same hours as the winery. Very popular spot for the Waiheke visitor. The rambling and rustic cellar door and café building offers views from the terrace over the vineyards. Renowned for excellent food — guests dine outside in summer months or inside near the roaring fire in winter. Menu has local and organic fare wherever possible. Starters: cheeses, bruschetta, tasting plates around $12. Mains: lamb shoulder rack infused with organic espresso, on a rosemary pear and potato gratin, pomegranate and baby spinach salad wilted with Stonyridge Jus around $30. Sides of salad and potato etc. are $7. Not surprisingly, the wine list features Stonyridge wines.

Vineyard dog

Norton — black lab (bird control).

Vineyard cat

Morris (dog control).

Onetangi Road Vineyard

82 Onetangi Road
Onetangi Valley
09 372 1014 www.onetangiroad.co.nz
Open seven days October–April 11.00 am–6.00 pm, May–September 11.00 am–4.00 pm

George and Debbie Craddock have been the owners since 2000 and they oversee a vineyard planted in French red grape varieties. Waiheke Island Brewery also trades onsite, with their dark ale, wheat beer, malt beer, baroona german style and a non-alcoholic ginger beer.

Notable wine

Cabernet/Merlot blend.

Food

Jester Café

Onsite café/tasting room where platters and a bistro blackboard menu are on offer.

Accommodation

One-bedroom country cottage sleeps two. BBQ and tennis court await you.

Miro Vineyard

> Browns Road
> Onetangi
> 09 372 7854 www.mirovineyard.co.nz
> Open Labour weekend–Easter 11.30 am–4.00 pm, rest of the year by appointment only

Cat Vosper and Barnett Bond named the vineyard after their daughter Miro. Cat (Catherine) Vosper is a past president of the Waiheke Winegrowers' Association and she manages the day-to-day running of the vineyard. Barnett is a medical doctor. The tiny 4.2-hectare (10-acre) vineyard specialises in Bordeaux-style reds and produces around 800 cases of wine per year.

Notable wines

The Miro blended red of Cabernet Sauvignon, Merlot, Cabernet Franc, Malbec ($36).

Food

The restaurant serves tapas-style food by chef Sarah La Touché and is open Labour Weekend to Easter. Open 11.30 am–4.00 pm or by appointment.

Events

Miro Vineyard has established a reputation amongst the Waiheke community as a place that knows how to entertain. Guests are treated on a yearly basis to at least one major culinary and cultural attraction, the latest featuring Gary McCormick, Sam Hunt and Tim Shadbolt.

Vineyard dog

Coke — bad habits: surfing and catching birds.

Accommodation

New separate two-person villa in French Provincial style, with views of Onetangi beach. All goodies included — chef's kitchen, complete with Italian espresso machine and gas range, plus breakfast supplies ($220 per couple). Also B&B accommodation in the main house ($90 for one to two persons).

Te Motu Vineyard

76 Onetangi Road
Onetangi Valley
09 372 6884 www.temotu.co.nz
Opening hours change seasonally, and are subject to change, call for enquiries

Terry Dunleavy, former wine industry leader, started things off about ten years ago. Nowadays, his two sons John and Paul have taken over day-to-day business. Previously, Terry was manager of the New Zealand Wine Institute and is now editor of the *New Zealand WineGrower* magazine. In his spare time, he is director of the Royal Easter Wine Awards. It's no wonder that the kids had to take over.

Just two wines are made from red varieties cabernet sauvignon, merlot, cabernet franc, malbec and syrah. The premium wine is Te Motu, a blended red Cabernet/Merlot ($80). The Dunleavy ($40) contains all of the grapes grown on Te Motu Vineyard that are not in the Te Motu blend.

Food

The Shed Restaurant

Another popular spot for dining, The Shed features rustic ambience and vineyard views. The wine list features their own wines, plus some premium French Champagnes, New Zealand sparklers and still whites. Entrées all $17.50. Mains about $35. Desserts around $15. How does Catalan seafood chowder (stew of mussels, cockles, fish and prawns with saffron, almond and parsley) for $37 sound? To finish, baked ginger cheesecake with crystallised ginger and butterscotch sauce, $14.50.

Waiheke weekend two — Sunday

Saratoga Estate Vineyard

72 Onetangi Road
09 372 6450 www.saratogaestate.com
Open summer months Saturday and Sunday 11.00 am–5.00 pm

Formerly Thabo Vineyard, new owners changed the name when they took over in 2002. Not a bad idea. They have 4 hectares (10 acres) of grapes, growing cabernet sauvignon, cabernet franc, merlot, malbec and sangiovese (a rarity). The Spanish Mission-style winery can be booked for weddings and private functions. Tours of Saratoga Estate are by appointment during summer, call Kathy on 0275 658 531.

Notable wines

Bell Tower Cabernets ($35).

Food

Platters and antipasti goodies.

Poderi Crisci

205 Awaawaroa Road
Awaawaroa Bay
09 377 7648 www.podericrisci.co.nz
Open Saturday and Sunday 11.00 am–4.00 pm

Antonio Crisci is bringing a taste of Italy to Waiheke, having just bought the former Christensen Estate property. Ten hectares (25 acres) are exclusively planted in merlot. Visitors are welcomed by a bronze sculpture by Paul Dibble — a female nude who sits and surveys the vineyard.

Notable wines

Wait and see!

Food

Light snacks and good coffee are available.

Passage Rock Wines

438 Orapiu Road
Te Matuku Bay
09 372 7257 www.passagerockwines.co.nz
Open 12 October–24 December Friday–Sunday 12.00 noon–4.00 pm, 27 December–end January seven days 12.00 noon to 4.00 pm, February and March Wednesday–Sunday 12.00 noon–4.00 pm, and April weekends only 12.00 noon–4.00 pm, closed May, June and July

Founders David and Veronika Evans Gander first had the vision of starting a vineyard back in 1991 while touring the Perth wine region of Australia. By 1994, the first vines were planted on Passage Rock Vineyard — located in what their website describes as 'isolated splendour' at the eastern end of Waiheke. Since then, their wines have been awarded many trophies. Their syrah is recognised as one of New Zealand's best, if not the best, and has been awarded six Gold medals. *Cuisine* magazine has also ranked it in New Zealand's top five syrahs for the last three years. David is the winemaker, and produces a blended red, chardonnay, merlot, viognier and syrah.

Notable wines

Viognier (28), Forte blended red ($35). The two Syrahs, standard ($35) and Reserve ($50), were awarded five stars by Michael Cooper.

Food

The café has a pizza menu at about $23, including kids' pizzas for $12. Starters about $15. Platters $28. Mains about $30. Sides about $10. How's roast Marlborough salmon, grilled summer vegetables, local watercress, salmon caviar and lemon ($30), with a side of rocket, pear and parmesan salad ($12)? Dessert: brandied strawberries with meringues and fresh cream ($12).

Things to do

Waiheke Jazz Festival

www.waihekejazz.co.nz

Traditionally held over Easter weekend, featuring the best of New Zealand's jazz musicians, the festival also hosts musicians from all over the world. A must-see for the jazz enthusiast. Five days of local and international jazz acts.

Waiheke Community Cinema

2 Korora Road
09 372 4240 www.wicc.co.nz

Relax on comfy couches and watch a variety of movies in this newly renovated complex.

Ostend Market

Ostend Road
Every Saturday from 8.00 am–12.00 noon
Arts and crafts, homemade preserves, food stalls, jewellery and clothing, books, new and second-hand goods, plus plants, herbal products, soaps, organic products.

Stony Batter

Stony Batter gun emplacement is a 1.3-kilometre walk from the gate. The bottom, eastern end of Waiheke offers great walks out over the Batter with views of Coromandel and several Hauraki Gulf islands. Explore the network of tunnels with a flash light. Or don't. It's your choice. But I'd be packing a cut lunch and compass. Optional tours for cowards like me are available. Total length of the tunnels is about half a mile.

Art

Similar to the alternative and artistic community of Nelson, Waiheke is a focus for artists and craftspeople. Painters, sculptors, potters and many others contribute to Waiheke's lively arts scene.

Places to stay

The Boatshed

Corner Tawa and Huia Streets
Little Oneroa
09 372 3242 021 512 127 www.boatshed.co.nz

High-end luxury accommodation right on the beach at around $600 per night. Choose between a three-storey Lighthouse suite, the Boatsheds right on the beach, or The Bridge — a Super-King suite with spectacular views of Oneroa and the Hauraki Gulf.

The Strand Apartments

Onetangi Beach
09 372 3003 0274 372 333

Purpose-built for optimum privacy and best beach views, these are stylish self-contained luxury apartments with generous decks and patios. Relax with a glass of wine and enjoy the stunning sunsets across the bay. Onetangi Beach with squeaky white sands is just across the road. Some of the island's best bush walks are minutes away at the Forest and Bird Reserve. Tariff: $200–$350 per night.

Island Time Studio Apartment

09 372 3003 0274 372 333

Luxurious studio apartment with spectacular gardens and a path to the sea just minutes from your accommodation. Tariff: $165 for a double.

Connells Bay Cottages and Sculpture Park

Cowes Bay Road
Connells Bay
09 372 8957 www.connellsbay.co.nz

The 100-year-old, self-contained guest cottage is just metres from the beach and nestled among native trees on a 24-hectare (60-acre) property featuring tranquil bush and rolling farmland. Tariff: $350 per couple per night and $50 each extra guest.

An onsite sculpture park is the culmination of John and Jo Gow's vision to unite art and nature by planting sweeps of native trees and creating special spaces for site-specific commissioned New Zealand sculpture. (Open by prior appointment only.)

Giverny Inn

44 Queens Drive
Oneroa
09 372 2200 www.giverny.co.nz

Giverny Inn's guest suite, Bacchus Villa, is a restored, 1939 heritage building with polished wood floors and soft-coloured plastered walls reminiscent of a Tuscany villa. The suite comprises a Queen bedroom, ensuite bathroom, kitchenette and lounge. The villa has a large deck and private garden where guests can pick their own vegetables and herbs. Qualmark 4-star-plus. Tariff: around $400 a night depending on the season. This includes a four-course breakfast, pre-dinner drinks and hors d'oeuvres.

Waikato

Waikato is a small producer (about one per cent of New Zealand's total), but just the same the region has a wine history to contribute to the bigger picture, and also produces some significant wines. In 1903, the New Zealand Viticulture Research Station was established at Te Kauwhata.

Viticulturalist Dr. Richard Smart conducted numerous trial plantings there in the 1980s. This site went on to become Rongopai Wines.

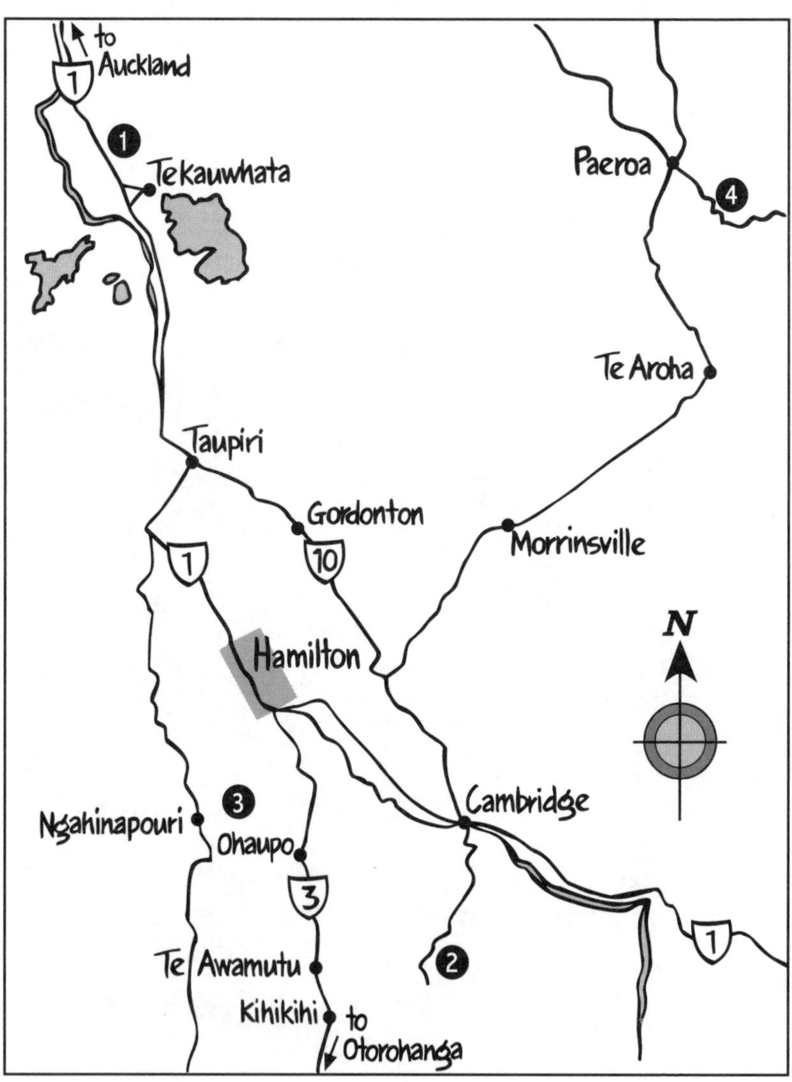

to Auckland
1
Tekauwhata
Paeroa
4
Te Aroha
Taupiri
Gordonton
Morrinsville
1
10
N
Hamilton
3
Ngahinapouri
Ohaupo
Cambridge
3
1
Te Awamutu
2
Kihikihi
to Otorohanga

Cook's Landing

Paddys Road (off State Highway Ten, ten kilometres south of Mercer, about 1.5 kilometres north of Te Kauwhata)
07 826 0004 www.cookslanding.co.nz
Open Monday–Thursday 10.00 am to 3.00 pm, Friday–Sunday 10.00 am–late

Situated in the Old Cook's Winery in Te Kauwhata.

Notable wines

Old Vines Chardonnay and Sauvignon Blanc — made from 30-year-old vines on the property.

Food

Café lunch menu includes panini, pasta, pizza, quiche and open sandwiches for around $14. Dinner menu at around $21 is more restaurant-style fare, such as whole chicken breast stuffed with feta and sun-dried tomatoes on potato rosti, with sides such as fries and salad at about $5.

Events

Check their website for Music in the Vines, St. Patrick's Day Dine and Dance, Harvest Week festival and more.

Judge Valley Vineyard

178 Judge Road
Puahue
Te Awamutu
0800 25 83 43 www.judgevalley.co.nz
Open seven days 10.00 am–5.00 pm, but phone ahead in case they are holding a function

Between Cambridge and Te Awamutu, the Judge Valley Vineyard is nestled in a valley, protected from cold southerlies. Owner and manager Kevin Geraghty established the vineyard in 1997, with a commitment to producing Bordeaux-style reds.

First release was in 2001 and saw many medals awarded. Merlot, malbec and cabernet franc are planted on sloping, north-facing hillsides. A large function centre caters for weddings and events.

Notable wines

Judge Valley Four Daughters ($60), Judge Valley Summer Rains ($65) — both blends of cabernet franc/merlot/malbec.

Vineyard dog

Brandy — border collie cross. Only three legs, as a result of his habit of nipping tyres, mudflaps and bumpers in motion. He also thinks the vineyard tractor is alive, and continually bursts out of hiding places to scare it. Kevin admits that it gets rather tiresome as Brandy leaps out of every single vineyard row — all 240 of them.

Accommodation

Cabernet Chalet offers one double bedroom, plus a double bed/settee, full cooking facilities, spa pool, shower and living room. A full country breakfast is complimentary. Other meals on request.

Proudly offers no TV, no internet access or any other worldly distractions. Complimentary bottle of bubbly included to sip in the spa. Tariff: $150 per night.

Vilagrad Winery and 3 Brothers Winery

702 Rukuhia Road (a few kilometres south of Hamilton towards Te Awamutu)
Ohaupo
07 825 2893 www.vilagradwines.co.nz
Open seven days 9.00 am–5.00 pm

Tasting $10 per person (reduces to $5 if you stay on for the Sunday lunch at $34.50 per person). This includes a vineyard tour, history and winemaking education, wine museum tour and comprehensive tasting.

Ivan Milicich Senior began growing grapes in 1906 on his small dairy farm at Ngahinepouri in the Waikato, and by 1922 was licensed to make and sell wine. This was the beginning of a family business that is now in its fourth generation. Ivan's granddaughter Nelda, and her husband Pieter Nooyen, are the present owners. The Vilagrad label uses grapes grown on the original property. A new label — 3 Brothers — has been added, using grapes from the major New Zealand wine growing regions.

Notable wines

Vilagrad Chardonnay/Gewürztraminer blend ($18).

Food

Sunday lunch all year round 12.00 pm–4.00 pm. Hearty traditional Dalmatian food with an international twist — spit roast pork and lamb, fish marinated in white wine and a cream sauce, salads and roast vegetables. Desserts, tea/coffee included. Kids aged 5–11 can dine for $17. Under fives are free.

Events

The winery has expanded into a café and functions facility, catering to locals and beyond for weddings, corporate events, dance parties, concerts and the Te Awamutu Food and Wine Festival.

Ohinemuri Estate

Moresby Street (between Paeroa and Waihi)
Karangahake Gorge
07 862 8874 www.dreamland.co.nz/ohinemuri
Open seven days October–May 10.00 am–5.00 pm, rest of year Wednesday–Sunday 10.00 am–4.00 pm

Horst and Wendy Hillerich bought their Karangahake property in 1989, with the intention of establishing their own boutique winery and restaurant. They began making wine almost immediately with grapes from Gisborne, Hawke's Bay and Marlborough. German born Horst was trained in the Rheingau region of Germany. The slightly out-of-the-way café and winery is deep in the Karangahake Gorge, nestled in the bush.

Notable wines

Patutahi Chardonnay ($24), Matawhero Gewürztraminer ($23), Patutahi Riesling ($19), Gimblett Syrah ($25).

Food

The restaurant was once horse stables and has a restored timber interior with a charming courtyard for outdoor dining. The seasonal menu has Mediterranean influences, and features platters, seafood, venison, soups, vegetarian dishes and also their famous winery pies. All the food is made in the restaurant kitchen, right down to the herb butters, vinaigrettes and the pickles on the platters.

Accommodation

A loft apartment sleeps four people and is situated in the original hayloft.

There is a large studio area that has a Queen-sized bed, a couch, a kitchenette and dining area. All meals are available by arrangement from the restaurant. Tariff: $110 per couple per night, $10 each extra person.

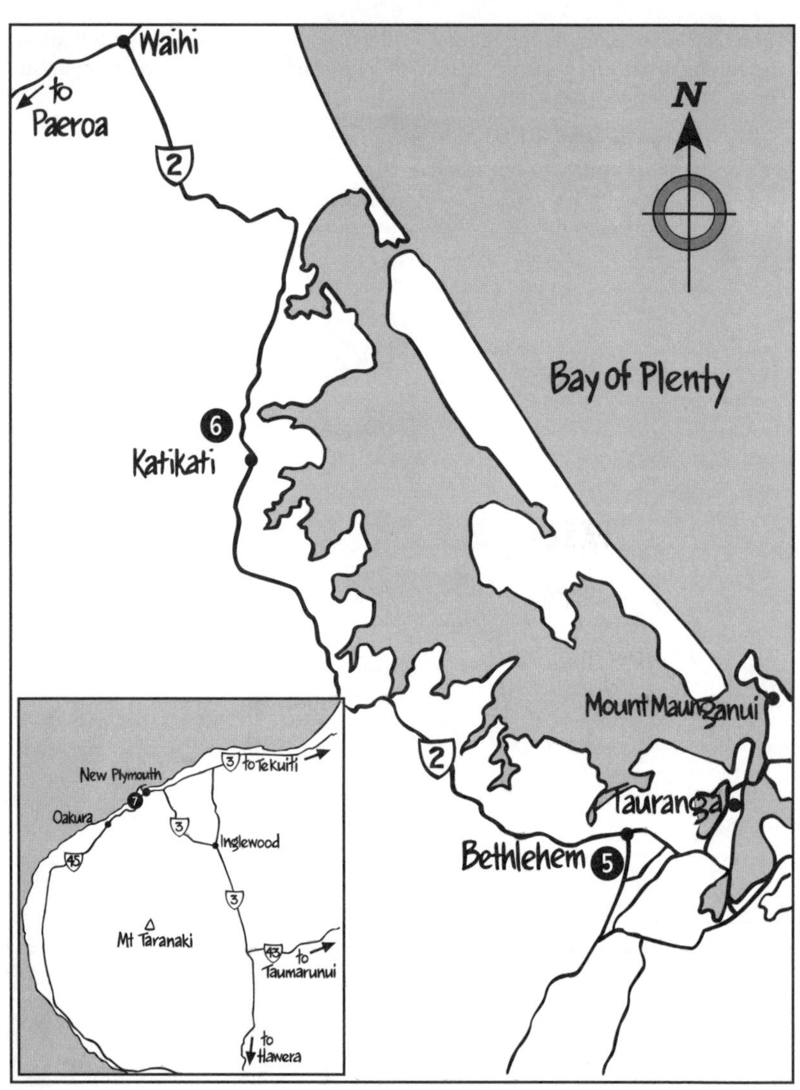
Waihi
to
Paeroa
2
N
Bay of Plenty
6
Katikati
Mount Maunganui
2
Tauranga
Bethlehem
5
New Plymouth
3
to Te Kuiti
7
Oakura
3
Inglewood
45
3
Mt Taranaki
43
to
Taumarunui
to
Hawera

Bay of Plenty

Just three in this neck of the woods, but all quality producers. The Bay of Plenty region is sunny, mild and warm, and experiences a wide variation in temperatures over the course of day and night (known in the trade as diurnal variation). A hot day of 23°Celsius may be followed by a night time low of one degree. This variation is suited to growing chardonnay and pinot noir.

Waikato weekend — Sunday

Mills Reef Winery and Restaurant

143 Moffat Road
Bethlehem
Tauranga
07 576 8800 www.millsreef.co.nz
Open seven days 10.00 am–4.00 pm

Completed in 1995, the Art Deco-style winery and restaurant architecture are a reflection of Napier's reputation as the Art Deco capital of the world. Set on eight hectares (20 acres) of landscaped grounds, the complex has full winemaking and bottling facilities, two underground barrel cellars, an aged wine cellar and an impressive tasting room. Also, the 150-seat restaurant is open for lunch all week. Grapes are all grown in Hawke's Bay, and winemaking is by founder Paddy Preston and his son Tim.

Elspeth is their top-end label — handpicked only in the best vintages. Numerous awards have justified their commitment. An outdoor concert venue onsite hosts large events at the winery.

Notable wines

Reserve Chardonnay ($20), Elspeth Chardonnay ($30), Hawke's Bay Sauvignon Blanc ($16) and Reserve Sauvignon Blanc ($21), Elspeth Cabernet/Merlot ($40), Elspeth Cabernet Sauvignon ($40), Reserve Malbec ($23), Elspeth Malbec ($40), Reserve Merlot ($23), Reserve Merlot/Malbec ($23), Elspeth Syrah ($40), Elspeth One Bordeaux blend ($50).

Food

Fine-dining restaurant open seven days for lunch. Dinners by appointment. On sunny days the outdoor dining area is extremely popular, as is the eight-metre, solid wood feasting table which is ideal for a large group or for several smaller groups to share and make new friends. Starters — tiger prawn on kaffir lime gazpacho, seared mahi mahi on smoked salmon risotto cake and scallops on pesto ($22). Mains — osso bucco of venison with lemon, capers and parsley on potato puree ($27). Sides available — asparagus, fries, salads ($6). To finish — nectarine and honey spring rolls, rolled in cinnamon sugar and served with home-made vanilla ice cream ($14).

Morton Estate

Cellar Door
State Highway Two
Katikati
07 552 0795   0800 667 866   www.mortonestatewines.co.nz
Open seven days 9.30 am–5.00 pm

I always think of Morton Estate in relation to their sparkling wines — good value, reliable champagne-style sparklers at around $20. However, they have a wide range of wines both red and white, with fruit sourced from either Hawke's Bay or Marlborough. Their 1995 Black Label Hawke's Bay Chardonnay won the 'Best Chardonnay in the World' trophy in the London International Wine Challenge in 1997. And their Sauvignon Blanc won the trophy for 'Best Sauvignon Blanc in the World' at the London International Wine Challenge 2003.

Established in 1975, it is still privately owned by businessman John Coney. The restaurant was previously open to casual diners but is now only available for functions for up to 100 guests.

Notable wines

Coniglio Hawke's Bay Chardonnay ($80), Hawke's Bay Chardonnay ($20), White Label Chardonnay ($17), Private Reserve Pinot Gris ($23), Stone Creek Riesling ($20), Rail Bridge Sauvignon Blanc ($23), Black Label Methode Sparkling ($33), IQ7 = Improving Quietly for Seven Years, Sparkling ($50).

Food

N/A (restaurant for functions only).

And if you've got heaps of time . . . head towards Taranaki.

Okurukuru Wines

738 Surf Highway 45 (on the coast, just off the main highway between New Plymouth and Oakura)
06 751 0787 www.thevineyard.co.nz
Open seven days in summer 10.00 am–7.00 pm, six days in winter (closed Mondays)

Exhibits a name with way too many 'u' vowels for the average Pakeha, Okurukuru (pronounced: Or-koo-roo-koo-roo). Enjoy outstanding coastline views from Oakura to the Sugar Loaf Islands, and Cape Egmont to New Plymouth. You may even be lucky enough to spot some whales off the coast.

Gisborne

Known as the Chardonnay Capital of New Zealand, and the first city in the world to see the dawn, Gisborne produces over 26,000 tonnes of grapes and is our third largest wine region. Right on the Pacific east coast, Gisborne is a mecca for surfers, scuba divers and fishermen, as well as a few intrepid wine fans. Wine tourism is pretty well in the early stages, but this is a region to watch — and one that will get better as time goes on.

The region's wine history began in 1850, with the arrival of a Marist priest, Father Lampila, and two others. They were originally heading for Hawke's Bay, but (whoops, what the . . . ?) their ship was blown off course and they landed in Poverty Bay. Anyway, they decided to stay on and planted vines to make sacramental wines for Mass.

It was in Gisborne that Captain Cook made his first landfall on New Zealand soil in 1769, naming it Poverty Bay after deciding it had nothing to offer. Bad call, James. Anyway, a monument to Cook can be found at the foot of Kaiti Hill, near the spot on which he first set foot.

Then, in the early twentieth century, German immigrant Friedrich Wohnsiedler pioneered commercial winemaking in Waihirere, where he made ports and sherries. Later, in the 1960s, Corbans and Montana extensively planted in the region for müller-thurgau and other bulk wines. Then chardonnay took off in the 1970s thanks largely to innovative wine pioneers such as Denis Irwin (founder of Matawhero Wines) and Montana's Peter Hubscher.

Quite a few of the good wineries in the region require booking ahead by appointment, but they are definitely worth seeking out, and the owners are very welcoming. Fine dining is pretty thin on the ground, but hearty local restaurant fare will do the job if you want a good simple feed. Everything comes with chips.

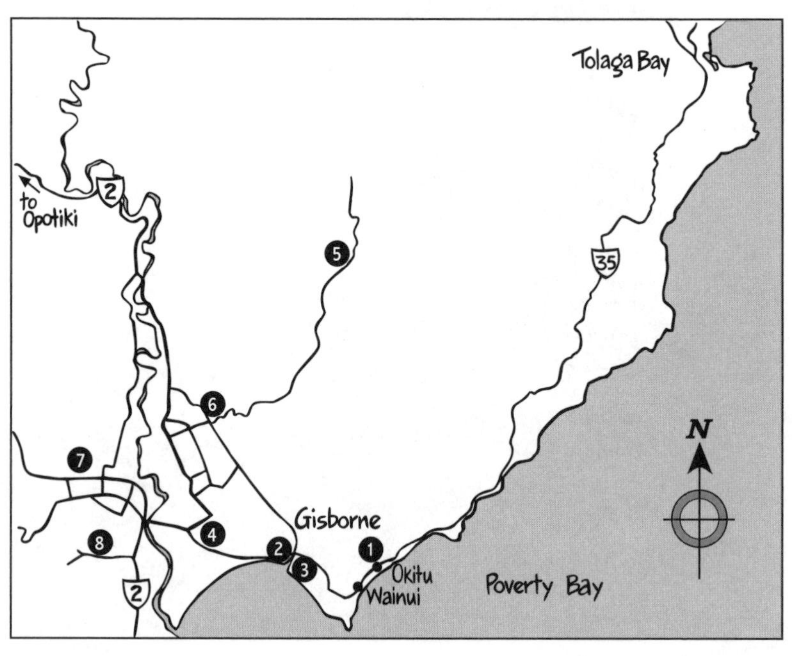
Tolaga Bay
to
Opotiki
2
5
35
6
N
7
Gisborne
4
8
2
1
3
Okitu
Wainui
Poverty Bay
2

Gisborne weekend — Saturday

Starting out on a limb at beautiful Wainui Beach . . .

Amor-Bendall Wines

24 Moana Road
Wainui Beach
06 868 0928 021 859435 www.amor-bendall.co.nz
Open seven days 8.00 am–6.00 pm

Located out on a limb at Wainui Beach, Noel Amor and his partner Alison Bendall kicked things off in 1988. At present, the tasting facility is part of a large space in a converted petrol service station, opposite the beach at Wainui, and they plan to relocate. Amor-Bendall don't own any vineyards, but get fruit from contract growers and do whole-bunch pressing right in the vineyard, with a mobile wine press. Annual production is about 12,000 cases.

Notable wines

Unoaked Chardonnay ($20), Pinot Gris ($25), Nelson Sauvignon Blanc ($25).

Food

N/A

Then head back into Gisborne.

The Lindauer Cellars

Solander Street
Gisborne
06 868 2757 www.montanawines.co.nz
Open seven days 10.00 am–5.00 pm

Lindauer Cellars opened in December 2002. The Lindauer Cellars stock a range of Montana products. In the grounds there is a BBQ area, shade sail and petanque court. 'Sumptuous à la carte menu' turned out to be minimal: garlic bread, bruschetta, dessert plate.

Tasting options: still or sparking, $5 a head, refundable on purchase. There is nowhere to spit out wine, so the plants get a good watering. (Beware of drunkenly leaning ponga ferns.) This is an okay place for a short break, but also pretty disappointing when it's our largest producer. They could do better (but things may have changed since my visit).

And, while you're in town . . .

The Cidery

Customhouse Street
Gisborne
06 868 8300
Open Monday–Friday 9.00 am–5.00 pm, Saturday 10.00 am–3.00 pm

There are tastings and cellar door sales and a new cider-making facility that produces Bulmer Harvest ciders and scrumpy. Also on sale: honey mead and other goodies, plus T-shirts, caps etc. Cidermaker Dennis Greeks oversees the large operation, which can be seen from an upstairs viewing room. Up to 70,000 litres of cider may be sitting in the stainless steel tanks at any one time. Bring your togs.

Then, head out into the region proper . . .

Bushmere Estate

166 Main Road
Matawhero
06 868 9317 021 946 301 www.bushmere.com
Open October–December Friday–Sunday 11.00 am–6.00 pm, January February Tuesday–Sunday 11.00 am–6.00 pm, March–May Friday–Sunday 11.00 am–6.00 pm, June–September by appointment only, generally it pays to phone ahead

David and Shona Egan are the owners and have been growing grapes for over 30 years. Once you have deciphered the opening hours — well worth a visit.

Notable wines

Chardonnay, Gewürztraminer (around $20). Stone Bridge Wines are also available at the cellar door.

Food

Small café serves renowned platter-style food, plus desserts, coffee and tea. Vineyard accommodation also available.

Tiritiri Vineyard

Waimata Valley (25 kilometres from Gisborne)
Gisborne
06 867 0372 www.tiritiriestate.com
Open generally 10.00 am–5.00 pm, phone ahead

Possibly New Zealand's smallest commercial vineyard, it covers only 0.27 hectares (about half an acre). Duncan and Judy Smith exclusively grow organic chardonnay grapes and produce only 50 to 200 cases per year. Their first vintage was in 1998. Winemaking is by renowned winemaker John Thorpe.

Notable wines

Reserve Chardonnay ($50), Gisborne Chardonnay ($40).

Food

N/A

TW Wines (Tietjen-Witters)

1121 Back Ormond Road
Gisborne
021 864 818 027 4502 339 www.twwines.co.nz
Open by appointment, phoning ahead is highly recommended

Formerly growers for other labels including Nobilo and Montana, Geordie Witters and Paul Tietjen launched their TW label in 1998. Using a small amount of high-quality grapes from both their Ormond Road vineyards they produced a premium chardonnay. Today, the range also includes malbec/merlot, viognier, a chardonnay/viognier blend, and a rosé called Lilly. Winemaker is Anita Ewart-Croy of KEW wines.

Tastings are very informal, well worth booking in advance, and take place outdoors on a large concrete table, in a glade surrounded by tall macrocarpas. Surely New Zealand's most unique tasting room.

Notable wines

Growers Selection Viognier, Chardonnay and Chardonnay/Viognier blend. Prices very reasonable at around $20 a bottle. My pick — Viognier, weighty and rich.

Food

N/A

While you're out that way, and well worth the drive . . .

Eastwoodhill Arboretum

2392 Wharaekopae Road
Ngatapa
06 863 9003 www.eastwoodhill.org.nz
Open seven days from 9.00 am–5.00 pm
Entrance fees for adults is $10. Children accompanied by adults free. Note: no dogs and no smoking.

A reasonable drive (30 minutes from Gisborne) but well worth the effort. Planted by First World War veteran Thomas Cook in 1918, this unique forest and garden contains New Zealand's largest collection (over 5000) of mature northern hemisphere trees and shrubs. Set among 135 hectares (334 acres) of hills, valleys, formal gardens and ponds, there is a network of easy walking tracks — from a 30-minute stroll to the four-hour circuit. Tracks are marked and colour coded, but I got lost after wine sampling at TW wines. Budget accommodation by prior arrangement. Special events are held throughout the year.

7

Kirkpatrick Estate Winery (KEW)

569 Wharekopae Road
Patutahi
06 862 7722 www.kew.co.nz
Open in winter by appointment, autumn and spring Friday–Monday 12.00 pm–4.00 pm, summer open seven days 11.00 am–4.00 pm

A very appealing, elevated terrace tasting area with comfy cushions greets the visitor to KEW, with sweeping views over the Patutahi Plateau. Simon and Karen Kirkpatrick bought the vineyard in 2003 and winemaker is Anita Ewart-Croy. The winery is nestled close to where the Kirkpatrick families have farmed for 150 years. Rugby legend, Ian Kirkpatrick is a relative.

Notable wines

A very good line-up of chardonnays, rosés, merlots and malbecs around $20. My pick — Unwooded Chardonnay and the Reserve Merlot.

Vineyard dog

Harry — schnauzer — obsessed with hitching rides on quad bikes.

Food

Antipasto platter: olives, freshly made onion marmalade, beetroot chutney, sundried tomato, chorizo, fruit, dukka and Repongaere olive oil, served with freshly toasted bread.

8

The Millton Vineyard

Papatu Road
Manutuke
Gisborne
06 862 8680 www.millton.co.nz
Open Monday–Saturday 10.00 am–5.00 pm, seven days in January

On first inspection, the vineyards look a tad messy, with a profusion of what look like weeds growing wildly among the vines. But it's all done on purpose — complementary planting to lure beneficial bugs, or scare away nasty ones. James and Annie Millton run their vineyards according to Steiner biodynamic principles — no artificial herbicides, fungicides, insecticides or fertilisers. Millton is the first certified organic vineyard in New Zealand and the fifth eldest in the world. Their wines have achieved great acclaim and Michael Cooper rates their Te Arai Chenin Blanc as one of New Zealand's classics. Prices are around the mid $20 mark, with the top shelf Clos de St. Anne range around $50.

Notable wines

Te Arai Chenin Blanc, Riverpoint Chardonnay, Gewürztraminer.

Food

N/A but you are welcome to bring your own picnic and relax in the garden.

Places to eat

Not much in the way of high-end dining, but still a few places with good food.

Colosseum

4 Riverpoint Road
Matawhero
06 867 4733

My pick as the best food and wine combination in Gisborne. Denis Irwin, local identity and former owner of Matawhero Wines, recently opened this Romanesque café and wine bar, which does brunch, lunch and dinners. Wines are available from Denis' back catalogue of fantastic aged wines. His selection includes gewürztraminer, chardonnay, sauvignon blanc, cabernet sauvignon, merlot and pinot noir. When I was there he had a stunning aged chenin blanc available. Food is simple but freshly prepared and utterly delicious. Dine inside or in the courtyard overlooking a cornfield. Rocky, a Papillon cross dog, may join you outside for lunch. He looks just like Gizmo from Gremlins.

Fettuccine Brothers

12 Peel Street
Gisborne
06 868 5700
Open seven days from 4.30 pm for dinner, fully licensed

Friendly, lively, and a bit noisy, with very bright lighting in a large spacious room. Good standard Italian-style food and a wine list to match, including many local wines.

World Café
663 Gladstone Road
Gisborne
www.worldcafe.co.nz
Open seven days 8.00 am–10.00 pm, fully licensed

Big hearty meals like open chicken sandwich, mixed grill, fish of the day, and pork sandwich. Has a large, open courtyard, baby changing facilities and friendly relaxed staff.

USSCo Bar and Bistro
16 Childers Road
Gisborne
06 868 3246
Open 10.00 am–late for brunch, lunch and dinner

Extensive grazing menu and kids menu. Medium priced. Lighting is a bit gloomy in the evenings.

Smash Palace Bar and Barbecue
24 Banks Street
Gisborne
06 867 7769   027 208 7545
Open seven days 3.00 pm–late weekdays, 12.00 pm–late on weekends, children welcome until 8.00 pm

An (ahem) unique dining experience. A real DC3 aeroplane stuck in the roof and an amazing collection of curios cover the walls and ceiling. Light bar food and flame-grilled pizzas available.

The Marina Restaurant and Bar
Marina Park
Gisborne
06 868 5919
Open Monday–Saturday, dinner only

Recommended fine dining, with seafood-oriented menu. Located in a restored

Victorian two-storey building in a picturesque river setting. View Gisborne's bridges by night.

Things to do

Dive Tatapouri

06 868 5153 www.divetatapouri.com

Variety of tours available — view marine life, feed stingrays, see penguins and dolphins. Also fishing charters and cage diving with Mako sharks. The base is situated on the waterfront at Tatapouri, State Highway 35, a ten-minute drive from Gisborne.

Freestyle NZ

127 Iranui Road
Gisborne
06 8688840 021 02568033 www.freestylenz.com

Freestyle New Zealand is a kite-surfing and adventure school, offering beginner to advanced lessons for kite-surfing and power-kite activities including the three-wheeled kite buggy and mountain board (large off-road skate board). They also run kayak and mountain bike tours around the Gisborne region.

Katapolt Kiteboarding

06 868 1517 027 446 9518 www.katapoltkiteboarding.com

Andy Lawton gives kiteboarding lessons and sells all the appropriate gear. Lesson fees start at $105 for one lesson one-on-one, to three lessons for $195. Two persons — one lesson at $75 each, $100 each for three lessons.

Sunride Surf School

021 133 2262 Email: sunridesurfschool@hotmail.com

Ex-Brit, Tyler White, liked Gisborne so much he decided to stay on. He offers affordable surfing lessons for the absolute grommet (beginner). Tyler also knows the best surf spots. Boards and suits if you need them are supplied. He operates from the City's Waikanae Beach. Lessons $40 one-to-one. More than one person $30 each.

Tourism Ngati Porou

06 864 8660 www.ngatiporou.com

Guided tours to the summit of Hikurangi, the sacred mountain of the Ngati Porou, and the first spot in the world to be touched by sun each day. At 1754 metres high, Hikurangi is the highest non-volcanic mountain in the North Island. Steeped in legend, Ngati Porou tradition says Hikurangi was the mighty fin of Te Ika Nui A Maui — the great fish of Maui — and was the first piece of land to be hauled out of the ocean by the legendary fisherman. Maui's bones lie on the mountain, with his canoe resting in Lake Takawhiti — near the summit. Local Iwi member Paora Brooking is your guide on a four-hour 4WD tour.

Golf

No less than 13 courses in the region, most with green fees of $5 to $10.

Places to stay

White Heron Motor Lodge

474 Gladstone Road
Gisborne
06 867 1108 0800 99 77 66 www.whml.co.nz

One-bed, two-bed and studio apartments are available, as well as honeymoon and executive suites. Qualmark 4-star plus. Guests receive complimentary corporate gym membership and a free round of golf at the Gisborne Park Golf Club. Wireless internet and broadband available. Tariff: from $115–$130 per person upwards depending on your choice of accommodation.

Coastland Motel

114 Main Road
Makaraka
06 868 6464 Email: coastlandmotel@xtra.co.nz

Budget option with Qualmark 3-star rating. Nine ground floor units and one four-bedroom motel house. City fringe, close to racecourse, golf, airport and only five minutes from city. Tariff: $65–$85 per night.

Repongaere Estate

30 Repongaere Road
Patutahi
06 8627515 021 375 387 www.repongaere.co.nz

Just 12 minutes from Gisborne, Repongaere is a boutique vineyard, olive plantation and luxury villa. Five brand new architect-cool, self-contained two-bedroom/two-bathroom villas with all the goodies — underfloor heating, kitchen, gas fires, broadband, washers and driers. Sample Repongaere's own olive oils and Chardonnay or indulge in a therapeutic massage. Tariff: around $200 per couple. Extra person or couple an additional $100. Seasonal rates apply.

Knapdale Eco-Lodge

114 Snowsill Road
Waihirere
06 862 5444 www.knapdale.co.nz

Kay and Kees Weytmans have won many environmental accolades for their luxury lodge, completed in 2004, and also for their adjacent 10 hectare (25 acre) forest. Structural timber was sourced from within a 20 km radius and was milled locally. Onsite are beehives, avocado orchard, deer, sheep, emus and highland stud cattle. Gourmet dinners, prepared by Kay, are available on request, accompanied by local chardonnays. Tariff: deluxe guest two-person room $275, romance room $330. Qualmark 4-Star plus.

The Beech Tree Farmstay

2060 Wharekopae Road
Ngatapa
06 8676 734 Email: dana@expresspr.co.nz

The Beech Tree Farmstay is set on 243 hectares (600 acres) of farmland 20-minutes from Gisborne and just down the road from the world renowned Eastwoodhill Arboretum. Luxury accommodation in a relaxed family atmosphere. King-size and Queen-size rooms available, including use of spa, pool and all other facilities. Breakfast is included and other gourmet meals are available on request. Tariff: $100–$120 per night.

Beachfront Wainui

11 Wairere Road
Wainui Beach
06 862 5661 021 222 0246

Beachfront holiday home, located right on Wainui Beach, and about ten minutes' drive from central Gisborne. Four bedrooms, sleeping up to eight people, plus a sleepout catering for four more. Includes a kitchen, plus lounge and sunroom opening on to the front deck. Sea kayak, crayfish pots and BBQ available. Tariff: Labour Weekend–30 April, $350 per night. 1 May–October, $250 per night. Prices based on four people, with extra people at $20.

Hawke's Bay

A large part of New Zealand's wine history began in Hawke's Bay. The Catholic church's Mission Vineyard was one of the first commercial vineyards in New Zealand, with first sales in 1895. Today, Hawke's Bay is renowned for its chardonnays, merlot, cabernet and syrah, with vineyards producing around 19 per cent of New Zealand's total grape harvest.

Also, it has New Zealand's first 'appellation' — the Gimblett Gravels. Established in 2001, Gimblett Gravels district, which includes Gimblett Road, has been building a reputation for producing high-quality wines from Bordeaux red varieties and syrah. The Gimblett Gravels appellation covers 800 hectares (over 970 acres), and is strictly determined by the extent of the old Ngaruroro River's gravel soils, which were exposed after a huge flood in the 1860s. High sunshine hours and dry summer heat make for some of our ripest grapes.

Napier's reconstruction after the massive 1931 earthquake left a legacy of one of the largest concentrations of Art Deco architecture in the world. In the depths of the Great Depression, Napier was rebuilt in just two years in the style of the 1930s. Nearby Hastings was also damaged severely and has its own examples of classic Spanish Mission and Art Deco style.

The landscape begins inland with the high, forested Ruahine and Kaweka Ranges. From there the land sweeps down towards the coast, flattening out to become the Heretaunga Plains. A number of wide rivers, excellent for fishing, run swiftly to meet the blue Pacific Ocean and glorious beaches which stretch from Mahia in the north to Porangahau in the south.

Hawke's Bay is very wine tourist-friendly — the region has plenty of great wine, restaurants, artisan food activities and accommodation.

It also boasts one of the longest place names in the world (in common usage): 'Taumatawhakatangihangakoauauotamateaturipukakapikimaungahoronukupokaiwhenuakitanatahu'.

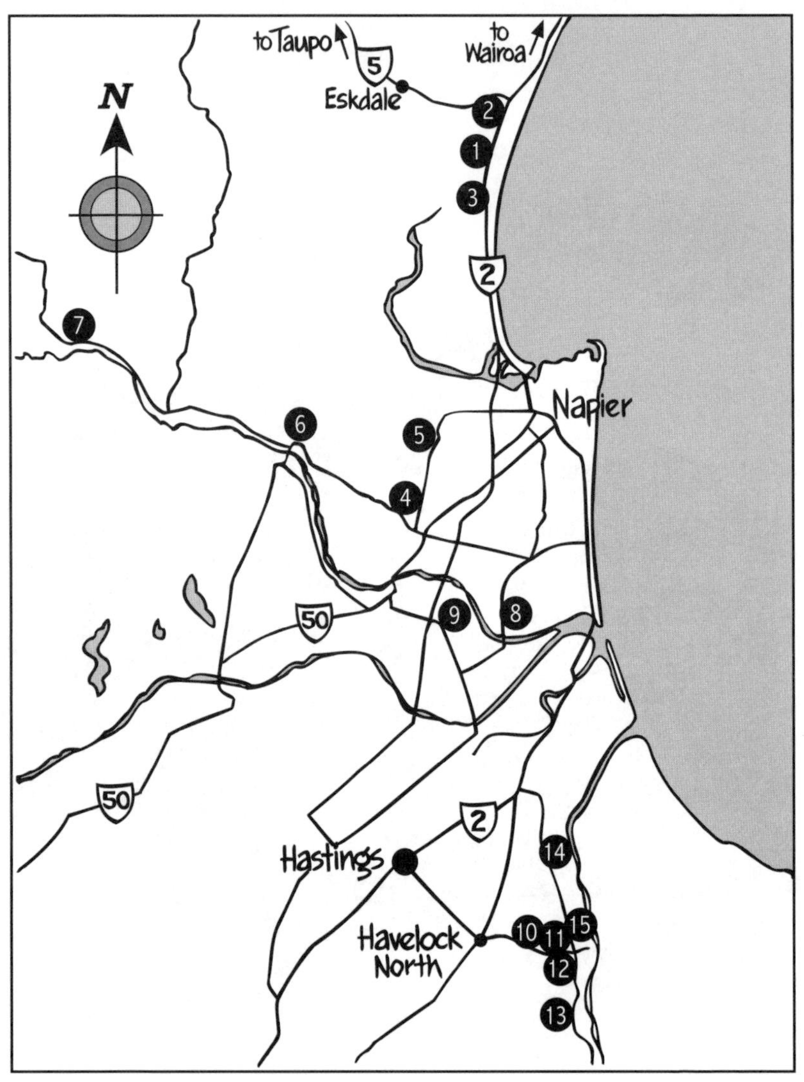
to Taupo
to Wairoa
5
Eskdale
N
2
1
3
2
7
Napier
6
5
4
50
9
8
50
2
Hastings
14
Havelock North
10
11
15
12
13

Esk Valley Estate

745 Main Road (north of Hawke's Bay at Bay View, just before the Napier-Taupo State Highway Five turn off)
Bay View
Napier
06 872 7430 www.eskvalley.co.nz
Winery/cellar door open seven days 10.00 am–5.00 pm

Esk Valley is one of Villa Maria's premium labels, consistently winning awards under the steady hand of winemaker Gordon Russell. The winery complex is a spacious white-painted building with a Mediterranean feel, with large terracotta planters and vine-draped terraces. Formerly the old Glenvale port and sherry winery, Esk Valley is now renowned for its white and red wines. Super premium Bordeaux-style blended red, The Terraces, sells for about $100 a bottle.

Notable wines

They are all great. Prices are $19–$50 for the main range. Three levels: Black Label, Reserve, and The Terraces, named for the steeply pitched vineyard where the grapes are grown. Wines include Sauvignon Blanc, Verdelho, Chardonnay, Pinot Gris, Riesling, Chenin Blanc, Merlot, Merlot/Cabernet Sauvignon and Syrah.

Food

N/A

Vineyard cat

Muscat — calico breed. A trophy hunter who relaxes by curling up in the yucca plant pot in the cellar door.

Eskdale Winegrowers

Eskdale Lane
Main Road
Eskdale
06 836 6302   Email: salonius@xtra.co.nz
Open seven days 9.00 am–5.00 pm

Colourful Canadian character, Kim Salonius, is the owner/winemaker of this small operation on the Napier-Taupo Highway, a little further on from Esk Valley. His wines are generally described as idiosyncratic — big bold and hearty. He has been growing grapes since the 1970s — chardonnay, gewürztraminer, malbec, cabernet franc, and cabernet sauvignon.

Food

N/A

Crab Farm Winery

511 Main Road
Bay View
Napier
06 836 6678   www.crabfarmwinery.co.nz
Open Thursday–Monday 10.00 am–5.00 pm

Retired surgeon James Jardine named his vineyard Crab Farm in memory of the mud crabs that occupied the site until the 1931 Napier earthquake lifted the land three metres above sea level.

His son Hamish Jardine has carried the business from grape growing to making its own wines. The cellar door is in a rustic building with exposed timber and wine-barrel furniture. Red wines are the focus here, with pinot noir, merlot, cabernet franc and cabernet sauvignon in the line-up.

Notable wines

Chardonnay, Pinot Noir, Merlot, and the Merlot/Cabernet/Malbec blend.

Food

Platters available.

Northern Hawke's Bay and Taradale — Sunday

Church Road Winery

150 Church Road (the Church Road Winery lies at the foot of Sugarloaf Hill in Taradale, a 15-minute drive from both Hastings and Napier)
Taradale
06 844 2053 www.churchroad.co.nz
Open seven days 9.00 am–5.00 pm

Yet another chunk of Hawke's Bay history. Former Marist brother Bartholomew Steinmetz established Church Road in 1897. Steinmetz returned to his native Luxembourg in the 1920s, leaving his winery in the hands of his assistant, 19-year-old Tom McDonald. McDonald went on to make some iconic Hawke's Bay cabernet blends, now commemorated in a premium red, aptly called Tom, which retails for about $120. Montana's Church Road label is now part of the Pernod Ricard (formerly Allied Domecq) portfolio. Definitely Montana's star winery, Church Road has three tiers of wines: Church Road label ($25), Church Road Reserve ($35), and a label for experimental wines — Church Road Cuvé Series ($40). The tasting room and restaurant have an upmarket barn feel —

large wooden doors opening onto terracotta floor tiles and subtle décor.

Notable wines

The lot. They're all great. Look out for the Cuvé Series wines — some are only sold from the cellar door. I tried the Cuvé Viognier a few years back — it was a stunner. Wish I'd bought 12 bottles.

Food

Church Road Winery Restaurant. Open seven days for lunch from 11.30 am. Voted one of the top five restaurants in the country by *Lonely Planet New Zealand Travel Guide*.

Mission Estate Winery

198 Church Road (corner of Avenue and Church Roads)
Taradale
06 845 9350 www.missionestate.co.nz
Open Monday 9.00 am–5.00 pm, Sunday 10.00 am–4.30 pm

Formerly a seminary for Marist priests, and now Hawke's Bay's largest winery, Mission Estate features historic grounds, huge Phoenix palms and elegantly restored buildings. The gracious, two-storeyed wooden homestead dates back to 1851 and many original features have been retained. Wines are in four labels: Estate, Vineyard Selection ($18), Reserve ($24) and the premium Jewelstone range (around $34).

The restaurant is superb (but do book ahead). Swiss Ewalt Jaritz is the ultimate maître d'.

Also look out for summer concerts held outdoors in the natural amphitheatre. Past performers have included Dame Kiri Te Kanawa, the Doobie Brothers, Rod Stewart and Dionne Warwick. See www.missionconcert.co.nz.

Notable wines

All three chardonnays: Vineyard Selection, Reserve and Jewelstone labels. Also Hawke's Bay Gewürztraminer, Vineyard Selection Sauvignon Blanc, Jewelstone Cabernet Sauvignon, Jewelstone Syrah.

Food

Restaurant open for lunch and dinner. For reservations call 06 845 9354.

Moana Park

530 Puketapu Road
Taradale
06 844 8269 www.moanapark.co.nz
Open seven days from summer Labour Weekend–Queens Birthday 10.00 am–5.00 pm, winter 12.00 noon–4.00 pm

Grape vines were established in 1979 by Ron Smith and, since 2000, wines have been under their own label, gaining a number of awards. He has four vineyards in the region including Gimblett Gravels and Bridge Pa — where broadcaster Paul Holmes spectacularly pranged his biplane on New Year's Eve 2004. Another unique feature of Moana Park is that they are certified by the Vegetarian Society, as they use no animal products in their winemaking. The cellar door is in a red barn-style building, and tastings can be had on the exterior paved area bordering the vineyard estate.

There are three tiers of wine: Vineyard Selection (about $17), Vineyard Tribute (about $28), and two flagship wines (around $35) — Moana Park Symphony (blended red), and Moana Park Concerto (blended from three chardonnay clones).

Notable wines

Dartmoor Chardonnay, Vineyard Selection Sauvignon Blanc, Vineyard Selection Merlot/Malbec, Tribute Syrah.

Sacred Hill Wines

1033 Dartmoor Road
Puketapu (which translates as 'sacred hill')
Napier
06 844 0138 www.sacredhill.com
Open seven days December–February 11.00 am–5.00 pm

Tony Bish is the very successful winemaker here and oversees production from four vineyards owned by the company. Aside from three in Hawke's Bay, (Rifleman, Dartmoor and Gimblett Gravels), they also have Hell's Gate Vineyard in Marlborough. The Mason family has owned it since launching in 1986, and it is headed by David Mason. Prices start at around $20 then take off to around $60 for some of the reserve wines. The cellar door has rustic charm and is constructed from old bridge and wharf piles.

Notable wines

Rifleman's and Wine Thief Chardonnay, Estate Gewürztraminer, Marlborough Sauvignon Blanc, Helmsman Cabernet/Merlot, Brokenstone Merlot, Deerstalker's Syrah.

Food

Deli goodies for sale at the cellar door, to be enjoyed at leisure in the expansive grounds among mature trees.

Brookfields Vineyards

376 Brookfields Road
Meanee
06 834 4615 www.brookfieldsvineyards.co.nz
Open seven days 11.00 am–4.30 pm

Brookfields is a well-known stop, not only for its red wines, but also for its restaurant. More at the boutique end of the market, they produce between 8000 and 10,000 cases of wine per year, and have no plans to increase production. In 1977 Peter and Sharon Robertson took over the old 1937 winery, which is constructed of handmade concrete blocks. Surrounding rose gardens add to the charm.

Notable wines

Marshall Bank Chardonnay, Ohiti Gewürztraminer, Ohiti Riesling, Sauvignon Blanc, Gold label Cabernet/Merlot, Burnfoot Merlot.

Food

The restaurant has a variety of menus. Mains are from about $16–$28.

Park Estate Wines and Restaurant

2087 Pakowhai Road
Napier
06 844 8137 www.parkestate.co.nz
Open seven days: cellar door and coffee 10.00 am–5.00 pm, lunches 11.00 am–3.00 pm

Owen and Diane Park run the winery and restaurant in a Spanish Mission-style building on the main road between Hastings and Napier. Formerly a fruit orchard, the property now produces a range of wines including the French Beaujolais grape — gamay. A large range of their own fudge, chutneys and organic juices are available at the cellar door.

Food

The restaurant features Italian/Mediterranean food with mains around $25. There is also a kids' menu for $8.50.

Bradshaw Estate Winery and Restaurant

295 Te Mata Rd
Havelock North
06 877 5795 www.havelocknorth.com/bradshaws
Open seven days November–March 10.00 am–4.00 pm, April–October Tuesday–Sunday 10.00 am–4.00 pm

Owned by Wayne and Judy Bradshaw, the winery is on the historic site of the old Vidals No. 1 Vineyard. It features attractive yellow ochre, Tuscan-style buildings with terracotta tile roofs, surrounded by shrubs. Wines include a Reserve Chardonnay, syrah and a dessert-style red.

Food

The restaurant is open for lunch all week and for dinner Friday and Saturday. While away the afternoon on the weatherproof terrace looking over the vines towards Mahia Peninsula. In winter you can enjoy a cosy lunch by the fire. The menu features local meats, seafood and seasonal produce. It also caters for conferences and functions. Booking is recommended.

Te Mata Estate

349 Te Mata Road
Havelock North
06 877 4399
0800 83 6282 www.temata.co.nz
Open Monday–Friday 9.00 am–5.00 pm, Saturday and Public Holidays 10.00 am–5.00 pm, Sunday 11.00 am to 4.00 pm

Yet another Hawke's Bay icon, Te Mata produces internationally famous labels such as the Coleraine and Awatea Cabernet/Merlots, Bullnose Syrah, and Elston Chardonnay. Owner John Buck is something of an industry legend and also claims to have the oldest winery in New Zealand (along with Mission Estate and Auckland's Pleasant Valley). With no less than ten Hawke's Bay vineyards, plus their newish Woodthorpe Estate, they have a solid portfolio of wines.

The cellar door is a striking white building designed by Wellington architect Ian Athfield. It features curved, Art Deco-inspired lines, a 'veranda', and a tall chimney.

Notable wines

Elston and Woodthorpe Chardonnay, Woodthorpe and Cape Crest Sauvignon Blanc, Awatea Cabernet/Merlot, Woodthorpe Cabernet/Merlot, Coleraine (blended red), Bullnose and Woodthorpe Syrah. Prices range from $30–$65.

Accommodation

Vineyard cottages

Two adjoining cottages are available — the studio and the vineyard flat. They are each intended ideally for one couple, but can expand to accommodate four people. Tariff for both: peak $245 per night, off-peak $210 per night. A third choice is the Woodthorpe Cottage, overlooking the Dartmoor Valley. Two luxury bedrooms, fully equipped kitchen and designer décor. Tariff $225 per night for two people.

And while you're in the area check out . . .

Te Mata Cheese Company
393 Te Mata Road
Havelock North
www.tematacheese.co.nz
Open seven days 10.00 am–4.30 pm

This is an artisan cheese factory where you can see cheese production and sample cheeses from cow, sheep and goats milk. There is a licensed café onsite and retail sales of cheese and local deli goods.

Napier and Havelock North — Sunday

Black Barn Vineyards

Black Barn Road (five minutes from the village of Havelock North, on the right, just past Lombardi on Te Mata Road)
Havelock North
06 877 7985 www.blackbarn.com
Open seven days 10.00 am–5.00 pm

With just over 20 hectares (50 acres) planted, the main focus is on premium Bordeaux-styled red varieties such as merlot, cabernet sauvignon and cabernet franc, but award-winning whites include chardonnay and sauvignon blanc. Owners (for about ten years now) are Andy Coltart and Kim Thorp, and winemaker is Dave McKee.

Black Barn also features a concert amphitheatre (see website for concert dates), Farmers' Market, Bistro and a choice of eight 'retreat' accommodation options, plus luxury spa treatments. Move in permanently — you'll never need to leave.

Notable wines

Barrel Fermented Chardonnay, Sauvignon Blanc, Merlot.

Food

Bistro: open for lunches from 12.00 noon Wednesday to Sunday. Booking recommended. Light seasonal café-style food with wines to match. A paved courtyard, overhung with drooping green vines is used in summer for dining al fresco.

Farmers' Market: open from 9.00 am till noon every Saturday of summer, starting in November. Just follow the line of cars down Black Barn Road to the carparks and you'll see the market under the trees, beside the underground cellars. The market season kicks off early November with new season asparagus, strawberries and artichokes and finishes, as summer comes to an end, with stonefruit, peppers and beans.

Events

Previous concerts held at Black Barn have featured Hayley Westenra and Dave Dobbyn, Anika Moa and Goldenhorse.

Accommodation

The Retreats: eight separate properties from around $100 per night per person. Different locations provide many options for beach, riverside or vineyard.

Craggy Range Vineyards

253 Waimarama Road
Havelock North
06 873 7126 www.craggyrange.com
Open seven days from 10.00 am

Craggy Range is a serious producer and the winery buildings seem to say, 'This is no hippy boutique, rosé outfit, mate.' It can be a tad intimidating with its massive fortress-like stone walls and high ceilings. The tasting room is a bit sterile. $5 for tastings (refundable on purchase).

Notable wines

Chardonnays — the lot. Te Muna Riesling. Sauvignon Blancs — the lot. Gimblett Gravels Merlot, Gimblett Gravels Syrah, Le Sol Syrah. Prices: $30 plus.

Food

Terroir Restaurant: fine dining in French Châteaux-inspired dining room with high vaulted ceiling, stone floor and wood-fired kitchen. Finalist in the *Cuisine* 2006 Restaurant of the Year Awards. Entrees around $20, mains around $30.

Open for lunch Tuesday–Sunday 12.00 noon onwards, open for dinner Tuesday–Saturday 6.00 pm onwards. For bookings call 06 873 0143.

Accommodation

The Cellar Master's Cottage — sleeps four — is nestled in amongst the chardonnay vines, and offers luxury self-contained accommodation with two double rooms, both with ensuite and views of Te Mata Peak. Tariff: $350 per night.

Askerne Estate Winery

267 Te Mata Mangateretere Road (turn left at the end of Te Mata Road)
Havelock North
06 877 2089 www.askerne.co.nz
Open seven days mid-December–end of February 10.00 am–5.00 pm, open weekends and Public Holidays from March–mid-December 1.00 am–5.00 pm

Another young winery, Askerne Estate has been going since 1993 and is situated on the east Heretaunga Plains, where sheep used to graze and asparagus grew. John Loughlin and his wife Catherine are the owners. Winemaker since 2002 is Craig Thomas. Prices around $20–$30.

Notable wines

Standard and Reserve Chardonnays, Gewürztraminer, Botrytis Dessert Chardonnay, Reserve Cabernet/ Merlot/ Cabernet Franc.

Accommodation

The Vineyard Cottage is set in 20 hectares (50 acres) of vineyard, and five-minutes' drive from Havelock North. It sleeps up to six. Breakfast provisions supplied. Modern amenities include Sky TV, DVD and internet access. For winter visits, underfloor heating and a log fire provide heating. Tariff: $295 per night (minimum of a two-night stay).

Akarangi Wines

103 River Road
Havelock North
06 877 8228 Email: akarangi@paradise.net.nz
Open seven days January 10.00 am–5.00 pm, weekends and Public Holidays only rest of the year

In this tiny vineyard of just three hectares (7.5 acres), clinical psychologist Morton Osborne is winemaker and owner. The cellar door is an old church building onsite.

Food

N/A

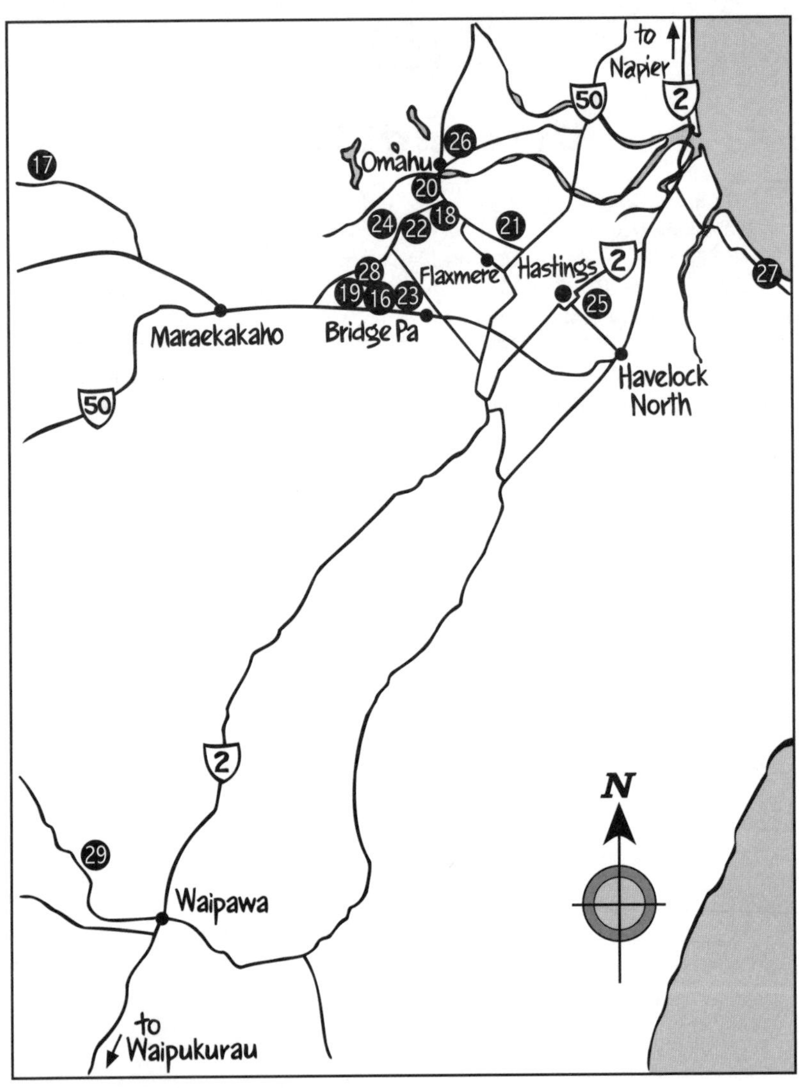
to Napier
50
2
26
17
Omahu
20
24
22
18
21
28
Flaxmere
Hastings
2
27
19
16
23
25
Maraekakaho
Bridge Pa
Havelock North
50
2
N
29
Waipawa
to Waipukurau

Alpha Domus

1829 Maraekakahoe Road
Hastings
06 879 6752 www.alphadomus.co.nz
Open seven days October–April 10.00 am–5.00 pm, open May–September Friday–Monday 10.00 am–4.00 pm

The Ham family have owned this winery since 1991. It has a small output — about 30,000 cases per annum and they are renowned for their top tier reds, The Aviator and The Navigator, as well as a glorious Noble Sémillon dessert-style and Viognier. Tastings are hosted in the winery plant surrounded by large, handsome polished oak fermentation tanks and stainless steel winery equipment.

Notable wines

AD Chardonnay, The Pilot Sauvignon Blanc, AD Aviator Cabernet dominant red, AD Navigator Merlot dominant red. Prices: mid $20–mid $60. I loved the dessert wine when I was there last (Late Harvest Sémillon $20).

Food

N/A. Picnickers are welcome.

Kemblefield Estate

Kemblefield Terrace (off State Highway 50, turn into Kereru Road, next right into Aorangi, then right into Kemblefield Terrace)
Hastings
06 874 9649 www.kemblefield.co.nz
Open Monday–Friday 9.00 am–5.00 pm, Saturday and Sunday 10.30 am–4.30 pm

Famous for introducing New Zealand to the great American red, zinfandel, Kemblefield produce some award-winning wines from their stunning winery on the far bank of the Ngaruroro River. The large spacious building and grounds feature a lot of local river stone, and there is a fountain and courtyard. Americans John Kemble (winemaker) and Karr Field started things off in 1992. John Kemble brought winemaking expertise from Sonoma, California, and also imported zinfandel rootstock from America. Their first vintage was in 2000. At a tasting in 2007, I found the Kemblefield 'zin' a fantastic ripe and spicy fruity red, more subtle than the American version.

Notable wines

Distinction Chardonnay ($22), Distinction Pinot Gris ($22), Reserve Zinfandel ($50).

Food

Picnic platters and estate olive oils.

Matariki Wines

52 Kirkwood Road (on Kirkwood Road on the edge of Gimblett Gravels, close to Hastings and ten kilometres from Napier)
Hastings
06 879 6226 www.matarikiwines.co.nz
Open seven days in summer 10.00 am–5.00 pm, winter Monday–Friday 10.00 am–5.00 pm, weekends 11.00 am–4.00 pm

Matariki is the Maori name for the legendary mother in the small cluster of seven stars (also known as the Pleiades) in the Taurus constellation. The six other stars are believed to be her daughters. In Maori culture, the appearance of Matariki near the shortest day in June is cause for the celebration of new growth and expectation of a plentiful harvest. This latterly has become celebrated as the Maori New Year. Former rugby international John O'Connor and his wife Rosemary chose the name to reflect New Zealand's bicultural nature. In 1981 they bought a parcel of land on what has now become the Gimblett Gravels region, and lived in a tin garage onsite while they developed the vineyard. They now own 230 hectares (570 acres). Most noted for their big red wines, the flagship is Quintology, a blend of five red varieties. Also onsite are pinot noir, syrah and sangiovese. Prices start at about $20 for the entry level Aspire range, and up to $40 for the Estate wines.

Notable wines

Chardonnays — all three. Estate Sauvignon Blanc, Reserve Cabernet Sauvignon, Aspire Syrah, Quintology.

Food

Matariki Dinner, a gourmet, three-course meal is matched with Matariki's wines, and over 120 guests are entertained by performers.

Vineyard dog

Flynn — German shorthaired pointer — welcoming committee.

Sileni Estates

2016 Maraekakaho Road
Bridge Pa
Hastings
06 879 8768 www.sileni.co.nz
Open seven days 10.00 am–5.00 pm

Graeme Avery, former medical publisher, started things off in 1997 with winemaker/manager Grant Edmonds. The initial 120 hectares (296 acres) were developed and then other local vineyard blocks added. Some sauvignon is now sourced from Marlborough contract growers. The wide driveway, flanked with vineyards, leads to the sprawling symmetrical main building, which bears the Sileni trademark triangle within a circle. Not content with making great wines, Sileni also has a cellar door, very popular restaurant, a gourmet food store and a culinary school. Wines are in three tiers — Cellar Selection (about $25), Estate Selection (about $35), and EV for Exceptional Vintage (about $65).

Notable wines

The Lodge Chardonnay, EV Chardonnay, Cellar Selection Pinot Gris, Cellar Selection Riesling, Cellar Selection Merlot, Plateau Pinot Noir.

Things to do at Sileni

The Wine Discovery Centre has many tour options: vineyard and winery tour and tastings daily at 11.00 am and 2.00 pm, $12 per person; gourmet wine and cheese match; the village press tour and tasting (estate grown olive oils); gourmet wine, cheese & olive oil tasting; wine and food experience degustation discovery; and degustation discovery (lunch or dinner).

Food

Restaurant open seven days, all year round, for lunch from 11.00 am. From October to April open for dinner Thursday, Friday and Saturday evenings.

Stonecroft Wines

121 Mere Road
Hastings
06 879 9610 www.stonecroft.co.nz
Open weekends only 11.00 am–5.00 pm

One of the Gimblett Gravels pioneers, Stonecroft is a small winery with an early mission statement proposing to 'produce full-bodied, elegant, fruit-driven wines'. Dr Alan Limmer (a doctor of science) and his wife Glen struggled and battled with the local council in order to establish their first plantings, way back in 1982, in what was to become premium New Zealand red wine terroir. (See their 'About Us' page on the website for the full and ludicrous story, dryly and hilariously related by Alan). This was back in the old days when the local council saw the future of the area as gravel quarrying and a rubbish dump. Stonecroft is now one of our most prestigious producers, with a reputation for long-lasting, exquisite wines, and also the first growers of what is now an increasingly popular New Zealand red — syrah. Expect to pay $35 plus.

Notable wines

Chardonnay, Gewürztraminer, Late Harvest Dessert Gewürztraminer, Syrah.

Food

N/A

C J Pask

1133 Omahu Road
Hastings
06 879 7906 www.cjpaskwinery.co.nz
Open Monday–Friday 8.00 am–5.00 pm, Saturday and Public Holidays 10.00 am–5.00 pm, Sunday 11.00 am–4.00 pm

Omahu Road has a slightly industrial feel to it, and this winery is in a plain no-nonsense building. General Manager and winemaker, Kate Radburnd, has steered CJ Pask through some major international awards, particularly for her red wines. Founded by top-dresser pilot, Chris Pask, the label pioneered growing premium red wines in the Gimblett Gravels. They also have some renowned chardonnay.

Notable wines

Wines come in three tiers — Roy's Hill (around $15), Gimblett Road (around $23) and the premium Declaration red (cabernet, merlot and malbec blend), and Declaration Chardonnay (both around $50).

Food

N/A

22

Te Awa Winery

2375 State Highway 50
Hastings
06 879 7602 www.teawa.com
Open seven days 9.00 am–5.00 pm

Te Awa is another winery with highly acclaimed wines and restaurant food. Bordeaux-style blended reds and pinotage are the flagship wines, made by Jenny Dobson, winemaker since the very first vintage. The buildings are rustic in style, with a casual feel.

Notable wines

Te Awa Chardonnay and Left Field Chardonnay, Sauvignon Blanc (oak aged), Te Awa Boundary (mainly merlot with cabernet sauvignon and cabernet franc), Zone 10 Cabernet Sauvignon, Longlands Merlot, Te Awa Syrah. Prices around $30.

Food

Restaurant open daily for lunch only from 12.00 noon–3.00 pm. Relaxed dining both inside and on the terrace under shady trees (weather permitting). Entrée: duck and oyster mushroom spring rolls with Te Awa sweet chilli sauce ($16). Main: sumac-dusted cervena, parsnip skordalia, medley of baby spring vegetables, macerated prunes and tamarillo chutney ($31).

Triangle Red

217 Ngatarawa Road (opposite Bridge Pa Vineyard)
Bridge Pa
Hastings
0800 494 637
Open seven days Boxing Day–end February 11.00 am–4.00 pm, March 1–Queens Birthday Friday–Sunday 11.00 am–4.00 pm, October 20–Christmas Eve Friday–Sunday 11.00 am–4.00 pm

Three local producers have banded together to establish a one-stop cellar door that represents all of them. Located at Bridge Pa Vineyard, Unison, Bushhawk and Bridge Pa wines are all available for tasting. With a focus on red wines, visitors have the opportunity to take part in the Triangle Red Experience, a flight of seven wines served with fresh bread for $9.

Notable wines

Bridge Pa Merlot/Malbec/Syrah, Unison Marie's Vineyard Merlot, Bridge Pa Louis Syrah, Unison Hawke's Bay Syrah. Prices: $30–$45.

Food

Deli lunches and authentic Italian wood-fired pizza are available to accompany wine in the vineyard café. Children are welcome and they also offer a healthy kids' platter.

Trinity Hill

2396 State Highway 50 (on the left between Gimblett Road and Ngatarawa Road)
Hastings
06 879 7778 www.trinityhill.com
Open seven days Labour Weekend–after Easter 10.00 am to 5.00 pm, after Easter–Labour Weekend 11.00 am to 4.00 pm

Owned by three families (hence the name Trinity Hill) and fronted by energetic Aussie John Hancock, this label has been very successful with red wines and also for introducing some new varieties to New Zealand. Now noted for their syrah and Bordeaux-style red blends, they have pioneered other varieties such as Italian red, montepulciano; Italian white, arneis; French white, viognier; Spanish red, tempranillo, and Portuguese red, touriga nacional. They have three tiers of wines: Trinity Hawke's Bay (around $20), Gimblett Gravels (around $35), and their ultra-premium Homage series at around (deep breath) $120 a bottle.

The winery building is Auckland architect Richard Priest's interpretation of a Hawke's Bay farm building. The large square concrete complex has an upstairs balcony which offers wide vistas over the Gimblett Gravels vineyards and the Western Heretaunga Plains towards Te Mata Peak.

Notable wines

Gimblett and Homage Chardonnays, Hawke's Bay Pinot Gris, Gimblett Cabernet Sauvignon, Gimblett Road Cabernet Sauvignon/Merlot, Gimblett Merlot, Gimblett Syrah, Hawke's Bay Montepulciano, Gimblett Tempranillo, Trinity Hill Homage — The Gimblett.

Food

Deli selection and platters available.

Vidal Wines

913 St Aubyn Street East
Hastings
06 872 7441 www.vidal.co.nz
Open Labour Weekend–Easter Monday Saturday 10.00 am–6.00 pm, Sunday 10.00 am–5.00 pm, Easter Monday–Labour Weekend seven days 10.00 am–5.00 pm

This is yet another historic New Zealand winery. José (Joseph) Soler arrived from Spain, and made his first wines in 1869 in Wanganui. He was later joined by his nephew, Anthony Vidal, and their relationship led to the establishment of Hawke's Bay's Vidal Wines in 1905. Now it is part of the Villa Maria group and under winemaker Rod McDonald (winemaker of the year 2006). The very top-level wines are under the prestigious Soler label — a syrah and a cabernet sauvignon, both at $40. Their other two labels are Vidal Estate (about $19) and Reserve (about $40).

Notable wines

Reserve Chardonnay, Marlborough Riesling, Marlborough Sauvignon Blanc, Reserve Cabernet Sauvignon, Reserve Merlot/Cabernet Sauvignon, Stopbank and Marlborough Pinot Noirs, Reserve and Soler Syrah.

Food

The restaurant is open seven days for lunch and dinner. This was New Zealand's first official vineyard restaurant, and is located in the former winery stables. Old photographs and memorabilia are displayed. It is fully licensed and the menu features fresh and often organic produce. Entrées are about $16, mains around $30, sides an extra $6, cheese board and desserts are about $13.

Crossroads Winery

1747 Korokipo Road
State Highway 50
Fernhill (near Taradale)
06 879 9737 www.crossroadswinery.co.nz
Open seven days Easter–Labour Weekend 10.00 am–5.00 pm, 11.00 am–4.00 pm rest of the year

Crossroads is a medium-sized winery, begun in 1990 a few years after old mates Lester O'Brien and Malcolm Reeves' paths literally crossed while in Europe. In Fernhill, near Taradale, the Spanish Mission-style winery is surrounded by farmland. New investment has allowed them to plant further vineyards in the Gimblett Gravels region and also Marlborough. Wines are $25–$30.

Notable wines

Talisman (a six-grape secret red blend, which Michael Cooper gives four stars). Also Destination Gewürztraminer, Destination Riesling, Destination Sauvignon Blanc.

Food

N/A

Clearview Estate Winery

194 Clifton Road (on the road to Cape Kidnappers)
Hastings
06 875 0150 www.clearviewestate.co.nz
Open seven days Labour Weekend–Easter 10.00 am–5.00 pm for brunch and lunch, wine, coffee and sales, dinner from 6.00 pm, December–February Friday–Tuesday 10.00 am–5.00 pm for brunch and lunch, wine, coffee and sales

Clearview is well known for its wines and restaurant, which in summer has long private tables amongst the grapevines for groups, umbrella tables in the courtyard, and a more casual drinks area near the children's playground.

Notable wines

Beachhead and Reserve Chardonnay, Reserve Sauvignon Blanc, Noble Harvest Dessert Chardonnay, Des Trois Pinot Noir.

Food

The restaurant is highly recommended. Chef Kerry McKay oversees the kitchen. Brunch dishes are about $16, pasta and mains about $27.

Ngatarawa Wines

305 Ngatawara Road
Bridge Pa
Hastings
06 879 7603 0508 782 2537 www.ngatarawa.co.nz
Open seven days Labour Weekend–Easter 10.00 am–5.00 pm, after Easter–Labour Weekend 11.00 am–4.00 pm

Ngatarawa Wines is by far one of the most friendly and approachable of the wineries in the area — nice people, great wines, great location, unpretentious. Alwyn Corban and Garry Glazebrook established their venture in former racing stables back in 1981. Garry's background was horse racing; Alwyn has a long history of winemaking, going back to his West Auckland Lebanese forebears. The Glazebrooks have now sold their share to Alwyn's cousin, Brian.

The cellar door and winery are located in charming old wooden stables, and there is an ornamental lake on the property. Wines are in four levels. Entry level is Stables range (about $16), then Silks (about $20), Glazebrook (around $27), and finally the top shelf Alwyn series (up to $60). A new range has just been released — Farmgate — available from the cellar door or online only in a four-pack ($25 a bottle).

Notable wines

Glazebrook Reserve Chardonnay, Alwyn Chardonnay, Stables Sauvignon Blanc, Glazebrook Reserve Merlot, Glazebrook Martinborough Pinot Noir, Alwyn Reserve Late Harvest Dessert Riesling, Glazebrook Reserve Syrah.

Food

N/A

And 40 minutes south of Hastings . . .

Lime Rock Wines

601 Tikokino Road
Waipawa
Central Hawke's Bay
06 8578247 www.limerock.co.nz
Open November–end of February Saturday and Sunday 11.00 am–4.00 pm (tastings by appointment)

Lime Rock Wines takes its name from its limestone-based vineyards. The cooler temperatures and soil types are ideally suited to growing sauvignon blanc. And in the tasting room you can see examples of ancient marine fossils, dug from their own limestone soil. Established in 2000 by winemaker Rosie Butler, her husband Rodger Tynan and brothers Peter and Warwick Butler. Rosie was a winemaker back in the 1970s for Montana and has also done vintages in Petaluma winery in South Australia.

Notable wines

Sauvignon Blanc, Pinot Noir.

Food

N/A

Things to do

Art Deco Weekend

Usually held on the second weekend in February. Visitors and locals dress in 1930s fashions and celebrate all things Art Deco. Organised through the Art Deco Trust, their website www.artdeconapier.com gives background on history and events and even a detailed section on how to dress in Deco style.

Deco Decanted Jazz Festival

Usually in the second week of July. See: www.artdeconapier.com

Vintage Deco Car Tour

A one-hour tour in a restored vintage Buick visits the National Tobacco Company Building, the Deco houses and gardens in the suburb of Marewa, and the grand Edwardian Hawke's Bay Club. $130 for up to three passengers. For bookings call: the Art Deco Shop on 06 835 0022.

Guided Art Deco Tours

Accredited guided tours take an easy stroll through the compact Art Deco Quarter in the city centre. Walks are held twice daily year-round, rain or shine. Bookings are not necessary. Children free.

Morning walk: 10.00 am, $14 per person (one hour), starts at the Napier Visitor Information Centre, (next to the Sound Shell) and ends at the Art Deco Shop. Refreshments and a movie screening are available afterwards.

Afternoon walk: 2.00 pm, $20 per person (two hours) and includes some interior visits and a 30-minute introductory slide show. Optional 30-minute presentation. Start and finish at the Art Deco Shop.

Hastings and Napier Farmers' Markets

Marine Parade
Napier
Both markets are on every weekend of the year, rain or shine.

The Hastings Market is on Saturdays from 8.00 am–1.00 pm in the Civic Square in Hastings' city centre.

The Napier Market is every Sunday from 8.30 am–1.30 pm near the Sound Shell on Napier's Marine Parade.

Marineland

290 Marine Parade
Napier
www.marineland.co.nz
Admission $10 adult and $5 child. 10.00 am–4.30 pm seven days a week. Dolphin shows daily 10.30 am and 2.00 pm.

Napier's Marineland is a marine zoo and wildlife centre. It features several species of native marine wildlife, including the Common dolphin, the New Zealand fur seal, the Leopard seal, and Little Blue penguin. Also available are Behind the Scenes Tours, the Penguin Recovery Workshop, and the Swim with the Dolphin programme.

Hawke's Bay Museum and Art Gallery

65 Marine Parade
Napier
Open 10.00 am–6.00 pm every day except Christmas Day. Adults $7.50, children under 15 free

The exhibition programme has a variety of changing exhibitions including the 1931 Napier Earthquake and Art Deco Style. The Museum Shop has a range of New Zealand art and design related merchandise.

The Century Cinema, onsite, screens art-house movies. The 330-seat theatre has good acoustics, and state-of-the-art sound.

The Faraday Centre

1 Faraday Street (off Carlyle)
Napier
www.hawkesbaymuseum.co.nz
Open Monday, Wednesday, Friday and Saturday 9.00 am–11.30 am, the last Saturday of each month 9.00 am–3.00 pm, $7 per adult, children under 15, just $1

Hawke's Bay's Museum of Technology and Science features household gadgets that have now disappeared from use. Listen to the hit and miss motors, the hot air engine and the power plant that lit Nelson Park in the aftermath of the 1931 Earthquake.

Arataki Honey Centre

66 Arataki Road
Havelock North
0800 272 825
Open Monday to Friday 8.00 am–5.00 pm

This interactive honey visitors centre is 20-minutes' drive from Napier and just minutes from Havelock North. Tastings are available and guided tours are by arrangement. Live bee display and retail sales.

Cape Kidnappers Gannets

Migratory seabirds, Australasian Gannets have a wingspan of nearly 1.8 metres (six feet). They nest on flat ground, taking turns to incubate and feed the sole chick from the breeding season. A number of guided tours to the colony are available over the breeding season (July–March).

Cape Kidnappers International Golf Course

448 Clifton Road
Te Awanga

This *Travel and Leisure Golf*'s '2004 Golf Course of the year' is 140 metres above Hawke's Bay, and designed by Tom Doak as a sister course to American billionaire Julian Robertson's Kauri Cliffs estate. Green fees: Affiliated, around $200, Non-affiliated, around $350. Contact: Jeremy Carlson Phone: 06 875 1900.

Places to stay

Harvest Lodge

23 Havelock Road
Havelock North
06 877 9500 www.harvestlodge.co.nz

This Qualmark 5-star motor lodge at reasonable tariff in the heart of Hawke's Bay features air-conditioning, double spa baths, flat screen TV, wireless broadband, DVD players, patios and King-size beds. Tariff: starts at $150 for a studio; up to $200 for a two-bedroom unit.

Wine Country Lodge

Corner Te Mata and Arataki Roads
Havelock North
0800 877110 www.winecountrylodge.com

This is a motor lodge in close proximity to local vineyards (Craggy Range, Black Barn, Te Mata, Lombardi) with Bradshaw Estate Winery and Restaurant just 200 metres away. Qualmark 4-star-plus: compact kitchen, wireless broadband and complimentary coffee and tea. Tariff: studio unit from $130. Two-bedroom spa unit from $170.

Mangapapa Petit Hotel

Halfway between Napier and Hastings on State Highway Two
06 878 3234 www.mangapapa.co.nz

This boutique luxury hotel is the former estate of canned-food magnate, Sir James Wattie. A sprawling estate with peach and apple orchards and eight hectares (20 acres) of manicured gardens brimming with roses and established trees. Indulge with an in-house day spa, heated pool, and seasonal degustation menu, by the in-house chef. Tariff: varies wildly depending on the season. Don't expect much change out of $1000 a night. Check the website for specific rates.

Elmore Lodge Motel

301 Omahu Road
Hastings City
0800 35 66 73   www.elmorelodgemotel.co.nz

Expect no frills, but comfort and reasonable rates. All units have Sky TV, a hair-dryer, iron and ironing board. Cot and highchair available. Qualmark 3-star-plus. Tariff: studio, one bedroom and two-bedroom units, $85–$140.

Olea Cottages

101 Ru Collin Road
Hastings
06 879 7674   www.oleacottages.co.nz

With these individual self-contained cottages you will receive goodies like complimentary continental breakfast supplies for the first two mornings, fresh flowers, local wine and fresh fruit, and fine bed linen. Within a five-minute drive there are seven wineries, two championship golf courses, the Equestrian Park and Bridge Pa Aerodrome. Qualmark 4-star-plus. Tariff: one bedroom cottage from $220 per night. Two bedroom cottage $320 per night (two couples). $30 service charge for one-night stays.

Omahu Motor Lodge

327 Omahu Road
Hastings City
0800 166 248   www.omahumotorlodge.co.nz

Very new, it opened in October 2005. Nineteen ground-floor units have wireless broadband internet. Fully air-conditioned. 17-inch LCD widescreen TVs. Seven Sky channels and teletext. Spa baths. Complimentary access to full gym and lap pool. 500 metres to restaurants and bars. Qualmark 4-star-plus. Tariff: $120–$170 per night (two people), extra person $20. Seasonal rates apply.

Martinborough and the Wairarapa

Around 15 years ago, word started spreading about some excellent wines from just over the winding road of the Rimutukas, north of Wellington. DSIR scientists had discovered a climate and soil type similar to the classic French region of Burgundy that was suitable for growing pinot noir and a few other grape varieties.

Now the Wairarapa, and Martinborough in particular, is one of our top boutique regions, producing not only internationally acclaimed pinot noir but also sauvignon blanc, riesling, pinot gris and even some big reds like syrah and blended reds.

Famous wineries like Dry River, Ata Rangi, Martinborough Vineyard, Palliser and Te Kairanga all hail from this region. Great food and upmarket accommodation has made this one of our main wine tourism regions for locals and foreigners alike. The broad, flat plains bake in the summer months, but in winter the Wairarapa becomes a misty, dreamy adventureland of fine wines and excellent food. Whatever the season — it's just right for a weekend away.

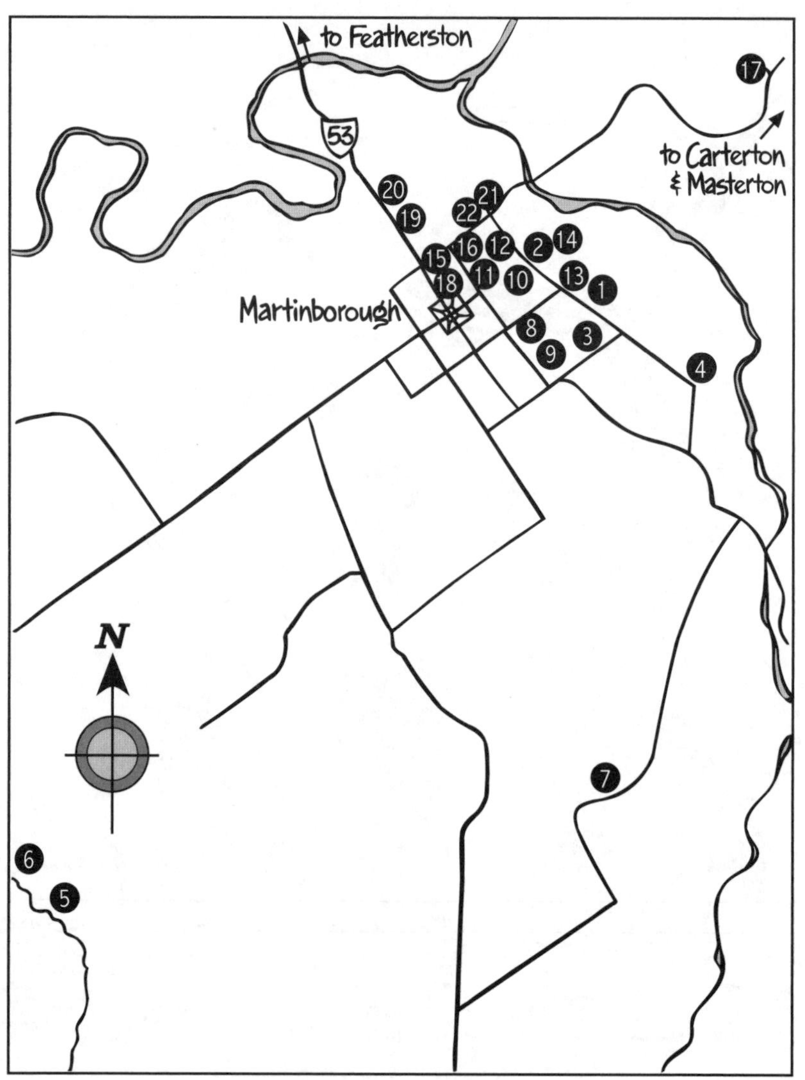

to Featherston
53
to Carterton
& Masterton
Martinborough
N
17
20
19
21
22
16
12
2
14
15
11
10
13
1
18
8
3
9
4
7
6
5

Martinborough

If you get your timing right, and you're in the region on the third Sunday in November, you'll be in time for the highly popular Toast Martinborough festival. Your festival ticket gives you a tasting glass, access to all the participating wineries and food stalls, and unlimited use of the shuttle buses that circulate the festival route.

Martinborough weekend one — Saturday

Tirohana Estate

Puruatanga Road
Martinborough
06 306 9933 www.tirohanaestate.com
Open seven days 9.00 am–6.00 pm

Tirohana is a boutique producer of pinot noir, sauvignon blanc, riesling and chardonnay. The wines are sold via the onsite cellar door or exclusively through Kirkcaldie and Stains in Wellington.

Notable wines

Standard and Reserve Pinot Noir.

Accommodation

The Qualmark 5-star, luxury accommodation (self-contained and serviced) overlooks the vineyard. The four luxury suites feature original New Zealand artworks and antique furniture. Tariff: $250 per night for two adults. Additional adults $65 per person per night.

Food

Platters and snacks available.

Alana Estate Limited

Puruatanga Road
Martinborough
06 306 9784 www.alana.co.nz
Cellar door open seven days 10.30 am–5.00 pm

The state-of-the-art, three-level winery is built on a gravity feed system, where minimal pumping and handling ensure high quality grape and wine management. The first vintage was in 1998.

The restaurant — Alana Estate Wine and Food Experience — features a menu that matches wines to each course. Chef Ian Garner is formerly from Wellington's renowned Petit Lyon.

Notable wines

At Alana Estate they grow four varieties of grape — pinot noir and chardonnay (the star varieties with many accolades), riesling and sauvignon blanc.

Food

Reasonably priced with mains around $25. For example, the pinot noir match is lamb loin rolled in spices and grilled pink, served with Bourguignon-style sauce of mushrooms, bacon and pinot noir with prunes and potato. Desserts are around $10.

Stonecutter Vineyard

Todds Road
Martinborough
06 306 9871   www.stonecutter.co.nz
Open Saturday and Sunday 11.00 am–4.00 pm

Stonecutter is a tiny estate — just three hectares (8 acres) — specialising in pinot noir and pinot gris, but with a few hundred plants of merlot, gewürztraminer and sauvignon blanc. Roger Pemberton and Lucy Harper planted Stonecutter Vineyard in 1995. Their first vintage was in 1999.

Notable wines

Pinot Noir has been the major success, picking up medals and accolades.

Food

N/A

Te Kairanga Wines

Martins Road
Martinborough
09 306 9122   www.tekairanga.co.nz
Open seven days 10.00 am–5.00 pm, winery tours every Saturday and Sunday at 2.00 pm

Second largest of the Martinborough wineries after Palliser Estate, Te Kairanga — or TK as it is nicknamed — is a publicly listed company formerly owned by Tom Draper. Six Martinborough vineyards produce sauvignon blanc, pinot gris, riesling, chardonnay, pinot noir and merlot; with grapes also sourced from Gisborne for chardonnay and merlot.

In addition to being a big part of the Toast Martinborough festival, TK has its own annual food and wine event, 'TK Day' which is held on the Sunday of Wellington Anniversary Weekend. This is more of a child-friendly family event, with music, food and wine. Bookings are essential.

Notable wines

Chardonnay and Pinot Noir, especially the Reserve labels. Note particularly the John Martin Reserve ($50 a bottle).

Food

Selection of packaged snacks available.

Martinborough weekend one — Sunday

Murdoch James Estate

Dry River Road
Martinborough
06 306 9165 www.murdochjames.co.nz
Open seven days from 11.00 am–5.30 pm

Eight kilometres south of Martinborough, Murdoch James winery produces a broad range of whites and reds. Roger and Jill Fraser planted some of the earliest local vines in 1986, and believe firmly in bio-sustainable, low-ecology-impact winemaking practices.

Notable wines

Blue Rock Riesling, Unoaked Chardonnay Sauvignon Blanc, Murdoch James Fraser Pinot Noir.

Food

Riverview Café looks across the Dry River Valley, and further afield to Lake Wairarapa and the Tararua Mountain Range. It features rustic Italian-inspired dishes, with local produce to the fore.

Open winter April–November Friday–Sunday 11.00 am–3.30 pm. In summer the café is open 12.00 noon–3.00 pm every day except Wednesday.Platters are available in the tasting room when the café is closed.

Accommodation

Winemaker's Cottage: self-contained, renovated original homestead cottage. Breakfast supplies and complimentary bottle of wine included. Tariff: $180 per night for a couple, $230 for two couples. $30 for each additional person. Children under two are free. Children aged 3–15, $25 each.

Coney Wines

Dry River Road
Martinborough
06 306 8345 www.coneywines.co.nz
Open for tastings and lunch in summer Friday–Sunday and Public Holidays, in winter Saturday, Sunday and Public Holidays

Tim Coney (older brother of international cricketer Jeremy) and his wife Margaret are the owners of 5.5 hectares (14 acres) of riesling, pinot gris, syrah and pinot noir. Tim has been known to burst into song to entertain his guests and, whether solicited or unsolicited, all Coney café guests receive a Basil Fawlty-style tasting from him at the table.

Notable wines

Attention to detail has ensured consistent high quality across the range. As the family are music fans, the wines have appropriate names: Pizzicato Pinot Noir and two Rieslings — Rallentando (dry and zingy) and Ragtime (fruity off-dry). There is also a Rosé.

Food

Tim's wife Margaret, a serious foodie, runs the café, offering medium-priced meals with international influences.

Te Hera Estate

Te Muna Road
Martinborough
06 3069018 www.tehera.co.nz
Open Monday–Friday 10.30 am–2.30 pm while stocks last, or by arrangement

John Douglas and wife Katherine Goldstone have five hectares (12 acres) of pinot noir and 0.4 hectares (1 acre) of riesling. They have received excellent accolades from local and overseas critics, including Britain's famous Jancis Robinson. Te Hera — the sail — is symbolic of the heroic voyages of our forebears, both Maori and European.

Notable wines

Pinot Noir and Riesling.

Food

N/A

Stratford Wines

115 New York Street
Martinborough
06 306 9257 www.stratford.co.nz
Open Saturday, Sunday and Public Holidays 10.30 am–5.00 pm

Roving winemaker Strat Canning and his wife Carla Burns had their first release in 1998. Strat also makes wine for Margrain and Haythornthwaite. 'Stratford', Strat's full given name, has been a family moniker since the first Stratford de Redcliffe Canning born in 1662.

Here they grow just pinot noir and riesling, the chardonnay having been pulled out after the 2002 vintage.

Notable wines

Both the Pinot Noir and Riesling have done very well. The 2000 Pinot Noir won the Champion Pinot Noir trophy at the Royal Easter Show in 2001.

Food

N/A

Canadoro Wines

125 New York Sreet
Martinborough
06 306 8801
Open seven days 11.00 am–4.00 pm, or by appointment

Golden retriever breeders Greg and Lesley Robins run the show and the name Canadoro comes from the Italian *Cane d'Oro* — golden dog. Contrary to the local pinot noir obsession, they have gone out on a limb with cabernet sauvignon. Theirs is routinely described as powerful and gutsy. They also produce chardonnay, sauvignon blanc, pinot gris and riesling.

Notable wines

Canadoro Cabernet Sauvignon. Michael Cooper gives it three stars and describes it as gutsy and harmonious. Also Chardonnay and a sweet, late harvest sauvignon blanc.

Food

N/A

Ata Rangi

Puruatanga Road
Martinborough
06 306 9570 www.atarangi.co.nz
Open weekdays 1.00 pm to 3.00 pm, weekends 12.00 noon–4.00 pm

Ata Rangi means 'new beginning' and this iconic Martinborough vineyard was started in 1980 by dairy farmer Clive Paton and his wife Phyll Pattie. It now produces about 11,000 cases a year.

Notable wines

Top critic Michael Cooper gives both Ata Rangi Pinot Noir and Craighall Chardonnay five stars. Crimson is a second tier pinot with a proportion of profits going towards protection of our pohutukawa trees.

Food

N/A

Martinborough weekend two — Sunday

Benfield & Delamare

35 New York Street
Martinborough
06 306 9926 (after hours) www.benfieldanddelamare.co.nz
Open Labour Weekend–Easter 1.00 pm–5.00 pm

Bill Benfield and Sue Delamare specialise in merlot dominant, Bordeaux-style blended reds. They have a very small output and an uncompromising approach to quality has ensured excellent results. The 2001 vintage picked Silver medals at both Vinales International in Paris and at the International Wine Challenge in London 2004.

Notable wines

Just two styles — the flagship Benfield & Delamare at $55 and a second tier label A Song for Osiris at about $25.

Food

N/A

Vineyard dogs

Harry, Lucy and Molly — Australian terriers.

Schubert Wines

57 Cambridge Road
Martinborough
06 306 8505 www.schubert.co.nz
Open most days 11.00 am–3.00 pm

German-born winemaker Kai Schubert and his partner Marion Demling export their wines to 23 different countries. They have three vineyards — Martinborough, East Taratahi (Wairarapa) and one in the Gimblett Gravels region of Hawke's Bay.

Notable wines

Quite a large line-up of reds and whites from the three vineyards, but the stars would be the Wairarapa Pinot Noir, Hawke's Bay Cabernet and a European-styled white blend called Tribianco (Chardonnay, Pinot Gris and Müller-Thurgau).

Food

N/A

Vynfields

Omarere Road (off Puruatanga Road)
Martinborough
06 306 9901   www.vynfields.co.nz
Open seven days January–February 11.00 am–5.00 pm

Vynfields is a certified organic producer of pinot noir and riesling. Kaye McAulay and John Bell are the owners of this 5.3-hectare (13 acre) property and their homestead is a relocated historic building from Lyall Bay in Wellington. Schubert Wines are the winemakers.

Notable wines

Reserve Pinot Noir.

Food

Snacks available over summer.

Accommodation

Luxury villa and cottage at $280 per night for two, and $50 per extra person. Includes complementary wine and generous breakfast provisions.

Haythornthwaite Wines

Omarere Road
Martinborough
06 306 9889 www.haythornthwaite.co.nz
Open Saturday, Sunday and public holidays 11.00 am–5.00 pm

The first release in October 1998 — their Pinot Noir — collected a Silver medal at the Air New Zealand Wine Awards. The owners are Mark Haythornthwaite, who grew up in Namibia, and his wife Susan, but the winemaking is by local busy bee winemaker Strat Canning. There are four varieties planted — sauvignon blanc, pinot gris, gewürztraminer and pinot noir.

Notable wines

Gewürztraminer and Pinot Noir.

Food

N/A

Accommodation

Self-contained Old Café Cottage, renovated to open plan. Sleeps three to four. Minutes' walk to the town square. $140 per night for two adults for the first two nights, then $100 per night for consecutive nights.

Winslow Estate

Princess Street
Martinborough
06 306 9648 www.winslowwines.co.nz
Open seven days 10.30 am–5.00 pm, in winter closed for tastings unless by appointment

Steve Tarring, an ex-marine biologist, changed tack in 1985 when he and his wife Jennifer established Winslow Estate. It is a family owned and operated boutique winery producing a limited volume of premium wines. All their wines are the product of handpicked single estate grapes, grown in Martinborough. Interestingly, they have opted out of the great cork versus screwcap debate and gone with a high-end, American-developed synthetic inert resin closure called Neocork.

Notable wines

For a relatively cool climate region winery, Winslow has done very well with its bolder hot climate reds. The Petra 2003 Cabernet Sauvignon and premium flagship Turakirae Reserve 2001 (Cabernet Sauvignon/Cabernet Franc/Merlot) have been very well received by critics. The Riesling has also had good press.

Food

N/A

Muirlea Rise

50 Princess Street
Martinborough
06 306 9332 Email: murilea.rise@xtra.co.nz
Open six days 11.00 am–5.00 pm, closed Wednesdays

Founded by the late Willie Brown, in the late 1980s and now run by his son Shawn, this winery has a very small production.

Notable wines

Pinot Noir has been very successful for this label, but they also do a fortified port style called Après.

Food

N/A

Margrain Vineyard

Corner Ponatahi and Huangarua Roads
Martinborough
06 306 9292 www.margrainvineyard.co.nz
Open summer Friday–Sunday 11.00 am–5.00 pm, winter Saturday and Sunday only

Husband and wife Graham and Daryl Margrain planted their first grapes in 1992 on their 10-hectare (25-acre) site. They have a philosophy of low-cropping, and producing premium wine only, from a wide number of grape varieties. Local winemaker Strat Canning contributes his experience in the production of their wide range of wines. Home Block Pinot Noir is the flagship wine, getting a Silver in the Air New Zealand Wine Awards for the 2004 vintage.

Notable wines

Home Block Pinot Noir (from 14-year-old vines), Chardonnay, Chenin Blanc (28-year-old vines), Gewürztraminer, Pinot Gris, and sweet dessert wines.

Food

Old Winery Café
06 306 8333
Open for lunches Saturday, Sunday and public holidays

Local produce and seasonal vegetables are a feature. On a sunny day you can sit outside and admire the vineyard views. Often there's live music on Sundays and you can even book an old London taxi to transport you there and back.

Accommodation

Don't drive home — stay the night. There are 14 studio villas, three-bedroom units, and one suite — designed by Wellington architect Roger Walker. Tariff: bedroom units $120, studios $165, the suite $365 a night.

Palliser Estate

Kitchener Street
Martinborough
06 306 9019 www.palliser.co.nz
Open seven days 10.30 am–4.00 pm

Palliser Estate is just outside Martinborough, located minutes from the town square. Managing director and marketing whiz Richard Riddiford heads the company, the largest producer in the region. The first vines were planted more than 20 years ago, in 1984, and they now export 60 per cent of their production, mainly to Britain. Two brands — Palliser Estate and Pencarrow — offer a comprehensive portfolio of wines, including chardonnay, méthode traditionelle, noble chardonnay, pinot noir, riesling, sauvignon blanc and pinot gris.

Palliser Estate is one of the major venues for the Toast Martinborough festival.

Notable wines

Their Sauvignon Blanc Riesling and Pinot Noir continue to pick up accolades and awards.

Food

N/A

Croft Wines

59 Kitchener Street
Martinborough
0508 457 638   Email: sales@croft.co.nz
Open Thursday–Sunday 10.00 am onwards

May Croft (an Anglican minister), husband Peter and their children Hannah and James, began the venture in 1997 with a small block in Kitchener Street. Wanting to expand, they found an ideal 10-hectare (25-acre) vineyard site, perched on the eastern Martinborough terraces. First planted was pinot noir, quickly followed by chardonnay, pinot gris and sauvignon blanc.

Notable wines

A new kid on the block, award-winning wines are Sauvignon Blanc and Chardonnay.

Food

N/A

The Cabbage Tree Vineyard

52 Kitchener Street
Martinborough
06 306 8178 www.thecabbagetreevineyard.co.nz
Open most weekends and public holidays 11.00 am–5.00 pm, sometimes open on Friday evenings

This is a tiny winery with just 1.2 hectares (3 acres) of vineyard started by ex-Wellington City Councillor David Bull and his wife Winifred. First vintage was in 2001.

Notable wines

In 2003 the Chardonnay and Pinot Noir picked up a Gold and a Silver medal respectively, in the Bragato Wine Awards.

Food

In summer, tasting platters are available with smoked chicken and fine cheeses, accompanied by chutneys and pickles etc.

Martinborough Vineyard

Princess Street
Martinborough
06 306 9955 www.martinborough-vineyard.com
Open seven days from 11.00 am–3.00 pm

Martinborough Vineyard is the producer of another iconic New Zealand pinot noir. Derek Milne, one of the founders was a soil scientist, and his 1978 DSIR soil research was crucial to identifying pinot as a potentially successful grape in the region. Derek and five other enthusiasts bought 6.5 hectares (16 acres) in the zone and started Martinborough Vineyard in 1980. Their wines did so well that, in London in 1997, they won a trophy for the Best Pinot Noir Worldwide at the prestigious International Wine and Spirit Challenge. Michael Cooper puts their pinot noir in his New Zealand Super Classic category.

Notable wines

Pinot Noir, of course. Also highly acclaimed are Pinot Gris and Chardonnay. There is a second tier label called Te Tera, which is great value Pinot Noir at about $25 a bottle.

Food

N/A

And right on the property . . .

Burnt Spur Wines

Martinborough Vineyard
Princess Street
Martinborough
06 306 9955   www.burntspur.co.nz
Open seven days 11.00 am–3.00 pm

Owned by the same parent company as Martinborough Vineyard, Burnt Spur is an entirely separate brand with its own winemaker and vineyards.

Notable wines

Sauvignon Blanc, Pinot Gris, Pinot Noir, Late Harvest Pinot Gris (dessert wine).

Food

N/A

Places to eat

In addition to the many fine cafes and restaurants attached to local wineries, there is some great food right in town.

The Village Café

6 Kitchener Street
06 306 8814
Open seven days 9.00 am–5.00 pm, breakfast 9.00 am–3.00 pm, blackboard lunch 12.00 noon–3.00 pm

Located in the Martinborough Wine Centre there is a laid back atmosphere here — no blaring techno or noisy baristas. Try the home-cured, manuka-smoked bacon and free range eggs or pure pork sausages. All their breads, scones, sauces, chutneys and smallgoods are made on the premises.

Taste of Martinborough Wine and Cheese Shop

8 Kitchener Street
Martinborough
06 306 8383

This café and store sells great coffee, deli foods and wine by the glass. They have a range of around 40 boutique cheeses from all over New Zealand, which you can sample, and have cut to order. Also on sale are local wines, olive oils, Schoc chocolates, pickles and jams, fudge and biscotti, and cider, plus French bread from Greytown's authentic French bakery.

Café Medici

9 Kitchener Street
Martinborough
06 306 9965
Open Wednesday to Monday 9.00 am–5.00 pm

Scenes of renaissance Italy decorate the walls. You will fine standard café fare here and the blackboard menu includes calzone, chicken salad and home-made bread.

The Martinborough

Peppers Martinborough Hotel
The Square
Martinborough
06 306 9350 www.peppers.co.nz/martinborough

This must-do, fully licensed restaurant with an extensive wine list, operates every day. It's superb food and service make it one of the best of New Zealand's provincial restaurants.

Est Wine Bar and Eatery

Situated in the nineteenth century Post Office building in Martinborough Square
06 306 9665 www.est.org.nz
Dinner Monday–Sunday 5.00 pm–late, lunch Saturday and Sunday 11.00 am–3.00 pm

A cosy little restaurant, right in the centre, specialising in contemporary New Zealand cusine, Est Wine Bar and Eatery has won awards for excellence in beef and lamb. It also offers venison, scallops etc. Their wine bar has a good selection of local wines to accompany tasting plates

The French Bistro

3 Kitchener Street
Martinborough
06 306 8863
Open Wednesday–Sunday for dinner, lunches Saturday and Sunday.

Jim Campbell and his wife, Cordon Bleu chef Wendy Campbell, run this renowned, stylish and cosy little bistro, decorated in chrome and black. French-inspired dishes are on offer with a selection of local wines. $20–$30 mains. Recommended.

La Mousse

3 Memorial Square
Martinborough
06 306 8224
Open seven days, wine bar from 4.00 pm, dinner from 6.00 pm, lunches Saturday and Sunday from 11.00 am

This French-style restaurant featuring traditional cuisine has a large courtyard for dining al fresco.

Things to do

Martinborough Wine Centre

6 Kitchener Street
Martinborough
06 306 9040 www.martinboroughwinecentre.co.nz
Open seven days 10.00 am–5.00 pm

The Martinborough Wine centre was established as a showcase for the wines and wineries of the region and has become the central hub of many of the local wine industry activities. Many local producers have their wines on display here, including a number that don't have door sales. These wines are all available for purchase and many are available for tasting. A large range of local produce is also available: local olive oils, lavender essential oils and related products, as well as the BeesOnline range of honey, soaps and oils, books, Icebreaker and Snowy Peak merino/possum-fur clothing, jams, chutneys and mustards.

Martinborough Country Market

Held every Sunday 10.00 am–2.00 pm behind The Village Café at the Martinborough Wine Centre

It provides a range of Wairarapa-grown seasonal produce, gourmet foods, handcrafts, artwork, jewellery, wool products, clothes, plus lemon, lavender and silk products, as well as rustic furniture, olive oils and preserves.

Circus Cinema

34 Jellicoe Street
Martinborough
06 306 9434 www.circus.net.nz/circus

Watch arthouse films in a relaxed and intimate environment. A licensed cafe and bar with cinema seating is custom designed for you to enjoy your food and drink during the film. How civilised. Drink local wines and imported beers.

Waiohine Gorge Suspension Bridge

Turn off State Highway Two just south of Carterton into Dalefield Road. Follow the road signs indicating Tararua Forest Park. The road-end car park is approximately 15 kilometres from State Highway Two.

DOC staff and contractors were involved in the design and construction of this bridge, built as a replacement for the 1982 original. It was completed at the end of July 2007 in order to cope with increasing numbers of trampers and picnickers. Supported by seven-metre-high towers, it is one of the longest and highest in the country, spanning 92 metres.

Cape Palliser

Allow half a day to drive the 40 km from Martinborough to the Lake Ferry Hotel Bar and Café for lunch. (Great food and they also provide accommodation). Then take the road to Cape Palliser — stopping at the Putangirua Pinnacles — and drive on along the coastal road through the small fishing town of Ngawi to the remote Cape Palliser lighthouse, the most southern point of the North Island.

Places to stay

BK's Chardonnay Motor Lodge

274 High Street
Masterton
06 377 7485   0800 222 880   www.bkschardonnay.co.nz

The brand new motel complex offers comfortable accommodation. There are18 luxury ground-floor units, seven with double spa baths. Breakfast and light meals are available on request. Qualmark 4-Star plus. Tariff: $100–$150 per night.

Acorn Estate Motel

Corner High and Manchester Streets
Masterton
06 377 0155   www.acornestate.co.nz

Qualmark 3-star plus. Good comfortable accommodation. Private spa pool, swimming pool, Sky TV or a video. All units are smoke free. Tariff: $89-$145 (2 persons). There is a five per cent discount for AA members.

Briarwood B&B

21 Main Street
Greytown
06 304 8336   www.briarwood.biz

This is a luxury option ranging from $190 for single ensuite to $350 for a two-bedroom suite. Meals are extra. The Qualmark 5-star rating reflects its elegance — Victorian themed, with all the indulgent goodies, including Egyptian cotton linen and double clawfoot baths.

Pinot Villas

4 Cambridge Street
Martinborough
06 306 9696   027 255 2708   www.pinotvillas.co.nz

The luxurious individual villas are just 50 m from the Square, hotels restaurants and cafés. Usual goodies, plus outdoor furniture, BBQ, bikes, petanque. Tariff: one-bedroom villa for a couple from $150; two-bedroom villas for four or five persons $260. Qualmark 4-star plus. Highly recommended.

Peppers Martinborough Hotel

The Square
Martinborough
06 306 9350   www.martinborough-hotel.co.nz

About as central as you can get — right on the Square — this elegant 1882 Victorian hotel has 16 individually themed rooms opening on to verandas or courtyards. Tariff: double room $295 for bed and breakfast; rises to $395 on Saturday night. There is also a fab restaurant, as mentioned previously.

Brackenridge B&B

Awhea Road (White Rock Road)
Martinborough
06 306 8115   www.brackenridge.co.nz

You have a choice of a studio or two-bed and four-bed colonial-style, nicely appointed luxurious cottages, each with fireplace. Can sleep up to eight people. Studio $190 per night. Individual cottages start at $215 per night for two persons. Prices include breakfast provisions.

The Old Manse B&B

19 Grey Street
Martinborough
06 306 8599   0800 399-229   www.oldmanse.co.nz

Originally the home of Presbyterian Ministers for the region, this restored villa provides the choice of five Queen-size rooms and a twin-room cottage. Tariff: $170–$210. Qualmark 4-star plus.

Wairarapa weekend — Saturday

After Martinborough, head back north on State Highway Two and take in the rest of the Wairarapa — Featherston, Greytown, Carterton and environs.

Featherston

There is not a whole lot going on in this township, but there are a few local spots of interest you shouldn't miss.

The Cider House Orchard

East Longwood Road
Featherston
027 308 8047

Penny Elliott and David Brosnan bought their 10-hectare (2 acre) block of land in 1992. They produce a range of ciders from traditional French and English cider apple varieties, fermented at their Cider House Orchard.

Fell Locomotive Museum

Corner State Highway Two and Lyon Street
Featherston
06 308 9379   www.fellmuseum.org.nz
Open seven days 10.00 am–4.00 pm

The Museum houses H199, the only locomotive of its type in the world, one of six designed specifically for the Rimutaka Incline where they climbed gradients as steep as one in 13. Exhibits include photographs, models, memorabilia, films and an audio-visual presentation.

Greytown

Historically New Zealand's first inland town, Greytown has lovely Victorian buildings in the main street, many of them housing very stylish foodie and speciality shops plus art galleries, antique shops and so on. Enjoy . . .

The French Bakery and Espresso Bar

81 Main Street
Greytown

Born in Brittany, French baker Monsieur Moise Cerson and his New Zealand fiancée have established a food lovers' Mecca with their bakery. They feature great coffee, breads, patisserie goodies, terrines and French cheeses.

The Greytown Butcher
Main Street
Greytown

If you're self-catering or just looking for something to go with that fab French bread, just along the road is The Greytown Butcher. They have a wide array of speciality meats and charcuterie, all displayed and beautifully presented in a spotlessly clean shop. Look for organic meats, ostrich ham and pastrami, venison, kangaroo and smoked meats.

Schoc Chocolates
177 Main Street
Greytown
www.chocolatetherapy.com

Drool over more than 50 flavours of chocolate in tablet or hand made form. How about walnut caramel — fresh local walnuts in a hard caramel, dipped in dark chocolate — or ginger and wasabi hand-rolled truffles?

Saluté Restaurant
83 Main Street
Greytown
www.salute.greytown.co.nz

At this highly acclaimed eatery they do mezze type starters, pizza, and Moroccan-influenced mains. Open for lunch and dinner Tuesday to Sunday. Brunch served Saturday and Sunday.

Main Street Deli
88 Main Street
Greytown

Renowned café food and extensive range of gourmet products for sale.

Carterton

Compared with Greytown and Martinborough, Carterton is rather the odd one out, despite being 'Daffodil capital of New Zealand'. It is very much a blue-collar rural town, with many boarded-up shops, and businesses selling farming equipment and supplies. When I was there, even the local wine shop was closed, doors firmly shut and a sign that said — 'Well we tried but it didn't work — go to the liquor wholesaler for wine'.

Masterton

Power on through on State Highway 22 to Masterton, and if you weren't all foodied out at Greytown, then head straight for the Farmers Market.

Masterton Farmers' Market

Solway Showgrounds every Saturday from 8.30 am

Stalls are set up in the old covered sheep pens, with woodchips on the floor. You can buy fresh seasonal vegetables and fruit, all kinds of dairy products, eggs, herbs, fresh-baked bread and flowers as well as olive oils, pickles, jams and fruit juices. There is also organic lamb and beef and ready-to-eat hot dogs, sausages and mint-and-lamb sausages — also organic, of course.

Kingsmeade Specialty Cheese

8B First Street
Masterton
06 378 7178

A bit of a diversion off State Highway Two, Kingsmeade specialises in sheep cheeses. Janet and Miles King run a large flock of milking ewes, which you can see being milked at their property nearby at 3.00 pm. The range includes havarti, haloumi, and gouda in addition to their Cygnet, Lark, and Wairarapa Jack cheeses. It pays to phone first before dropping in.

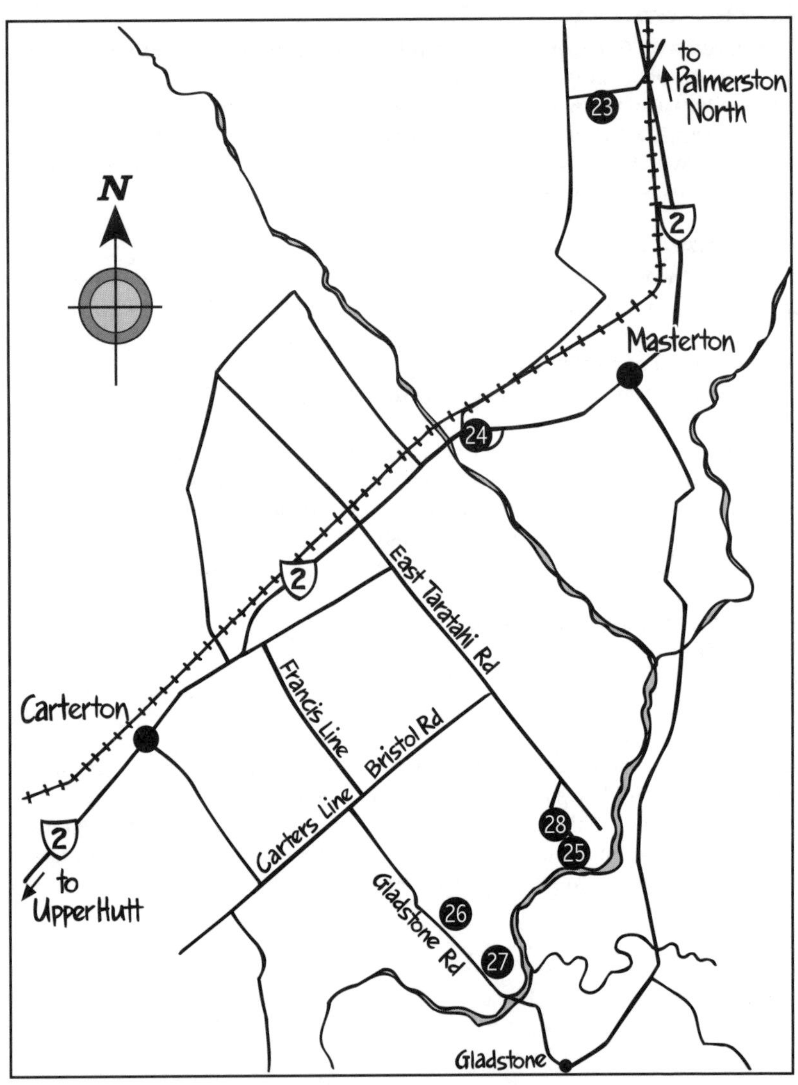
N
to
Palmerston
North
23
2
Masterton
24
2
East Taratahi Rd
Francis Line
Bristol Rd
Carterton
Carters Line
2
to
UpperHutt
28
25
26
Gladstone Rd
27
Gladstone

Now to the wine . . .

There are three local wineries in this neck of the woods.

Loopline Vineyard

42 Loop Line
Opaki
06 377 3353 www.loopline.co.nz
Open seven days 10.00 am–5.00 pm (but sometimes closed Tuesday and Wednesday)

The most northern Wairarapa winery five kilometres north of Masterton, on the Opaki Plains, Loopline was started by Frank and Bernice Parker, with the first vintage in 1995. Former beef and lamb farmers Ian and Jenny McGovern took over the reins in 1999.

Notable wines

Sauvignon Blanc, Riesling and Pinot Gris. Prices around the mid $20 mark.

Food

N/A

Solstone Estate

119 Solway Crescent
Masterton
06 377 5505 www.solstone.co.nz
Open seven days 11.00 am–5.00 pm

Elizabeth Barrett-Hackel and her Canadian-born husband Lloyd have been the owners since 2001. Local winemaker Bernard Newman has worked in Masterton since 1991 and relishes the opportunity to work on Solstone's unique vineyard — one of the oldest in the valley. Plantings date back to 1981, in narrow rows with low trellising, as is the French tradition in Bordeaux.

Notable wines

Cabernet Franc and Pinot Noir.

Food

The Vintage Room restaurant has simple, hearty country fare. Lunch Monday–Sunday 11.00 am–3.00 pm, dinner available in summer but closed June 1–September 1.

Johner Estate

40a Dakins Road
Carterton
04 498 2109 www.johner-estate.com
Open Monday–Friday 10.00.am–4.30 pm

German-born winemaker Karl-Heinz Johner and son Patrick started this winery in 1998 — their second venture as the family also owns a winery in the Baden wine-growing region in Germany. In Dakins Road, they concentrate on sauvignon blanc and pinot noir, although there are new releases of pinot gris, riesling, syrah and a cabernet merlot/malbec.

Notable wines

Sauvignon Blanc and Pinot Noir are the mainstays, but look out for Noble Pinot Noir — a dessert wine made from botrytis-affected grapes. And no, it's not a red — the clear juice was pressed off soon after picking.

Food

N/A

Things to do

Aratoi Wairarapa Museum of Art and History
Bruce Street
Masterton
www.aratoi.co.nz
Open seven days 10.00 am–4.30 pm

Contemporary café, exhibits, local history and art. Check the website for regular updates on current exhibitions.

Wairarapa weekend — Sunday
Heading back from Masterton on State Highway Two towards Martinborough, hang a left at East Taratahi Road towards Gladstone.

Gladstone Vineyard

Gladstone Road
Carterton
06 379 8563 www.gladstone.co.nz
Open Tuesday–Sunday 11.00 am–5.00 pm, also Public Holiday Mondays

Gladstone Vineyard has been owner-operated by Christine and David Kernohan since February 1996. Both born in Glasgow, Scotland, they moved to New Zealand nearly 30 years ago. Christine is chief winemaker, while David is an architect, running his own business from the vineyard.

Notable wines

Sauvignon Blanc and Pinot Noir, but also a very nice Pinot Gris and a Bordeaux blended red. A second label — 12,000 Miles — is at a more affordable price range. (The name relates to the distance travelled from Glasgow to New Zealand).

Food

The Stoker's Café is open Thursday–Sunday and Public Holiday Mondays 11.00 am–3.00 pm.

Accommodation

The luxury Gladstone Vineyard apartment sleeps two to four. The tariff includes country breakfast supplies, complimentary wine and a winery tour. $225 for the first night, $415 for a two-night weekend stay with late check-out. Prices are negotiable midweek out of season.

Fairmont Estate

Gladstone Road
Carterton
06 379 8498 Email: pinot@xtra.co.nz
Open Monday–Sunday 10.00 am–5.00 pm

Right next door to Gladstone Vineyard, Fairmont Estate had its first crop in 1997. Winemaker and owner Jon McNab makes one of the best Wairarapa pinot noirs, outside of Martinborough. Michael Cooper, top critic, gives it four stars.

Notable wines

Pinot Noir obviously, but their Pinot Gris and Sauvignon are also doing well.

Food

N/A

Borthwick Estate

Dakins Road
Gladstone
06 372 7512 www.borthwick.co.nz
Open only by appointment, barrel tasting only, no purchases onsite

The first vintage was in 1999. Paddy Borthwick, a graduate of the wine institution, Roseworthy College, in South Australia, has been in the wine industry since 1991, including winemaking in Marlborough, France, Switzerland, Australia and the United States. Plantings include riesling, sauvignon blanc, chardonnay, pinot noir and very rare in New Zealand, the Italian chianti grape — sangiovese.

Notable wines

Wairarapa Riesling, Wairarapa Sauvignon Blanc.

Food

N/A

Things to do

Stonehenge Aotearoa

027 246 6766 www.astronomynz.org.nz/stonehenge
Tours are available to the public at 2.00 pm Saturday, Sunday and Public Holidays (except December 24, 25 and 26), bookings essential

Ten minutes from Carterton by car, 'the henge' was built by members of the Phoenix Astronomical Society in order to create an open-sky observatory inspired by, and built on a similar scale to, the famous Stonehenge in England. Adults $12, children $6.

Hot Air Ballooning

09 478-6602 www.freemanx.co.nz

View the snow-capped Tararua mountains and the scenic Wairarapa countryside from a hot air balloon. Early morning flights, seven days a week, all year round (weather permitting) in balloons of various sizes.

Kahutara Canoes

06 308 8453 www.wairarapa.co.nz/kahutara

Local taxidermist, John McCosh, offers a variety of South Wairarapa canoe and kayak trips, on the Ruamahanga River, Wairarapa. Trips include stops for boiling the billy and can also include a BBQ lunch.

Marlborough

In 1973 Montana Wines' chief winemaker Frank Yukich — against the advice of the company board — planted trial grapes in Marlborough, convinced that its climate and soils could produce great wine. Cabernet sauvignon and müller-thurgau were trialled, with varying degrees of success. New Zealand's first commercial sauvignon blanc vineyards were planted by Montana in 1976 — and the rest is history. Marlborough is now New Zealand's star wine region, with almost 50 per cent of the country's grape harvest and around 12,500 hectares (31,000 acres) of vines. High sunshine hours and cool night temperatures, combined with old stony alluvial soils produce not only our internationally successful zingy Marlborough sauvignon blanc, but also very good chardonnay, riesling, pinot gris, pinot noir and traditional méthode traditionelle wines.

The broad alluvial Wairau Plains area, south of Blenheim, contains the bulk of plantings, but other sub-regions such as Fairhall, Hawkesbury and the Awatere and Waihopai valleys continue to develop, with their own distinct microclimates and wine styles.

In addition to wine, Marlborough is a gourmet food and wine lovers playground, with an abundance of vineyard restaurants and cafés, two summer farmers' markets and many boutique foodie outlets. One let-down is that evening dining seven days a week is almost nil. Just three vineyard restaurants, are open at present: Herzog, Gibb's, and Vintners Retreat. Of course, there's some good dining in Blenheim township, but to find a local dining experience right amongst the vines, your choice is very limited. For our largest and internationally famous region, Marlborough really should do better.

On the map, Marlborough does look dauntingly huge, but it is quite do-able in a series of trips. One weekend obviously wouldn't do the region justice.

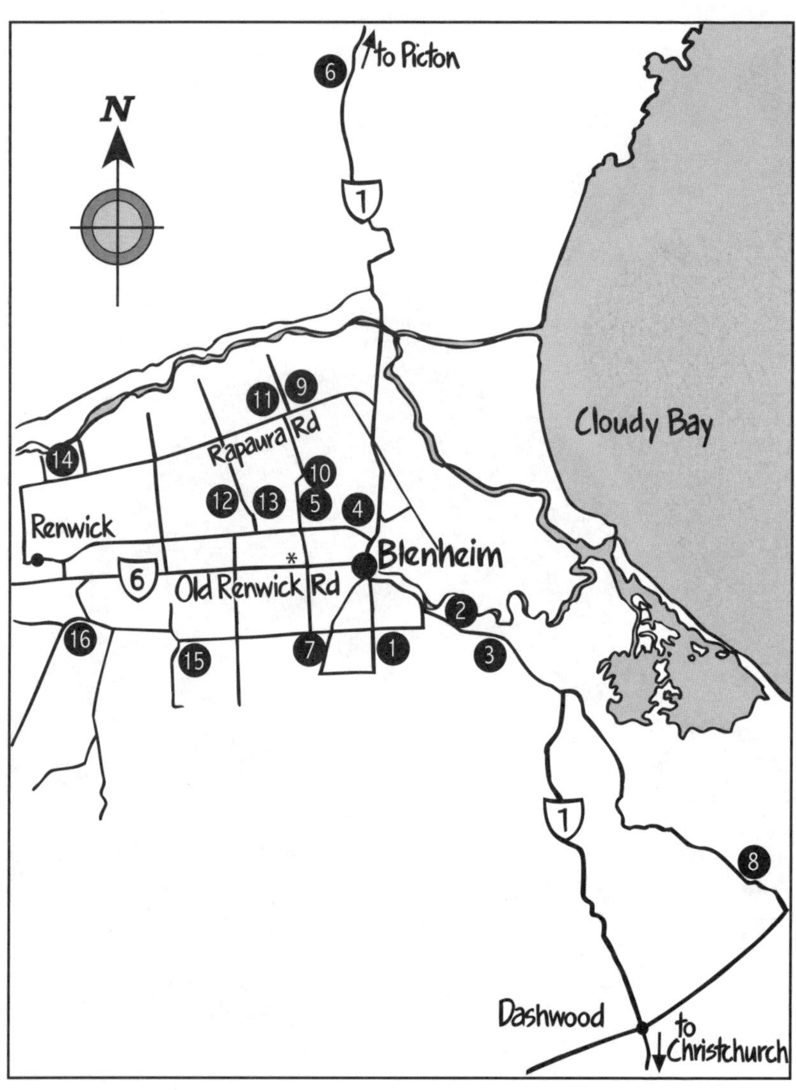
to Picton
6
N
1
Cloudy Bay
9
11
Rapaura Rd
14
10
12
13
5
4
Renwick
Blenheim
6
Old Renwick Rd
2
16
15
7
1
3
1
8
Dashwood
to
Christchurch

Lawson's Dry Hills

Alabama Road (on the eastern side of Blenheim about a kilometre from the Redwood Street roundabout intersection)
Blenheim
03 578 7674 www.lawsonsdryhills.co.nz
Open seven days 10.00 am–5.00 pm, closed Christmas Day, Good Friday

Lawson's Dry Hills was founded in 1992 by Barbara and Ross Lawson. Since launching the label they have gained a reputation for the excellence of their gewürztraminer and sauvignon blanc. The rustic cellar door gives a good view of the Wither Hills in the distance — hence the name.

Notable wines

Chardonnay, Gewürztraminer, Riesling, Limited Release Sauvignon Blanc.

Food

Cheese platters. Picnickers welcome.

Vineyard dog

Tomi — golden lab.

Mount Riley Wines

10 Malthouse Road
Riverlands
03 577 9900 www.mountriley.co.nz
Open seven days late October–March 10.00 am–4.30 pm, April–mid-October by appointment

A large producer with nearly 120 hectares (290 acres) in Marlborough, Mount Riley is a family owned New Zealand company established in 1992 by ex-Corbans Wines accountant John Buchanan. In 2004 John's youngest daughter Amy joined Mount Riley as sales and marketing director. Head winemaker Bill 'Digger' Hennessy has been leading Mount Riley's winemaking since 1998. Their 2006 Sauvignon Blanc has been a huge success at around $30. The premium Seventeen Valley range is $20–$40.

Notable wines

Seventeen Valley Chardonnay, Estate Pinot Gris, Seventeen Valley Sauvignon Blanc.

Food

N/A

Vineyard dog

Tisha — Rhodesian ridgeback.

3

Montana Brancott Winery

Riverlands
Main Road South State Highway One
Blenheim
03 577 5775 www.montana.co.nz
Cellar door open seven days 10.00 am–4.30 pm, winery plant tours on the hour 10.00 am–3.00 pm

A one-stop shop for wine tourists, Montana has spared no cash in setting up this cellar door complex in a French Châteaux-inspired building with vaulted, eight-metre ceilings. Here they provide tours, tastings, a restaurant and gift shop. If you have the time, take in the Odyssey Tour, which includes a tour of the vineyard and winery plant, a tasting and three-course lunch (bookings essential).

Notable wines

There are heaps to try but a standout is their own premium Letter Series Brancott 'B' Marlborough Sauvignon Blanc.

Food

A specialty is the Montana Terroir Platter designed to complement the wines. Relaxed café-style food and a children's playground make for a family-friendly winery visit. Open 10.30 am–3.00 pm.

Whitehaven Wine Company

1 Dodson Street
Blenheim
03 577 6634 Email: whitehavenreservations@xtra.co.nz
Whitehaven Conservatory Restaurant and Cellar Door: cellar door open seven days 10.00 am–4.00 pm, restaurant open seven days for lunch and dinner

Whitehaven Wine Company was established in 1994 by majority shareholders, (the late) Greg, and Sue White, and winemaker, Simon Waghorn. American company Gallo is also a partner in the company. The cellar door and restaurant are located in Dodson Street, where the original facility was set up. The vineyards are located some distance away. Whitehaven sources fruit from 40 acres of its own vineyards and from 30 contracted growers located in carefully selected vineyard sites across Marlborough's Wairau and Awatere valleys.

Notable wines

Gewürztraminer, Pinot Gris, Noble Dessert Riesling.

Food

Café-style cuisine, mains around $18.

Matua Valley Marlborough Cellar Shop
New Renwick Road
Blenheim
03 572 8642   www.matua.co.nz
Cellar door and gardens are open seven days

The cellar door offers a wide range of Matua wines to choose from and the selection available for tasting changes fortnightly. You can also purchase from a wide range of gifts and souvenirs.

Walnut Block

43 Blicks Lane
Blenheim
03 577 9187   021 734 475   www.walnutblock.co.nz

Specialising in pinot noir and sauvignon blanc, and headed by Clyde Sowman, Walnut Block is a small producer with just these two wines in the stable. Harrods of London is a customer, so they must be doing something right.

Accommodation

Two newly built, luxury one-bedroom, self-contained cottages situated on the 60-acre estate are open plan, with extensive views across vineyards to a mountain backdrop. Continental breakfast provisions are provided, including a selection of fruit, yogurt, cereals, jams, bread, tea and fresh-ground coffee. Tariff: $200 a night.

Johanneshof Cellars

State Highway One
Koromiko
03 5737035 www.johanneshof.co.nz
Open summer Tuesday–Sunday 10.00 am–4.00 pm, closed Saturday and Sunday in winter, best to phone ahead
(Don't miss the barrel cave tour and tasting at $10 per person — a candle-lit excavated magic wine tunnel.)

Out on a limb on State Highway One at the small village of Koromiko on the way from Blenheim to Picton, Johanneshof specialises in 'aromatic' German-style white wines. It is jointly owned and operated by Edel Everling (fifth generation winemaker from Ruedesheim, Germany) and Warwick Foley from Marlborough, who both trained in the famous wine area of Rheingau in Germany. Their oldest vines were planted 18 years ago.

The vineyard is located on a steeply sloping clay hillside with a 50-metre sandstone tunnel, 20 metres below ground and functioning as a barrel room. They also produce Edelbrand, a brandy from twice-distilled white wine that clocks in at 38 per cent alcohol.

Notable wines

Gewürztraminer, Sauvignon Blanc, Pinot Gris.

Food

N/A

Wither Hills

211 New Renwick Road
Blenheim
03 520 8270 www.witherhills.co.nz
Open seven days 10.00 am–4.30 pm

Founded by former winemaker Brent Marris and his father, but now part of Lion Nathan, Wither Hills specialises in just three grape varieties — sauvignon blanc, chardonnay and pinot noir. Around 300 hectares (750 acres) of vineyard provide the grapes. Ben Glover is now the chief winemaker (previously winery manager). The winery and cellar door is contained in a stylish building designed by Jasmax architects.

Notable wines

All three: Chardonnay, Sauvignon Blanc, Pinot Noir.

Food

N/A

While you're in the area . . .

Villa Maria Marlborough Cellar Shop
Corner Paynters and New Renwick Roads
Fairhall
03 520 8470 www.villamaria.co.nz
Open seven days 10.00 am–5.00 pm, May–October 11.00 am–5.00 pm (subject to change), complimentary wine tasting, winery tours by appointment. Indicated with a star on the map at the start of this section.

And if you're still in town during the week head for . . .

Vavasour Wines

Redwood Pass Road
Seddon
03 5757481 www.vavasour.com
Open Monday–Friday 10.00 am–4.30 pm, closed weekends and Public Holidays

Peter Vavasour was one of the founders back in 1986. A 20-minute drive south of Blenheim, will get you there — to a place where the climate is different and free from frost (the bane of most Marlborough growers).

In addition to the standard label (around $30) they produce two other ranges of wines — Dashwood and Redwood Pass (around $20).

Notable wines

Anna's Vineyard Chardonnay ($40), Marlborough Chardonnay, Awatere Pinot Gris, Marlborough Riesling, Awatere Sauvignon Blanc, Awatere Pinot Noir.

Food

N/A

St Clair Family Estate

Corner Rapaura and Selmes Roads
Riverlands
03 570 5280 www.saintclair.co.nz
Open seven days 9.00 am–5.00 pm

St Clair is owned by Neal and Judy Ibbotson, two of Marlborough's earliest vineyard pioneers, having planted their first vines in 1978. Their son, Sydney-based Tony, looks after their design and branding, while daughters Sarina and Julie both work in the business in sales and marketing. Their flagship wine is the Wairau Reserve Sauvignon Blanc, which has been awarded 20 trophies for consecutive vintages since 2000.

Notable wines

Omaka Reserve Chardonnay, All the Block series Chardonnays, Godfreys Creek Gewürztraminer and Pinot Gris, Block 9 Riesling, All the Block series Sauvignon Blancs, Wairau Reserve Sauvignon Blanc, Rapaura Reserve Merlot, Omaka Reserve Pinot Noir.

Food

Platters available.

Drylands Estate

Drylands Winery and Cellar Door Shop
Hammerichs Road
Rapaura
03 570 5252 www.drylands.co.nz
Open seven days 10.00 am–5.00 pm

Darryl Woolley is the winemaker at Drylands, part of the Nobilo group, which took over the former Selaks Estate in 1998. Very distinctive intense fruit-flavoured wines come from this single vineyard range. Their wines are competitively priced at around $22 — sauvignon blanc, pinot gris, dry riesling, chardonnay, pinot noir and merlot.

Notable wines

Dry Riesling, Sauvignon Blanc, Pinot Noir.

Food

Yet another Swiss restaurateur, Dietmar Schnarre, runs the popular Drylands Restaurant, which features local produce matched with Drylands, Rose Tree Cottage, Nobilo and Selaks wines. Vegetarian and gluten-free dishes are also catered for. Mains are around $23. Lunch Wednesday–Sunday, dinner Wednesday–Saturday.

Hunter's Wines

Rapaura Road
Renwick
03 572 8489 www.hunters.co.nz
Open seven days 9.30 am–4.30 pm, closed Public Holidays

Jane Hunter OBE heads this very successful company that was founded by Jane and her late husband, Ernie, in 1983. Hunter's Wines have since won more than 100 Gold medals at national and international wine competitions. The winery and café are set among native gardens where a vine-covered trellised walkway links the café, wine shop and art gallery. The wines available for tasting include current vintages and 'library' wine tastings.

Notable wines

Marlborough Chardonnay, Marlborough Gewürztraminer, Marlborough Riesling, Kaho Roa Sauvignon Blanc, Marlborough Sauvignon Blanc, Marlborough Pinot Noir, The Hounds Pinot Noir.

Food

Café-style food — light meals around $15 and for the bigger appetite about $19. There is also a kids' menu . . . and some very tempting starters and desserts. Open seven days Monday–Friday 10.30 am–4.30 pm, closed Public Holidays.

Allan Scott Estates

Jacksons Road
Blenheim
03 572 9054 www.allanscott.com
Open seven days 9.00 am–5.00 pm, closed public holidays

Allan Scott is another of the region's pioneers, having been employed by Montana way back in 1973 when they were planting trial grapes at Fairhall. Two years later, he and his wife Catherine started their own vineyard, growing contract grapes. By 1990 they launched their own label, and have become one of the region's major producers. They remain steadfastly family-owned, with son Joshua winemaker, daughter Victoria running their popular restaurant, and younger daughter Sara as viticulturalist. The winery, built from rammed earth, also provides a rustic ambience for their popular lunchtime restaurant and cellar door tasting room. There are two ranges of wine — premium Prestige 'single vineyard' label and the standard Allan Scott label. Prices range from $20 to $30.

Notable wines

The Wallops Chardonnay, Marlborough Chardonnay, Marlborough Gewürztraminer, The Moorlands Riesling, The Hounds Pinot Noir.

Also for tasting: Josh makes a range of boutique beers under his Moa label. 750ml bottle for $12.50, or a champagne-cork-sealed magnum (1.5 l) for $25.

Food

Twelve Trees Vineyard Restaurant (03 572 7123). Open from 9.00 am daily. The restaurant's rammed earth construction makes it cosy in cold weather and pleasantly cool during Marlborough's hot summers. Also a leafy, shaded courtyard enhances outdoor dining. Highly recommended. They serve bistro-style food at around $19 a main. Food and wine matches are suggested.

Cloudy Bay Vineyards

Jacksons Road
Blenheim
03 520 9140 www.cloudybay.co.nz
Open seven days 10.00 am–5.00 pm, closed Public Holidays

Cloudy Bay is probably the most famous New Zealand sauvignon blanc in the key markets of America, Britain, Australia and Japan, and largely responsible for the worldwide awareness of Marlborough as a wine region. Started by Australian wine company Cape Mentelle in 1985, Cloudy Bay is now part of the international wine portfolio of Luis Vuitton Moët Hennessy. Winemaker Kevin Judd was headhunted from Selaks at the ripe age of 24 for the critical first vintage, and is now New Zealand managing director. In addition to sauvignon blanc, they also produce a super premium $45 sparkler Pelorus (Michael Cooper gave it five stars). There are friendly staff at the cellar door, no tasting fees and a wide list of wines on offer to sample.

Notable wines

Pelorus vintage and non-vintage. Also Chardonnay, Gewürztraminer, Riesling, standard label Sauvignon Blanc, and Te Koko (oak aged) Sauvignon Blanc, Pinot Noir.

Food

N/A

Herzog

81 Jeffries Road
Blenheim
03 572 8770 www.herzog.co.nz
Open Monday–Friday 9.00 am–5.00 pm, weekends 11.00 am–4.00 pm

Well known for their fine wines and also their multiple award-winning restaurant, Hans Herzog and his wife Therese had previously grown pinot noir and run a restaurant near Zurich, but felt the allure of the South Seas. Breaking a tradition (going back to 1482) they established an organic/biodynamic winery on the banks of the Wairau River. With just 11 hectares (27 acres), they produce around 6000 cases per year. Wines include montepulciano, a grape common in Central Italy, but only planted on about seven hectares (17 acres) in New Zealand.

Notable wines

Chardonnay, Pinot Gris, Viognier, Pinot Noir. Merlot/Cabernet blend, Montepulciano.

Food

Bring your chequebook. Entrées are around $25 and mains are up to the $100 mark. Still, that's what you get at a Michelin-rated luxury restaurant with international chefs. Specialities include Wagyu beef rib eye and whole crayfish. The wine list runs to 24 pages and includes fine wines from all over the world. Dessert wine? . . . May I suggest the Château d'Yquem, Sauternes Grand Cru Supérieur 1989 ($750). And — gloriously un-PC — they have a cigar list as well. Open for dinner October 16–mid May Tuesday–Sunday from 6.30 pm. Also onsite is the bistro, open from mid-October to mid-May Tuesday–Sunday 12.00 noon to 3.00 pm. This is affordable, and designed for the more casual diner. Entrées are about $18, mains around $25 including pasta, fish, poultry and fab desserts.

Highfield Estate

Brookby Road (turn off State Highway Six onto Godfrey Road, turn right into Dog Point Road and left into Brookby Road)
Blenheim
03 572 9244 www.highfield.co.nz
Open seven days 10.00 am–5.00 pm

Privately owned by two overseas directors, Shin Yokoi and Tom Tenuwera, Highfield Estate is one of the smaller premium producers in Marlborough. They have been awarded numerous international trophies for their wines. The winery and restaurant complex offers panoramic views of Marlborough's Wairau Valley. The structure is based on a Tuscan Terracotta building called Capaggiolo, complete with a tower. Obviously a very popular tourist lunch and tasting stop, it is looking a tad tired and could do with a spruce up.

Notable wines

Chardonnay, Sauvignon Blanc, Pinot Noir.

Food

The restaurant focuses on fresh local produce: lamb, beef, pork, salmon etc. Service is brisk and efficient. Entrées are around $20, mains around $28. Lunch is available from 11.30 am–3.30 pm while a light lunch menu is available from 3.30 pm–4.30 pm. Evening dining and functions can be made by arrangement, but for a minimum of 30 people.

Accommodation

Highfield's fully self-contained apartment has sweeping views and contains one double bedroom, open-plan living, a fully equipped kitchen, laundry, bath and shower, and air conditioning. Tariff: $250 a night.

Omaka Springs Estates

47 Kennedys Road
Blenheim
03 572 9933 www.omaka.co.nz
Open Monday–Friday 10.00 am–4.30 pm

Former airline pilot Jeff Jensen and his wife Robina started Omaka Springs in1992. They have two vineyards: one in Kennedys Road and the other in Falveys Road, totalling 72 hectares (177 acres). They also grow 2500 olive trees, which include 23 different varieties. Their olive oil is sold at the cellar door, and they are aiming to export overseas.

Notable wines

Pinot Gris, Falveys Sauvignon Blanc, Chardonnay.

Food

N/A

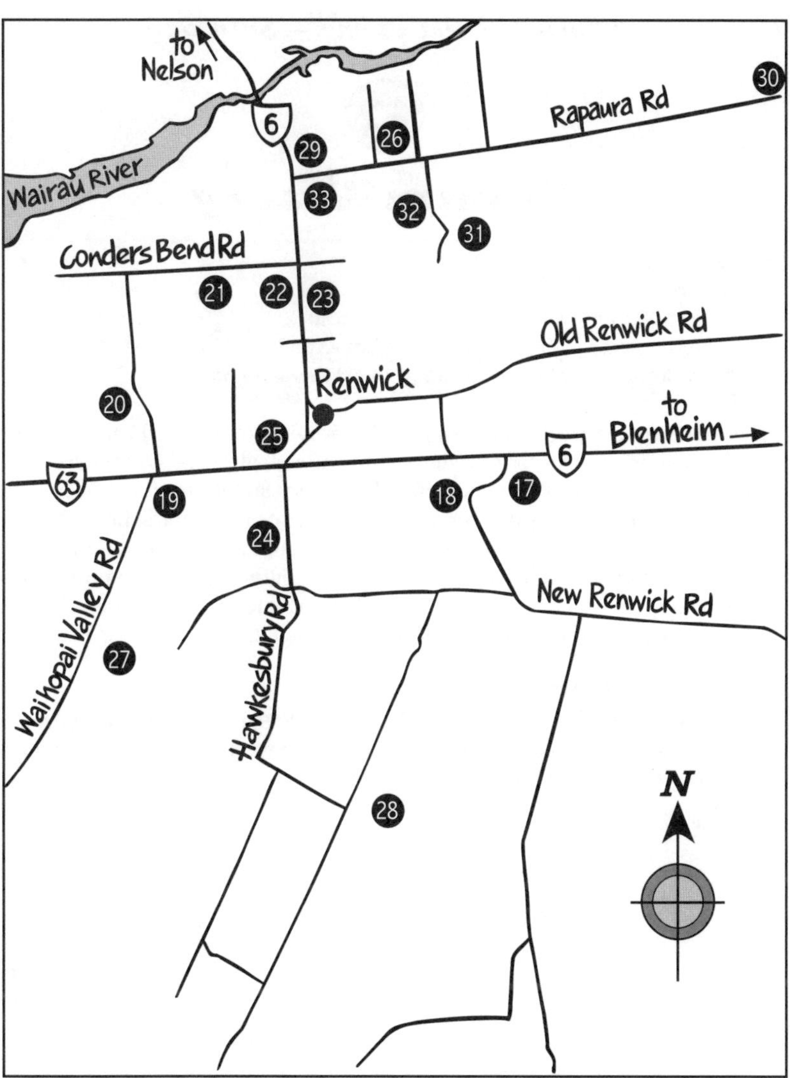

to Nelson
Wairau River
6
Rapaura Rd
30
29
26
33
32
31
Conders Bend Rd
21
22
23
Old Renwick Rd
Renwick
20
25
to Blenheim
63
6
19
18
17
24
New Renwick Rd
Waihopai Valley Rd
Hawkesbury Rd
27
28
N

Fromm Winery

Godfrey Road
Blenheim
03 572 9355 www.frommwineries.com
Open seven days from October–April 11.00 am–5.00 pm, May–September Friday–Sunday 11.00 am–4.00 pm

The name comes from its Swiss founder, winemaker Georg Fromm, whose experience dates back to four generations of winegrowers. La Strada means 'the way' and is a symbolic name for the winery and its wines, conceptually meaning 'to move forward'. Fromm is known for its pinot noirs, Bordeaux red varieties, and zingy low alcohol rieslings. Low cropping, sustainable viticulture, and hand-tending in the vineyard also contribute to the signature wines. Winemakers are Hätsch Kalberer and William Hoare. A strong Swiss German influence pervades. The website offers both languages.

Notable wines

Clayvin Chardonnay, Dry Riesling, La Strada Reserve Merlot, Marlborough Merlot/Malbec. All of the Pinot Noirs are fantastic. Sweet wines: Gewürztraminer late harvest, La Strada Riesling and Spätlese.

Food

N/A

18

Kathy Lynskey Wines

36 Godfrey Road
Blenheim
03 572 7180   021 608 554   www.kathylynskeywines.co.nz
Open summer seven days 10.30 am–4.00 pm, winter Wednesday–Sunday 10.30 am–4.00 pm

Formerly known as Wairau Peaks, the name has changed to Kathy Lynskey Wines. Kathy is Marlborough-bred and shares the running of her company with her Californian-born partner Kent Casto, who comes with 20 years' experience in the American restaurant scene.

Nine hectares (22 acres) of stony former-riverbed soil produces some full-bodied wines. With the exception of sauvignon blanc, their wines are all Single Vineyard or Reserve. Prices range from $25 to $55.

Notable wines

Casto Reserve Chardonnay, Godfrey Reserve Chardonnay, Gewürztraminer, Pinot Gris, Reserve Block 36 Pinot Noir.

Food

N/A

Grove Mill

Waihopai Valley Road
Renwick
03 572 8200 www.grovemill.co.nz
Open seven days 11.00 am–5.00 pm

Eco-friendly Grove Mill is a corporate-owned winery that is also situated in the Waihopai Valley. The mission is to produce high-quality wines with minimal environmental impact. The company mascot is the Southern Bell Frog, which lives in the winery wetland. Grove Mill's cellar door houses the Diversion Art Gallery featuring exhibits from some of New Zealand's leading artists and sculptors.

Notable wines

Estate Chardonnay, Marlborough Riesling, Estate Riesling, Marlborough Sauvignon Blanc, Wairau Reserve Pinot Noir.

Food

Cheese platters are available, but visitors are also welcome to picnic. The picnic area has tables under shade sails with views up the Waihopai Valley to the mountains and across the wetland to the Richmond Ranges.

20

Seresin Vineyards and Winery

85 Bedford Road
Blenheim
03 572 9408 www.seresin.co.nz
Open seven days 10.00 am–4.30 pm

Founded in 1992 by Britain-based director of photography Michael Seresin, the focus here is on high-quality winemaking practices — such as organic/biodynamic grape growing, plus hand-harvesting and low cropping levels. Winemaker is Clive Dougal, ex-Brit and former assistant winemaker at Pegasus Bay, Waipara. Colin Ross, an expert in organic growing, is viticulturist and estate manager formerly from . . . wait for it . . . Cowaramup, Western Australia. Give that cow a ram up.

A large sentinel stone marks the entrance to the winery, with the signature handprint logo representing the Seresin's gentle 'hands-on' approach to winemaking.

Notable wines

Reserve Chardonnay, Marlborough Gewürztraminer, Memento Riesling, Marlborough Sauvignon Blanc, Marlborough Pinot Gris. Pinot Noirs: Raupo Creek and Leah.

Food

N/A

Bladen Vineyard

83 Conders Bend Road
Renwick
03 572 9417 www.bladen.co.nz
Open seven days Labour Weekend–Easter 10.00 am–5.00 pm

In 1997 the first wines were produced under the Bladen label, by owners Dave and Christine Macdonald. They own a small eight-hectare (19-acre) vineyard, specialising in 'aromatic' wines — sauvignon blanc, gewürztraminer, riesling and pinot gris. However, they also do a pinot noir and a merlot/malbec blend. Their tiny tasting room welcomes visitors.

Notable wines

Tilly Block Gewürztraminer, Eastern Block Riesling, Sauvignon Blanc, The Setter Merlot/Malbec.

Food

N/A

Framingham Wine Company

Conders Bend Road
Renwick
03 572 8884 www.framingham.co.nz
Open seven days 11.00 am–4.00 pm

The estate produces a range of wines from six vineyards. The company derives its name from the village of Framingham, located in Southern Norfolk in

Britain — the small village that was the ancestral home of the company's founder, Rex Brooke-Taylor.

The vineyards date back to the early 1980s making them some of the oldest vineyards in the region. The first wine, a riesling, was released in 1994. Riesling is their flagship wine, with other whites, pinot noir and the Italian variety montepulciano completing the line-up. The very English entranceway garden features lavender and roses, giving way to a wood-panelled tasting room.

Notable wines

Marlborough Chardonnay, Marlborough Gewürztraminer, Classic and Dry Rieslings, Marlborough Sauvignon Blanc, Marlborough Pinot Gris.

Food

N/A

Forrest Estate

19 Blicks Road
Renwick
03 572 9084 www.forrestwines.co.nz
Open seven days 10.00 am–4.30 pm, wine tours of the vineyard and winery are also available by appointment, closed Marlborough Anniversary Day

Influential winemaker and former medical researcher, Dr John Forrest and his wife Brigid (also a scientist) established Forrest Estate in 1989. They now produce high-end wines from both the Renwick vineyard and a Hawke's Bay Gimblett Gravels property. An eye-catching riverstone wall marks the estate from the road.

Visitors can sample their delicate German-style wines at the cellar door's copper-clad bar, or take time out to relax and picnic in the gardens with marble sculptures among trees.

Notable wines

Marlborough Chardonnay, Marlborough Gewürztraminer, Marlborough Pinot Gris. Rieslings: Brancott, James Randall, The Doctor's. Also, James Randall Sauvignon, 'Bubbles for Brigid' Sparkling, and Brancott Pinot Noir. Prices around the $18 mark.

Food

N/A

Isabel Estate Vineyard

72 Hawkesbury Road
Renwick
Blenheim
03 572 8300 www.isabelestate.com
Open Monday–Friday 11.00 am–4.00 pm, Saturdays only November–end of February 11.00 am–4.00 pm, excluding Public Holidays

Isabel Estate currently produces five wines from six estate blocks: sauvignon blanc, chardonnay, pinot noir, pinot gris and riesling. In exceptional vintages, a botrytised dessert sauvignon blanc is produced. In 1982, former Air New Zealand pilot Michael Tiller and his wife Robyn established the vineyards and named them Isabel in honour of Michael's mother. Isabel remains one of the largest family-owned and operated wine estates in Marlborough.

Notable wines

Chardonnay, Pinot Gris, Pinot Noir.

Food

N/A

Accommodation

Isabel Lodge easily accommodates ten to 12 people and is especially suited to families and groups. The comfortable timber-clad lodge has three double bedrooms, plus TV, laundry and a large stone fireplace. Situated in the heart of the working vineyard. Tariff: about $45 per person per night. Children under 12, $20.

Renwick weekend two — Saturday

Te Whare Ra

56 Anglesea Street
Renwick
Belnheim
03 572 8581 www.te-whare-ra.co.nz
Open seven days September–May 10.00 am–5.00 pm, shortened hours June–August, phone ahead

The oldest boutique winery in the region, Te Whare Ra takes its name from Maori, meaning 'The House in the Sun'. Some vines were planted back in 1979. Owners Jason and Anna Flowerday have brought a wealth of experience to the winery since they took over in 2003. Jason has worked vintages for Selaks and Nobilo in New Zealand, and for Hardys Australia. Anna comes to Te Whare Ra after seven years with Hardys in Australia. They have two blocks in Renwick totalling about nine hectares (22 acres). A speciality is the blended (very unusual) white wine called Toru — 'three' in Maori — of gewürztraminer, riesling and pinot gris.

Notable wines

Chardonnay, Sauvignon Blanc, Pinot Noir, Toru blend, Noble Riesling.

Food

N/A

Huia Vineyards

22 Boyce Road
Renwick
Blenheim
03 572 8326 www.huia.net.nz
Open seven days 10.30 am–5.00 pm

In 1996 Mike and Claire Allan started Huia Vineyards with the intention of producing small quantities of premium wines. They both trained as winemakers at Roseworthy winemaking college in South Australia. The style of their wines is dry, subtle and elegant with the emphasis on mainly white aromatic grapes: gewürztraminer, riesling, and pinot gris. They also do chardonnay, sauvignon blanc and pinot noir, plus a champagne-style sparkler (Huia Brut). Prices are around the $25 mark. The cellar door is friendly with a relaxed style.

Notable wines

Huia Brut sparkling, Gewürztraminer, Riesling, Sauvignon Blanc, Pinot Noir.

Food

N/A

Spy Valley Wines

37 Lake Timara Road (off Waihopai Valley Road)
Renwick
Blenheim
03 572 9840 www.spyvalleywine.co.nz
Open seven days Labour Weekend–Anzac Day 10.00 am–4.00 pm

Taking its name as a sly dig at the local American Waihopai electronic eavesdropping station, Spy Valley is a stylish modern winery owned by the Johnson family. The vineyards are located on the southern side of Marlborough's Wairau Valley, nestled on the sunny terraces of the Omaka River. Eight varieties of grapes planted over 145 hectares (360 acres) produce premium quality fruit which has, in five short years, established the label as one of Marlborough's leading new wineries.

Notable wines

Marlborough Sauvignon Blanc, Envoy Chardonnay, Marlborough Riesling, Envoy Gewürztraminer, Echelon Méthode Traditional sparkling, Marlborough Merlot, Envoy Pinot Noir.

Food

N/A, unless you decide to stay . . .

Accommodation

Timara Lodge
Dog Point Road
03 572 8276 www.timara.co.nz

Exclusive (and that excludes me and anyone I know personally), luxury accommodation, plus breakfast and dinner prepared by Louis Schindler, head chef of Herzog Winery restaurant. Sounds fab. Win Lotto. Invite me along. Tariff: upwards of $750 a night per person . . . for a couple, yowch!

And if you're in town during the week . . .

Fairhall Downs Estate Wines

70 Wrekin Road
Renwick
Blenheim
03 572 8356 www.fairhalldowns.co.nz
Open Monday–Friday 9.00 am–4.00 pm

Located in the Brancott Valley, this 32-hectare (80-acre) family-owned winery produces sauvignon blanc, pinot noir, chardonnay and pinot gris.

Ken and Jill Small are former Southland farmers who began in 1982 as contract growers. Now they are highly regarded wine producers. Daughter Julie and her husband Stewart Smith have joined the company.

Notable wines

Sauvignon Blanc, Pinot Noir.

Food

N/A

Wairau River Winery

Corner State Highway six and Rapaura Road
Renwick
Blenheim
03 572 9800 www.wairauriverwines.com
Open seven days 10.00 am–5.00 pm

Phil and Chris Rose released their first wine in 1991 and the Wairau River label was born. With five estate vineyards, under family ownership, Wairau River is one of the largest independent wine estates in Marlborough. There are two tiers of wine — the Estate range (around $22) and the Home Block range (around $26). The latter consists of three single vineyard wines — sauvignon blanc, chardonnay and pinot noir. The cellar door and restaurant is built of local mud-brick blocks, each weighing 80 kilograms, and is inspired by the colonial homestead. Trellised sauvignon blanc vines surround the building.

Notable wines

Gewürztraminer, Riesling, Sauvignon Blanc, Home Block Pinot Noir.

Food

Relaxed bistro-style dining using fresh local produce. Finalist in the *Cuisine* Restaurant of the Year 2006 Awards — Best Winery restaurant category. Open 10.00 am–5.00 pm every day, lunch is served 12.00 pm–3.00 pm.

No. 1 Family Estate

169 Rapaura Road
Renwick
Blenheim
03 572 9876 www.no1familyestate.co.nz
Open seven days 11.00 am–4.30 pm

Champagne-maker, Daniel Le Brun, launched this family-owned méthode traditionelle-producing business back in July 1999, using the processes perfected by his Champagne-making family in France over 12 generations. The winery has been set up with state-of-the-art processing equipment, imported from the Champagne region. The company is owned by Adele and Daniel Le Brun, and their children Virginie and Remy. Virginie, has been a television presenter on 'What Now', and is totally drop-dead gorgeous. The winery is dedicated solely to the production of méthode traditionelle. The four méthodes produced at No. 1 Family Estate are Cuvée No. 1, a non-vintage Blanc, De Blancs (100 per cent chardonnay), a non-vintage blend, Cuvée Number Eight, a vintage blend (created in only the finest years), Cuvée Virginie, and Reserve Cuvée 10, celebrating the first ten years of No. 1 Family Estate.

Notable wines

All four méthode traditionelle wines.

Food

N/A

And while you're in the area . . .

The Vines Village
193 Rapaura Road
Renwick

This is a small rustic shopping complex that contains The Quilter's Barn (quilting supplies), Prenzel (schnapps, liqueurs), a café, the Olive Oil Shop (nine local oils for tasting, plus kitchen equipment, sauces, marmalades), and Bouldevines Wine Cellar which has tastings and sales of local labels without a cellar door — Clayridge, Terravin, Awatere Terrace and Bouldevines.

Lake Chalice Wines

93 Vintage Lane (turn south from Rapaura Road into Vintage Lane)
Renwick
Blenheim
03 572 9327 www.lakechalice.co.nz
Open summer Monday–Friday 11.00 am–4.00 pm, weekends by appointment, in winter phone ahead for opening times

Founded in 1989 by Chris Gambitsis and Phil Binnie, who were later joined in 1998 by winemaker Matt Thomson. Initially the vineyard was just 11 hectares (27 acres), but they now own four key vineyards as well as sourcing fruit from contract growers. Their company logo is the New Zealand native falcon, the Karearea. Lake Chalice sponsors the Wingspan Birds of Prey Trust, which works to preserve New Zealand's native raptors.

Notable wines

Platinum Chardonnay, Raptor Sauvignon Blanc, Platinum Merlot.

Food

N/A but picnickers welcome.

Domaine Georges Michel

56 Vintage Lane
Blenheim
03 572 7230   www.georgesmichel.co.nz
Open seven days October–April from 10.30 am

Another slice of France in the heart of Marlborough — Georges Michel and his wife Huguette acquired the vineyard in 1997 and have made their Gallic mark on the region. The company also owns wineries in Beaujolais and Burgundy, and their winemaking consultant visits each year from France. Winemaker is Georges' daughter, Swan Michel. They specialise in premium-quality chardonnay, pinot noir and an award-winning Marlborough sauvignon blanc. They also produce a brandy, named Marc of Marlborough, from the 40-year-old copper still on site.

Notable wines

La Reserve Marlborough Sauvignon Blanc, Reserve Chardonnay, Golden Mile Pinot Noir. Also look out for Autumn Folly — a 'vin doux naturelle' — a sweet dessert wine with added grape brandy to lift the alcohol level to 14.5 per cent.

Food

La Veranda Restaurant

La Veranda Restaurant serves brunch, lunch, salads, antipasti, and dessert boards. The current favourites are salt and pepper squid salad, French toast with crispy bacon, pumpkin pesto, and chilli jam, and the fab chocolate pudding.There are also fine French cheeses, from importer Maison Vauron, and locally roasted CPR coffee to finish off your meal. Bookings: 03 572 9177. Open 9.30 am–4.30 pm.

Nautilus Estate

12 Rapaura Road
Renwick
Blenheim
03 572 9364 www.nautilusestate.com
Open seven days in summer 10.00 am–5.00 pm, winter 10.30 am–4.30 pm

Nautilus has long been primarily associated with its premium méthode traditionalle sparkler, Nautilus Cuvée. Now the emphasis is on their pinot noir — with the plant divided into two separate wineries: a pinot winery and a white winery. Gravity feed and a hi-tech approach ensure minimal handling of grapes and juice in the pinot winery. Winemaker Clive Jones is a graduate in wine science from Charles Sturt University, New South Wales.

Notable wines

Chardonnay, Pinot Gris, Sauvignon Blanc, Pinot Noir.

Food

Cheese platters available or BYO picnic.

Places to eat

Rapaura region

Gibb's Vineyard Restaurant

258 Jacksons Road
Blenheim
03 572 8048 www.gibbs_restaurant.co.nz
Open for dinner November–April Monday–Sunday from 6.30 pm, May–October Tuesday–Saturday from 6.00 pm

The Vintners Room Restaurant and Bar

190 Rapaura Road
Blenheim
03 572 5094 www.mvh.co.nz
Open seven nights for dinner. Drinks from 4.00 pm and dining from 6.00 pm

Blenheim

Hotel D'Urville

52 Queen St
Blenheim
03 577 9945 www.durville.com
Open seven days a week, breakfast 7.00 am–10.00 am, lunch 12.00 noon–2.00 pm, dinner 6.00 pm onwards

Fine dining, interesting menu. Highly recommended.

Things to do

Marlborough Food and Wine Festival

Held in February each year. See: www.wine-marlborough-festival.co.nz. Experience highly acclaimed wines of the region and indulge in the culinary delights of local chefs plus a line-up of New Zealand's leading performers to keep you entertained throughout the day . . . and get a bit dizzy.

Pelorus Mail Boat Cruise

03 574 1088 www.mail-boat.co.nz

On Tuesdays, Thursdays and Fridays you have the chance to join one of the last remaining waterway mail delivery services in New Zealand. In the early years most of the goods carried were farming supplies and a few tourists. These days, tourists and the mail are the only passengers.

The Marlborough Farmers Market

A&P Showgrounds
Maxwell Road
www.mfm.co.nz
Every Sunday November–May 9.00 am–noon

Here you'll find the best Marlborough producers in one venue. Growers bring their produce to the A&P Park and sell direct to the public.

Makana Confectionery

Corner Rapaura and O'Dwyers Roads
03 570 5370 www.makana.co.nz
Open daily 9.00 am–5.30 pm

Visit a boutique chocolate factory. See how they make their chocolates, taste a few samples and, of course, shop for gifts and indulgences.

Dolphin Watch Eco-tours
Picton foreshore
0800 9453 5433   www.naturetours.co.nz

Enjoy stunning scenery on the way to the outer Marlborough Sounds aboard a high-speed catamaran. Experience close encounters with seabirds, seals and dolphins: endangered Hector's, Bottlenose and Dusky, according to season.

Omaka Aviation Heritage Centre
Aerodrome Road
Blenheim
Open seven days from 10.00 am–4.00 pm

One of the world's largest private collections of First World War aircraft will wow you with static and flyable displays of aircraft, rare memorabilia and cinematic and special effect presentations.

Places to stay

As with other regions, there is plenty of choice from motel, B&B and exclusive luxury accommodation.

Hotel D'Urville
52 Queen Street
03 577 9945   www.durville.com

Boutique lodging in what was the Public Trust building, a Blenheim Art Deco landmark. Tariff: around $200 in low season, about $330 in high season.

The Peppertree B&B
State Highway One (about five minutes drive south of Blenheim)
Riverlands
Blenheim
Ph 03 520 9200   0508 853 851   www.thepeppertree.co.nz

Swiss couple Heidi and Werner Plüss run The Peppertree, a gracious restored

1901 homestead. Five luxury suites with ensuite, phone and internet access are on offer. Free pick-up from Blenheim airport is included, if required. Activities available: croquet, petanque, swimming, wineries and vineyards, museum, golf courses and driving ranges nearby. Qualmark 5-star. Tariff: from $400 per night.

Old St Mary's Convent

Rapaura Road
Blenheim
03 570 5700 www.convent.co.nz

The restored 1901 convent building is set in 24.2 hectares (60 acres) of park-like grounds includes right in the heart of wine territory. It features lovely stained glass and lots of polished timber, including a kauri staircase. Accommodation includes five luxury rooms and a honeymoon suite. Qualmark 5-star. Tariff: $550–750 a night.

Waterfall Lodge

Le Grys Vineyard
Conders Bend Road
Renwick
Blenheim
03 572 9490 www.legrys.co.nz

Waterfall Lodge is a self-contained, cottage set amongst the vines at the Le Grys Vineyard. The cottage has a master bedroom with a Queen-size canopy bed and a second room with two extra-long single beds. It offers all the goodies — fine linen, fluffy towels and robes — plus a swimming pool. Breakfast provisions, wine and nibbles are supplied. Qualmark 4-star-plus. Tariff: $250 per night for two people, $50 per extra person (with a maximum of four persons).

Nelson

In addition to high sunshine hours and stunning scenery, Nelson has emerged as a significant wine region, despite its small output of around three per cent of New Zealand's total. Boutique is probably the word best used to describe the vast majority of the wineries, though there are some larger players based in Nelson such as Waimea Estates, Neudorf, Seifried and Kahurangi. There is a distinct German influence in the region with history going back to 1843, when German winemakers first tried to make a go of it in the Nelson soils. Not many stayed. Most left for South Australia where they pioneered the Barossa region. But other, newer wineries have continued to pop up in what has become a very trendy region.

Aside from wine, Nelson has many excellent cafés and restaurants, and a burgeoning art and craft scene. The region also boasts three national parks, including Abel Tasman, and has a plentiful supply of orchard fruits, shellfish and other seafood.

No clear regional wine speciality has emerged, but Nelson produces some award-winning sauvignon, pinot gris, gewürztraminer, chardonnay and pinot noir.

For the active traveller the greater Nelson region offers many outdoor activities: hiking, kayaking, mountain biking, seal swimming.

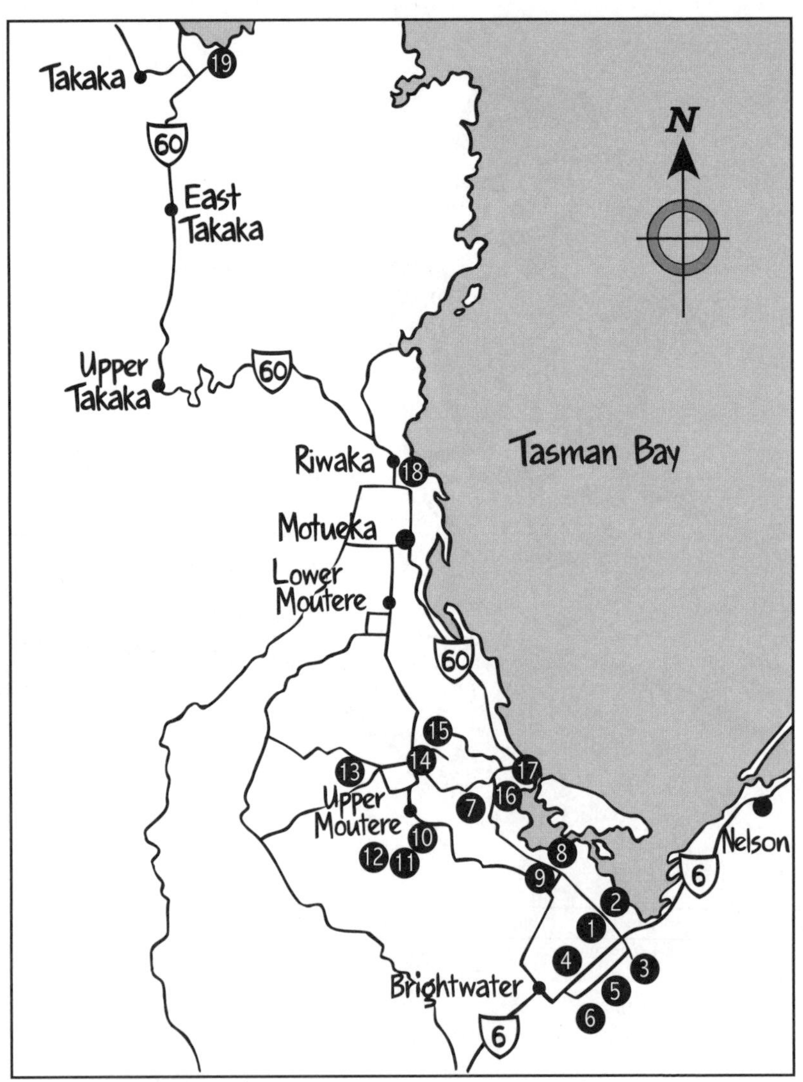

Takaka
19
60
East Takaka
Upper Takaka
60
N
Tasman Bay
Riwaka
18
Motueka
Lower Moutere
60
15
14
13
17
16
7
Upper Moutere
10
12
11
8
9
2
1
4
3
5
6
Brightwater
6
Nelson
6

Waimea Estates

Appleby Highway
Hope
03 544 4963 www.waimeaestates.co.nz
Open seven days Labour Weekend–March 11.00 am–5.00 pm, April–September Wednesday–Sunday 11.00 am–4.00 pm, $2 tasting fee refunded on wine or café purchase

Former orchardists Trevor and Robyn Bolitho have diversified from apples into grape-growing and winemaking. They now have the second largest wine operation in Nelson, with six vineyards and 80 hectares (200 acres) producing a range of grape varieties: sauvignon blanc, pinot gris, gewürztraminer, chardonnay and pinot noir. Their premium ranges are the Bolitho Reserve and Signature Vineyard series at around $25. Winemaker Michael Brown is a local boy who studied viticulture at NMIT in Blenheim, then went on to make wine in Spain, France and Argentina before moving on to Waimea.

Notable wines

Signature Gewürztraminer, Bolitho Pinot Gris, Nelson Sauvignon Blanc, Bolitho Reserve and Signature Chardonnays, Bolitho Pinot Noir.

Food

Top international chef Chris von Schreibern uses fresh local fare in his renowned café/restaurant 'Cafe in the Vineyard'. Nelson scallops, crayfish, Marlborough green lipped mussels and Neudorf cheeses all feature on the menu. Paved and trellised, it is a very enjoyable lunch stop with indoor/outdoor seating. Live music is on Sundays and there's a cosy fire in winter. Dishes are around the $20 mark. A full range of Waimea Estates wine is available, including some rare wines and back vintages.

Richmond Plains Wines

Grape Escape (Cellar Door)
McShane Road
Richmond
03 544 4054   027 4486 666   www.organicwines.co.nz

Lars Jensen bought the certified organic vineyard from Appleby Vintners David Holmes in 1995. He grows sauvignon blanc, chardonnay and pinot noir, organically with companion planting, similar to Millton Vineyards of Gisborne.

Tastings are at Te Mania and Richmond Plains cellar door, Grape Escape complex, off McShane Road.

Notable wines

Richmond Plains Reserve Pinot Noir.

Food

Also onsite is the café and wine bar Prenzel (where you can taste schnapps, liqueurs, brandies and infused olive oils). There is also the Escape Art Gallery, Cruellas Natural Fibre Boutique — a gift shop selling alpaca and natural wools — and Living Light selling handcrafted candles.

Accommodation

Vineyard Cottage

Contact: Lars and Samantha Jensen
03 544 2340 or 03 544 2345   Email: cottage@richmondplains.co.nz

Nestled next to the vines, and just a stroll away from the Grape Escape complex, the cottage sleeps two and is fully self-contained with all amenities. Complimentary bottle of wine and breakfast provisions.Tariff starts at $90 per person per night (off-peak) for two or more nights.

Fossil Ridge

Hart Road
Richmond
03 544 7459 www.fossilridge.co.nz
Open seven days November–Easter 11.00 am–5.00 pm

Darryl and Tranja Fry named their tiny three-hectare (7.5-acre) vineyard Fossil Ridge, after a rare mollusc fossil (*Monotis richmondiana*), found abundantly in the local soils. In just ten years, they have transformed bare land into a picturesque vineyard, with a mirrored duck pond and macadamia and olive trees. The small tasting room has decks overlooking the ponds. For $5 you get a tray of four wines to sample, plus a selection of their own olives and macadamias. Wines produced are chardonnay, riesling, and pinot noir.

Notable wines

The two Chardonnays (one unoaked) have picked up medals.

Food

N/A

Brightwater Vineyards

546 Main Road
Hope
03 544 1066 www.brightwaterwine.co.nz
Open seven days Labour Weekend–Easter 11.00 am–5.00 pm, other times at reduced hours

Gary and Valley Neale returned home from the big OE in 1992, determined to contribute to the growing worldwide reputation of New Zealand wines. Settling in Nelson, they began planting grapes the following year, and produced their first wines under the Brightwater label for the 1999 vintage. They have nine hectares (22 acres) of grapes in their vineyard — about 20 minutes' drive from Nelson. They produce a minimal 7000 cases a year.

Notable wines

Sauvignon Blanc, Riesling, Rutherford Chardonnay, Merlot, Pinot Noir. (Michael Cooper is a big fan.)

Food

N/A

Greenhough Vineyard

Patons Road
Richmond
03 542 3868 Email: greenhough.vineyard@clear.net.nz
Open seven days in January 1.00 pm–5.00 pm, Labour Weekend–Easter Saturday and Sunday 11.00 am–5.00 pm

Greenhough Vineyard and Winery was established by Andrew Greenhough and Jennifer Wheeler and has been operating since 1991 in the Waimea Plains, 20 minutes from Nelson. They are gaining an excellent reputation for their wines, particularly their chardonnay and Hope Vineyard Pinot Noir.

Notable wines

Riesling, Sauvignon Blanc, Chardonnay and Hope Vineyard Pinot Noir.

Food

N/A

Kaimira Estate

121 River Terrace Road
Brightwater
03 542 3491 www.kaimirawines.com
Open seven days Labour Weekend–Easter 11.00 am–5.00 pm

Situated on the banks of the Wairoa River near Brightwater, Kaimira Estate Winery is owned and operated by Ian Miller and June Hamilton. First vintage was in 1999. They produce sauvignon blanc, riesling, pinot gris, chardonnay, rosé and pinot noir. The use their own grapes for the top tier Brightwater label, and contract growers for the Nelson label. A new tasting room displays local art.

Notable wines

Brightwater Chardonnay, Brightwater Pinot Gris, Brightwater Riesling, Nelson Sauvignon Blanc.

Food

N/A

Woollaston Estates

School Road (off Old Coach Road)
Mahana
Upper Moutere
03 543 2817 www.woollaston.co.nz
Open seven days January–February 11.00 am–4.30 pm, March–December group tastings welcome by appointment

Ex-politician and son of famous New Zealand artist Sir Tosswill Woollaston, Philip, and his wife Chan, planted their first grapes at Wai-iti River Vineyard in 1993. In 2000 they brought in business partners Glenn and Renee Schaeffer, from Nevada, America, to fund development of three further local vineyards. The winery is built into the hillside over four different levels, allowing a natural gravity feed of juice and wine during winemaking, and making for minimal handling. The roof is planted with a garden of tussock and shrubs. Aside from great wine, many people make the journey from Nelson just to look at the feature 'Yantra for Mahana' sculpture by Marté Szirmay.

Notable wines

Nelson Riesling, Nelson Pinot Noir.

Food

Platters by arrangement.

8

Seifried Winery

Redwood Road (off State Highway 60 towards the Abel Tasman National Park, look for the winery on the right at the Rabbit Island turnoff)
Appleby
Richmond
03 544 1555 www.seifried.co.nz
Open seven days 10.00 am–5.00 pm all year round apart from Christmas Day, Boxing Day and Good Friday

In 1973 Austrian born Hermann Seifried and his New Zealand wife Agnes started what is now the Nelson region's largest producer. Their three children are also involved — winemakers Heidi and Chris, and marketing manager Anna. The Old Coach Road and Seifried labels are familiar to most New Zealanders, and now they have added a reserve selection of wines under the Seifried Winemakers Collection brand, with prices starting at around $18 and heading up to $35.

Notable wines

Reliable mid-priced wines in the main. Two notable rare Austrian grape varieties are grown: a white hybrid, würzer (floral and spicy); and a red, zweigeld (deeply coloured, earthy and spicy). Also noted — Pinot Gris, Nelson Sauvignon Blanc, Winemakers Selection Riesling and Winemakers Selection Pinot Noir.

Food

Expect simple but hearty food using local ingredients — pasta, steak etc. There are also picnic areas and a children's playground. Open all year round for lunches. Extended evening dining during summer. Closed Good Friday, Christmas and Boxing Day. Winter evening dining is by arrangement. Bookings: 03 544 1555 or restaurant@seifried.co.nz

Stafford Lane Estate

80 Moutere Highway (on the Moutere Highway eight kilometres north of Richmond)
03 544 2851 www.staffordlane.co.nz
Open seven days 11.00 am–5.00 pm

For $3 you get to taste three to five wines and have a platter of olive oils, dukkah, olives and gourmet chutney with bread. Spend over $15 and there is no tasting charge.

Mike and Carol McGrath took over a ten-hectare (25-acre) orchard and vineyard block in 2001. The winery takes its name from three-times Prime Minister of New Zealand, Edward William Stafford, who once lived on the property. Aside from wines they make 11 types of olive oils and marinated olives from a variety of olive trees on the property. The vineyard produces pinot gris, riesling, gewürztraminer, chardonnay, and pinot noir.

Notable wines

Reserve Nelson Pinot Noir.

Food

As above but only to take away. Extra virgin olive oil, marinated and pickled olives, dukkah made from their own hazelnuts. Also gourmet jams, jellies, feijoa chutneys, and mustards — all made using traditional recipes, without preservatives.

Now head out on to the Moutere Highway, to discover more treats . . .

Kahurangi Estate Ltd

Sunrise Road
Upper Moutere
03 543 2980 www.kahurangiwine.com
Open seven days 10.30 am–4.40 pm, tasting fee of $2 is refundable on purchase

Greg and Amanda Day bought the property from the Seifried family in 1998 and built a solid reputation to become one of the larger producers in the region.

Notable wines

Nelson Sauvignon Blanc, Nelson Pinot Gris, Reserve Moutere Riesling, Moutere Gewürztraminer, Mt Arthur Chardonnay, Heaphy Chardonnay.

Food

Their deli-café offers a range of fresh local produce and their own Kahurangi Olive Oil, plus good Atomic espresso coffee. Selections can be made to create your own personalised Kahurangi Platter (enough for two, $36) to enjoy in the open courtyard or to take away. Or how about Nelson scallops, with asparagus salad, a citrus chilli dressing on a ginger mash for $15.50? Open seven days from 10.30 am–4.30 pm.

Sunset Valley Organic Vineyard and Winery

Eggers Road
Upper Moutere
03 543 2161 www.sunsetvalleyvineyard.co.nz
Open seven days November–May 11.00 am–5.00 pm, winter hours by appointment

BioGro-certified winemakers Ian Newton and his partner Ros Squire have three hectares (7.5 acres) planted in sauvignon blanc, riesling, chardonnay, pinot noir and cabernet sauvignon. They established their vineyard after buying a rolling 25-hectare property in 1993.

Notable wines

Nelson Sauvignon Blanc, Nelson Pinot Noir.

Food

N/A

Vineyard accommodation

Self-contained vineyard chalet with plenty of room for a couple with two children, or for four adults. Tariff: $150 for the first night and $120 for each successive night (a minimum two-night stay is required).

Moutere Hills

Eggers Road
Sunrise Valley
Upper Moutere
03 543 2288 www.mouterehills.co.nz
Open six days (closed Mondays) Labour Weekend–Easter
11.00 am–5.00 pm

Simon and Alison Thomas started this venture in 1993 with three hectares (7.5 acres) of gently sloping vineyard and some old wool shed buildings. New owners since 2004, John and Ali Tocker, have just recovered from a disastrous cellar and winery fire, and are back on track and open for cellar door sales and café lunches. There are two ranges of wines — chardonnay, pinot noir and sauvignon blanc, plus an easy-drinker range: Hopsbarn Rose, Red and White at about $22.

Notable wines

Sauvignon Blanc ($25), Pinot Gris ($34).

Food

Café lunches.

Neudorf Vineyards

Neudorf Road
Upper Moutere
03 543 2643 www.neudorf.co.nz
Open seven days September–end of May 10.30 am–5.00 pm

Tim and Judy Finn are the owners, and have vineyards in two sites: the north-facing slopes of Moutere Valley, and at Brightwater — the stony alluvial area between the Waimea and Wai-iti rivers. They kicked things off in 1978, when their bank manager told them they'd be much better off sheep farming than growing grapes. Fortunately, they ignored his advice. Many international accolades have made them one of the region's star producers. Prices start in the mid-$20s for the savvy and are up to around $50 for the Moutere Pinot Noir.

Notable wines

Moutere Chardonnay, Nelson Chardonnay, Moutere Pinot Noir, Home Vineyard Pinot Noir, Moutere Riesling, Moutere Pinot Gris.

Vineyard dog

Pip — food-crazed bearded collie.

Food

N/A. (Sorry Pip —try the folks with the picnic baskets.)

While you're in the area visit . . .

Neudorf Dairy
230 Neudorf Road
Upper Moutere
03 543 2789 www.neudorfdairy.co.nz
Open five days Tuesday–Sunday, sheep milking season Tuesday–Sunday 3.30 pm

Call in for free cheese tastings, or to watch sheep milking or cheese making (phone to confirm times). The dairy is owned and operated by Brian and Sharon Beuke. The Beuke family (originally from Germany) have been farming their property at Neudorf for four generations since the 1860s.

Himmelsfeld Vineyard

Gardner Valley Road
Upper Moutere
03 543 2223 www.himmelsfeld.co.nz
Open seven days October–Easter, in winter most days or by appointment

Beth Eggers has a small 10-hectare (25 acres) site where she grows chardonnay, sauvignon blanc and cabernet sauvignon. She is a fifth-generation German descendant of Hans and Dora Eggers, who arrived in the Moutere in 1859. Her parents used to grow hops in nearby Sunrise Valley. Since her first vintage in 1997, Beth has picked up many awards for her wines which are grown in the Moutere clay soils of Himmelsfeld (translates from German as Heaven's Field).

Tastings are done in her wine loft, and onsite are 100 pet Romney 'lawnmower' sheep and a tiny chapel where traditional Christian festivals are celebrated throughout the year.

Notable wines

All three: Chardonnay, Sauvignon Blanc and Cabernet Sauvignon.

Food

N/A

Accommodation

A private lakeside cottage sleeps two.

Glover's Vineyard

Gardner Valley Road
Upper Moutere
03 543 2698 www.glovers-vineyard.co.nz
Contact the vineyard for details of opening hours

Dave Glover, a former Wellingtonian, spent 16 years in Australia where he gained a PhD in Algebra and worked for the Ministry of Defence. Now he makes a very small amount (around 1000 cases) of quite distinctive wines. Glover and his wife, Penny, planted their first vines in Gardner Valley Road in 1984. David is a great believer in the power of tannin in red wines and aims to extract as much as possible. His small vineyard produces riesling, sauvignon blanc, chardonnay, pinot noir, syrah and cabernet.

Notable wines

Moutere Cabernet Sauvignon.

Food

N/A

Rimu Grove Winery

Bronte Road East (off Coastal Highway 60, near Mapua)
Upper Moutere
03 540 2345 021 165 2767 www.rimugrove.co.nz
Open seven days Christmas–end February 11.00 am–5.00 pm, weekends only Labour Weekend–Easter 11.00 am–5.00 pm, other times throughout the year by appointment

Napa Valley-born winemaker Patrick Stowe and his wife Barbara bought what was an old apple orchard in the rolling hills of the Bronte Peninsula sloping down to the scenic Waimea Estuary. In 1995 they removed the apple trees and planted pinot gris, chardonnay and pinot noir. Patrick is an affable enthusiast and very passionate about his wines. Tasting is in the tiny winery building. If there's nobody to attend to you, use the walkie-talkie on the table.

Notable wines

Nelson Pinot Gris, Nelson Pinot Noir.

Food

You're welcome to picnic and enjoy the view.

Ruby Bay Lodge and Vineyard

271 Pomona Road
Ruby Bay
Nelson
03 540 3938 0274 540 393 www.rubybaylodge.co.nz
Open Thursday–Monday 11.00 am–4.00 pm, or phone to make an appointment

Scots couple Sam and Audrey Watt extend their warm hospitality and fine wines to visitors — either casual wine samplers or luxury B&B guests.

Notable wines

Riesling, Pinot Noir.

Food

B&B guests only.

Accommodation

The Vineyard Cottage is $300–$375 a night with a fully stocked chef's pantry and all the goodies. Vineyard lunch platter and wine are complimentary. Sleeping two to four guests, all rooms enjoy sea views.

The Lodge Suite is $375–$400 a night. For four guests, the lodge has two King-size bedroom suites, both with their own private access. Featuring native red beech floors, designer bathrooms and rain showers, each suite has its own covered balcony. Á la carte breakfast and lots of treats await your indulgence.

18

Anchorage Wines

47 Flett Road
Lower Moutere
Riwaka
03 526 7252 www.anchoragewines.co.nz
Open Wednesday–Sunday from 11.00 am

Chris Drummond and his forebears have been in Motueka since the 1840s. Fruit growers for many generations, they now grow grapes and make wines, having launched their Anchorage label in 2003. They have 25 hectares (62 acres) of vineyard that overlooks the Motueka River and Tasman Bay.

Notable wines

Nelson Sauvignon Blanc, Pinot Gris, Chardonnay.

Food

Antipasto platters for two and four people.

Golden Bay Wines

Abel Tasman Drive
Motupipi
Golden Bay (near Abel Tasman National Park)
03 525 9167 www.goldenbaywines.com
Open seven days in summer 1.00 pm–5.00 pm

Owned and operated by Peter and Katherine Orange, Golden Bay Wines is a small family-run vineyard and winery dedicated to producing small quantities of wines that demonstrate the distinctive style and character of the Golden Bay region. The vines are carefully tended by hand pruning, tucking and leaf plucking, and individual attention is given to each vine with grapes being selectively hand-picked.

Notable wine

Petros Sparkling Wine (about $30).

Food

N/A

Places to eat

The Smokehouse Café and Bar

Shed 3
Mapua Wharf
Nelson
03 540 2280 www.smokehouse.co.nz
Open seven days from 10.00 am

Just off the Coastal Highway on the old Mapua wharf looking over the Waimea Estuary, the Smokehouse is nestled between three national parks. It was voted 'Best Café' in Taste Nelson Awards for three consecutive years. Hot smoked seafood, poultry, New Zealand lamb, sausages and vegetables have become a speciality.

Morrison Street Café

244 Hardy Street
Nelson
03 548 8110 www.morrisonstreetcafe.co.nz
Open Monday–Friday 7.30 am–4.00 pm, Saturday 8.30 am–3.00 pm, Sunday and Public Holidays 9.00 am–3.00 pm

This is a fully licensed café with outdoor garden courtyard. The menu changes seasonally to feature available foods and includes a good selection of low-allergy dishes and dietary options. Children are well catered for.

Mot Valley Cafe

163 Motueka Valley Highway
Ngatimoti
Tasman
03 526 8834
Open Friday–Sunday 12.00 noon–11.00 pm

Recommended. The café food is French, German and Mediterranean.

Monterey House Cafe and Garden

Orinoco Valley
Motueka
03 526 8267

This highly regarded Motueka eatery offers high teas and good café food. Open seasonally.

Awaroa Lodge

Abel Tasman National Park
03 528 8758 www.awaroalodge.co.nz

Enjoy breakfast, lunch or dinner featuring organic greens, seasonal seafood and local produce, light snacks, natural juices, roasted coffee, regional beers and premium wines. Dine overlooking the wetland or in the courtyard listening to the tui calls. Accommodation is also available.

Things to do

Arts and crafts

Nelson has long been a mecca for creative and alternative people and has a burgeoning arts and crafts scene. The region is home to prominent painters, photographers, ceramicists, artists, glassmakers, sculptors, textile and furniture craftspeople, jewellery makers, and also has a lively festival and performance programme. There are way too many to list. It's probably best to visit the Nelson Arts Organisation site www.nelsonarts.org.nz for more information.

World of Wearable Art and Classic Cars Museum

95 Quarantine Road
Nelson
03 547 4573 www.wowcars.co.nz

The annual World of Wearable Art Awards Show started in Nelson, but was hijacked by the capital city Wellington. Anyway, the museum is still in Nelson and this gallery gives visitors a rare opportunity to view the historic garment collection. Mannequins twirl to inspired musical arrangements under theatre lighting. Enjoy and admire the detail and craftsmanship these designers put into their garments.

The Classic Cars Museum features a collection of over 50 classic cars from Edwardian times through to highly sophisticated, modern super cars. It also displays relatively modern cars destined to become classics.

Nelson Saturday Market

Montgomery Square
Nelson

This is an established market that showcases many of the region's artists. Art trails allow visitors to see potters, painters, sculptors, weavers and ceramicists at work. Also there are crafts, pottery, unique gifts, designer wear, woodwork, organic veggies, breads, fruit, cheeses and gourmet food stalls.

The Refinery

3 Halifax Street
Nelson
03 548 1778 www.refinerygallery.org
Open Monday–Saturday 10.00 am–3.00 pm

This gallery and workshop specialising in art using recycled materials has ten artists in residence sharing workshop space. Media range from copper and tiles, to old cutlery and timber.

Founders Organic Brewery

Founders Historic Park
Nelson
0800 2462739 www.biobrew.co.nz

In Australasia's first certified organic brewery, John Duncan, a fifth generation Nelson brewer, combines the brewing traditions of yesteryear with today's technology. Brewed on location are three styles of lager, plus an ale and a seasonal sparkling apple cider. Certified organic ingredients are used — hops from Tapawera near Nelson, pale malt grown and roasted in Canterbury, and other speciality malts imported from Germany.

The brewery's café and bar is open during the summer months after Labour Weekend, offering chowder, platters, burgers and paninis, plus a good kids' menu and weekend brunch specials.

Höglund Art Glass Centre

Landsdowne Road
Richmond
Nelson
03 544 6500 www.nelson.hoglund.co.nz
Open seven days 9.00 a.m–5.00 pm

Acclaimed artists Ola Höglund and Marie Simberg-Höglund showcase their work in this gallery. There is also a retail shop and guided tours are offered at $15 per adult. Child under 14 free with adult.

Brightwater Wine and Food Festival

Held annually early February
www.bwff.co.nz

The festival features a wide choice of local wines, olive products and boutique beers, complemented by an abundance of craft stalls. Some of Nelson's best restaurants provide food. Also cooking demonstrations are offered by renowned chefs. Music and activities for children are included.

Saurau Village on the Moutere Highway

This village complex has a picture-postcard German village feel with a spiky-towered Lutheran church at its centre. Check out The Old Post Office, here you will find goodies and knick-knacks including elderflower cordial, citrus passionfruit curd, olive oils, gourmet shortbread, chutneys, relishes, fruit cheeses, samples and sales of local Neudorf cheeses, plus retro-style kitchenware.

Motueka Sunday Market

In the carpark behind the visitor information centre in Wallace Street, Motueka, (rain or shine) you will find food, clothing, crafts, entertainment, produce and jewellery.

Anatoki Salmon Farm

McCallums Road
Golden Bay
03 525 7251 www.anatokisalmon.co.nz
Open all year round (except Christmas Day) 9.00 am–4.30 pm

Catch your own salmon. There is no charge for entry or for using their fishing gear. You only pay for what you catch. Also sample their salmon croquettes or classic smoked salmon. Bring a picnic and stay a while.

Places to stay

Torrent Bay Lodge

Within the Abel Tasman National Park
0800 223 582   Email: info@abeltasman.co.nz

Sitting on the edge of a golden beach, Torrent Bay Lodge has been the Wilson family holiday home for over 30 years. Their home has been extended and remodelled to share with visitors who stay to enjoy Abel Tasman guided walks and kayak excursions.

Meadowbank Homestead

Awaroa Bay (within the Abel Tasman National Park)
0800 223 582   Email: info@abeltasman.co.nz

Meadowbank was rebuilt as an eco lodge in 1994 using recycled timbers and featuring heirlooms representing eight generations of the Wilson family's association with the Nelson region. The homestead provides all the comforts of modern living while minimising the impact on the environment.

Muritai Manor B&B

48 Wakapuaka Road (seven kilometres north of Nelson on the road to Blenheim)
Wakapuaka
03 545 1189   0800 260 662   www.muritaimanor.co.nz

The Muritai Manor has five guest bedrooms, each with an ensuite, as well as a guest dining room, guest lounge, off-street parking, extensive gardens, solar-heated outdoor swimming pool and outdoor heated hot tub. Guests must be over 12 years old. Qualmark four-star plus. Tariff: Double room $310 per night.

Nelson City Holiday Park
230 Vanguard Street
Nelson City
0800 77 88 98 www.nelsonholidaypark.co.nz

This is the closest holiday park to Nelson's city centre and a short walk to Victory Square for shops, pubs and takeaway food. It's a great place to stay while exploring the Nelson region because the hosts are booking agents for Nelson and Abel Tasman National Park activities. Included free are a BBQ and TV room with internet access. Modern kitchen cabins, standard cabins, sites for campervans, caravans and small tents. Tariff: (two people) $32–$99. Minimum prices at peak time. Qualmark 4-star plus.

Pohara Beach Top 10 Holiday Park and Motels
Abel Tasman Drive
Pohara
Golden Bay
0800 764 272 www.poharabeach.co.nz

This Qualmark 4-star beachfront accommodation covers five hectares (12 acres). A variety of accommodation options are available: at the lower end, motorhome and tent sites are available, then comfortable, fully equipped kitchen cabins. At the other end, fully serviced, luxury motel units, including brand new, beachfront studios and cabins with ensuites are available. Local shops and licensed restaurants nearby. Close to Abel Tasman National Park, kayaking, and beaches. BBQ area, fully equipped communal kitchen, guest laundry and children's playground. Tariff: (two people) cabins/ensuite $50–$85, tent/power $32, motels $110–$150.

Richmond Motel and Top 10 Holiday Park
29 Gladstone Road
Richmond
Nelson City
0800 250 218 www.nelsontop10.co.nz

Located in Richmond opposite the Visitor Information Centre, Jubilee Park, badminton and tennis courts and a short walk to malls and the shopping centre, this park has nine motel units, ten self-contained units, seven kitchen units, five standard cabins and 40 sites. Bedding hire is available for the cabins. Swimming pool (in the summer), BBQ, laundry, playground and email facilities. A bed for every budget. Qualmark-4-star plus. Tariff: $25–$125.

Lemonade Farm Apartment

Roses Road
Upper Moutere
03 5432 686   www.lemonadefarm.co.nz

Enjoy this separate private apartment on a lemon farm in wine country. B&B rates include daily fresh towels, kitchen and bathroom servicing, a generous breakfast basket with homebaked bread, fruit, pastries, plus cook-your-own free-range eggs and home-cured bacon. Features stereo with MP3 player input, access to free wireless broadband, a private outdoor spa and BBQ.

Tariff: $200 per night per couple. $40 for each extra person. Children aged up to three years old are free and those aged 4–12 are $20 per night.

Farm dogs are available over the fence for endless games of fetch the deflated soccer ball, which they will obligingly drop on your side on return.

Kaikoura

Finally, as part of the Alpine Pacific Triangle touring route — which takes in Waipara, Hanmer Springs, and Kaikoura — is the Kaikoura Winery, about 120 kilometres north of Waipara.

You could easily spend a weekend here, whale watching, wine tasting and enjoying the local seafood and stunning scenery. As for accommodation and activities, a small sample is listed here. Other activities include seal watching, playing on quad bikes and horse riding.

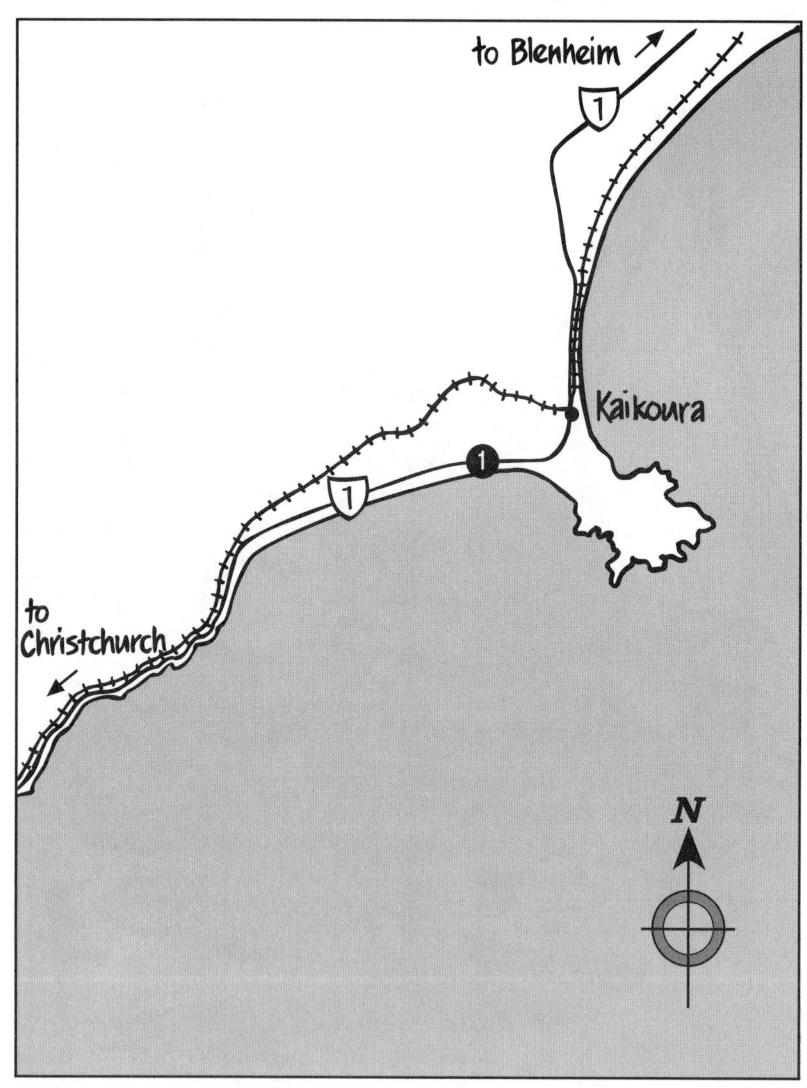

to Blenheim
1
Kaikoura
1
1
to
Christchurch
N

1

Kaikoura Winery

140 State Highway One (two kilometres south of Kaikoura)
03 319 7966 www.kaikourawinery.co.nz
Open seven days 10.00 am–4.00 pm, winery tours on the hour between 10.00 am and 4.00 pm daily

Kaikoura Winery has one of the most scenic vineyards in New Zealand, sheltered by the Kaikoura Ranges to the west, with vines planted on a limestone bluff overlooking the deep blue Pacific Ocean, where whales frolic and crayfish line up to be harvested.

The three-quarter-hour winery tour takes in the winemaking process and underground cellars, concluding with a tasting overlooking the coastline.

The tour and tasting is $9.50 per person. If you want to taste only, you pay $4 which is refundable on the purchase of three to six bottles. Shuttle from Kaikoura township, tour and tasting, $16.00. Tickets and departure from the information centre (Scenic Tours Shuttle, 0800 766 9626). Departs 15 minutes before the tour.

With the first vintage in 2004 the small four-hectare vineyard has been planted with pinot noir, pinot gris, chardonnay and gewürztraminer grapes. Other grapes come from North Canterbury and Marlborough. In 1999 the doors were first opened for tours and tastings.

Notable wines

Unoaked Chardonnay, Gewürztraminer Noble Riesling.

Food

Platters, soup, deli bar.

Winery cat

Pinot — fearless rabbit hunter and security guard.

Places to eat

There is not much in the way of fine dining here, which is surprising for a tourist mecca like Kaikoura. Casual dining seems to be the norm, with relaxed atmosphere and friendly service to the fore in the better eateries. 'Relaxed' service can merge into sluggish in some of the others. Cuisine — seafood seafood seafood . . .

White Morph Motor Inn Restaurant

92–94 The Esplanade
Kaikoura
03 319 5014 www.whitemorph.co.nz

Recommended by the locals as the best restaurant in town, it combines with five-star accommodation on the seafront. The restaurant menu features fresh fish, crayfish and Pacific Rim cuisine, complemented with a selection of local wines.

Green Dolphin Restaurant and Bar

12 Avoca Street
Kaikoura
03 319 6666

Recommended for night-time dining.

Aromas Café

13A West End
Kaikoura
03 319 5221

Offers good basic café food and coffee. Licensed and BYO.

Hislops Wholefoods Café

Beach Road
Kaikoura
03 319 6971 www.hislops-wholefoods.co.nz

This fully licensed cafe has a reputation for fresh, wholesome organic food and consistent quality. It provides breakfast, daytime blackboard and evening restaurant menus.

Cods And Cray Fish 'n' Chips

Classic takeaways.

Nin's Bin

The old caravan on the Coast Road — fresh crays, bro!

Black Rabbit Pizza Co

17 Beach Road
Kaikoura
03 319 6360

Well known for gourmet pizzas, pasta, salads and puddings.

Things to do

Whale Watch

03 319 676 www.whalewatch.co.nz

Aim for close encounters with giant sperm whales at all times of the year. Tours are at 7.15 am, 10.00 am and 12.45 pm daily. An additional tour at 3.30 pm is scheduled in the summer months (November–March).

Adults $130, children $60 (aged 3–15 inclusive). Children under three are not permitted on the tour.

A 95 per cent success rate means they guarantee an 80 per cent refund if your tour doesn't spot a whale. Purpose-built catamarans feature outside viewing decks, while inside, award-winning animations are shown on plasma screens.

Seal Swim Kaikoura

0800 732 579 www.sealswimkaikoura.co.nz

Shore-based and boat-based seal encounters, from $60 to $80 per person.

Wings Over Whales

Kaikoura Airfield (five kilometres south of Kaikoura on State Highway One)
03 319 6580 0800 226 629 www.whales.co.nz

See sperm whales, dolphins and seals from the air, as well as spectacular views of the Kaikoura mountain range and coastline. Operates seven days. Adults $145, children $75.

Maori Tours Kaikoura

10 Churchill Street
Kaikoura
03 319 5567 www.maoritours.co.nz

This award-winning boutique tour is by mini-coach, with a maximum of ten guests. Take this opportunity to learn of Maori customs and protocol, the local history, flora and environment. The tour was set up by Maurice and Heather Manawatu in 2001 as a family-owned and operated business. Tours depart twice daily, all year round at 9.00 am and 1.30 pm and last approximately 3.5 hours. They include light refreshments. Adults $95, children $55. Free pick-up service within five kilometres of the town centre.

Dolphin and Albatross Encounter
Encounter Kaikoura venue on the beachfront
96 The Esplanade
Kaikoura
0800 733 365   www.oceanwings.co.nz

Get up close and personal with dusky dolphins or albatross. A variety of tours includes swimming with the dolphins. From $130 for adults, $35 for children.

Onsite is the Encounter Café serving breakfast and lunch along with casual dining. On offer are local seafood, home-baked goodies, great coffee and an interesting list of local wines.

Kaikoura Golf Club
Five minutes' drive heading south of Kaikoura, the golf club is on State Highway One on the right-hand side
03 319 5628   www.kaikouragolf.co.nz
Open seven days from 9.00 am, green fees are $30

An inland 18-hole course with scenic alpine backdrop.

Places to stay

Lemon Tree Lodge Boutique B&B
31 Adelphi Terrace
Kaikoura
03 319 7464   www.lemontree.co.nz

This recommended medium-priced B&B overlooks the township of Kaikoura with spectacular views out across to the Kaikoura mountain range and the blue waters of the Pacific. Tariff: from $199 per couple in the high season.

Hapuku Lodge and Tree Houses
State Highway One (at Station Road 12 kilometres north of Kaikoura, midway between Christchurch and Picton)
Kaikoura
0800 KAIKOURA www.hapukulodge.com

Make a choice from the lodge, guest rooms, the large Olive House or a tree house. Tree houses are nested ten metres above the ground in the canopy of a native manuka grove. Each Tree House has spectacular views of Kaikoura's dramatic mountains and Pacific coastline. Tariff: $390–$780 a night. In-house chef Rod Ramsay (no *#*&ing relation to Gordon) makes the most of local seasonal produce.

Panorama Motel
266 The Esplanade
Kaikoura
03 319 5053 0800 288 299 www.panoramamotel.co.nz

A 22-unit complex comprising a mixture of studio, one-bedroom and two-bedroom ensuite units. This is an older style motel, but with the best sea views in town. Tariff: $110–$160 (one–two persons). Extra person $15.

Admiral Court Motel
16 Avoca Street
Kaikoura
03 319 5525 0800 555 525 www.kaikouramotel.co.nz

Comfortable accommodation offering a studio and three family units. Qualmark 4-star rated. Tariff: $110–$160 (one–two persons), extra person $15. Seasonal rates apply.

The Old Convent B&B
Mount Fyffe Road
Kaikoura
03 319 6603 0800 365 603 www.theoldconvent.co.nz

These restored convent buildings housed a French order of nuns back in 1911.

Ensuite rooms from $120 to $195, family suites $220, and a three-bedroom cottage is $240 for four persons. Four-minutes drive to Whale Watch. Breakfasts included and dinners available. Swimming pool, bicycles, and internet access are available.

Bendamere House B&B
37 Adelphi Terrace
Kaikoura
03 319 5830 0800 10 77 70 www.bendamere.co.nz

Situated in a prime location in Kaikoura directly overlooking the township and beach, this B&B is Qualmark 4-star rated. About $175 a night for two. Extra person, around $20. Continental breakfast provided.

Kaikoura Cottage Motels
Corner Old Beach Road, Mill Road and State Highway one
Kaikoura
03 319 5599 0800 526 882 www.kaikouracottages.co.nz

Individual cottages smartly furnished and within walking distance of the beach. Tariff: $85–$150.

Absolute Waterfront Apartments
9 Kaka Road
South Bay
Kaikoura
03 319 6881

Situated in popular South Bay looking directly out to sea, offers a choice of two apartments, the Waterfront (sleeps four), or the Waterside (for couples). Only five minutes by car to all the attractions, cafés and Kaikoura township, this complex also allows you easy access to the Kaikoura Peninsula walking track, and the foreshore walk to the seal colony is only metres away. Kayaks are for your use at no charge. Tariff: $90–$110.

Waipara

I think of Waipara as one of New Zealand's orphan wine regions. It tends to get overshadowed despite the fact that it produces some gorgeous wines (albeit with less than five per cent of New Zealand's total grape production). There are 69 vineyards with more than 1000 hectares (405 acres) planted, and 19 wine producers — all just 45-minutes' drive north of Christchurch. Locals call it Wiper-a. The phonetically correct would probably say Wai-Pah-Rah.

The Waipara Valley is wide and flat, in the lee of the Teviotdale hills that provide protection from cool easterly winds, but open to warming northwest winds. The valley has three general growing sites — valley floor, hill slopes or river terraces. It is a microclimate region, typically with warm dry summers and extended dry autumn weather. Wine varieties that are very successful in these conditions are riesling, chardonnay and pinot noir. And Waipara is home to some consistently award-winning wines like Pegasus Bay, Main Divide, Muddy Water, Daniel Schuster, Alan McCorkindale and Waipara Hills.

Unlike Martinborough, there is no real centre to Waipara, but, having said that, it's a charmingly laid-back area with wineries and local attractions no more than a short car ride away.

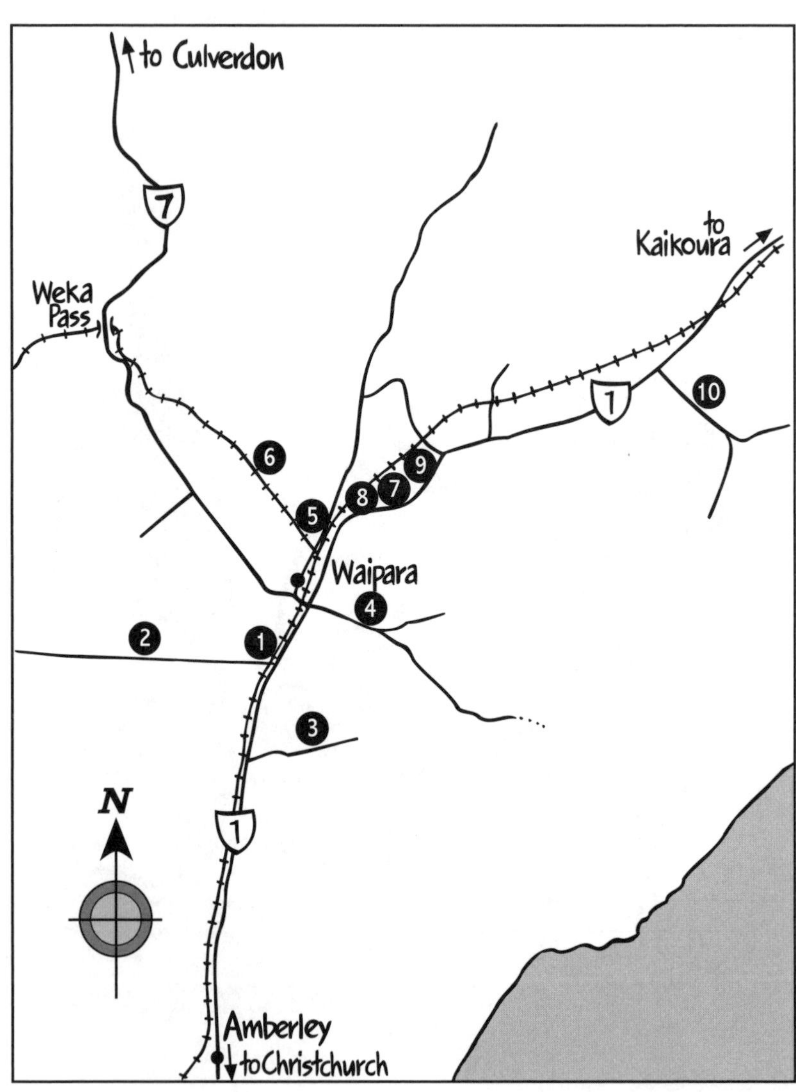
to Culverdon
7
to Kaikoura
Weka Pass
1
10
6
9
7
8
5
Waipara
4
2
1
3
N
1
Amberley
to Christchurch

The Mud House Winery and Café

State Highway One
Waipara
03 314 6900 www.mudhouse.co.nz
Cellar door and restaurant open seven days in June, July and August 10.00 am–4.00 pm, rest of the year 10.00 am–5.00 pm, lunch available 11.00 am–4.00 pm

Mudhouse Winery and Café is the latest incarnation of what has been formerly known as Canterbury House Winery, and Waipara Hills Winery and Restaurant. It all gets a bit confusing if you rely on old maps and reference material. Marlborough-based Mud House Wines was taken over by Waipara Hills in 2006, and they moved head office to this Waipara facility, but continue to market some wines under the Mud House label. However, the bulk of the wines available for tasting here are their own label. Grapes are sourced from Waipara, Marlborough and Central Otago. There are three labels — Regional (around $20), Waipara (up to $45) and Single Vineyard (over $50). Mud House label wines are also available for tasting.

Notable wines

All the aromatics have done very well, also the single vineyard Marlborough Simmond Pinot Noir and Méthode Traditionelle sparkler.

Food

The impressive tasting room and restaurant have a high vaulted ceiling. The restaurant offers standard New Zealand fare at about $25 a main.

Fiddler's Green Wines

Georges Road
Waipara
03 314 6979 www.fiddlersgreen.co.nz
Open October–April Saturday and Sunday 11.00 am–5.00 pm, other times by appointment

Approximately nine kilometres north of Amberley on State Highway One, take the turn off into Georges Road for a distance of 2.5 kilometres to reach the entrance to the vineyard on the right-hand side of the road.

Wines produced by Fiddler's Green are riesling, pinot noir, sauvignon blanc, chardonnay, pinot gris and gewürztraminer. The vineyard was established in 1994. Impressive double gates and an olive tree-lined driveway open up to a Mediterranean-style cellar door building set among the vines.

Notable wines

Sauvignon Blanc, Riesling, Pinot Noir, Chardonnay.

Food

N/A

Vineyard dog

Gem — border collie cross.

3

Pegasus Bay Winery

Stockgrove Road
Amberley
Waipara
03 314 6869 www.pegasusbay.com
Open seven days 10.30 am–5.00 pm, restaurant also open seven days 12.00 noon–4.00 pm, bookings recommended

Owned by the extensive Donaldson family, Pegasus Bay is the local star in Waipara, with their range of wines and superb restaurant having won many awards. Located six kilometres north of Amberley, they have 50 hectares (20 acres) of vineyard for their renowned Pegasus Bay label ($25–$45), and they also source grapes from Marlborough and Canterbury for the second tier Main Divide label (around $24).

Michael Cooper describes their Pegasus Bay Pinot Noir as one of Canterbury's greatest wines. Even the Main Divide range is extremely good and great value — especially the pinot noir and riesling.

Opera lover Christine Donaldson organises musical events at the winery and obviously had a hand in naming the premium wines: Aria late-pick riesling; dessert wines, Finale and Encore; Maestro Merlot/Malbec; two pinot noirs, Aria and Prima Donna, and also a chardonnay, Virtuoso. The large wooden-panelled tasting room features old premium wine bottles fashioned into chandeliers.

Notable wines

The lot. They're all fantastic.

Food

Pegasus Bay Winery Restaurant was awarded *Cuisine* magazine's Restaurant of the Year 2006 Award for Best Casual Dining (Regional) winner. Relaxed dining and a wide-ranging, sophisticated menu matching food to wines is the key to its success. Entrées are about $20, mains around $35, platters for two are $65, desserts are about $15.

Mount Cass Vineyards

133 Mount Cass Road
Amberley
Waipara
03 314 6834 www.mountcasswines.com
Open Thursday–Sunday 11.00 am–5.00 pm or by appointment

Mount Cass is another family-owned winery, one of the first three commercial vineyards planted in the Waipara Valley in 1982. Chris and Carol Parker have been sole owners since 2002.

They grow sauvignon blanc, chardonnay, pinot noir, cabernet sauvignon and a late harvest dessert chardonnay. A very laid back, corrugated iron tasting room displays their wines, alongside other items including 'movie pots' — ingenious planters and pots, created by Chris's brother-in-law and made from recycled movie reels.

Notable wines

Sauvignon Blanc ($18), Reserve Riesling and their stunning Pinot Noir ($24).

Food

N/A

Vineyard dog

Cassie — cross breed.

Torlesse Wines

Loffhagen Drive
Waipara (near Waipara Village, adjacent to State Highway One and 63 kilometres north of Christchurch)
03 314 6929 www.torlesse.co.nz
Open seven days and most Public Holidays 11.00 am–5.00 pm

The winemaker is Kym Rayner, a graduate of Roseworthy Wine College, South Australia, where he spent his early years honing his skills.The top level label is Omihi Road and the next step down, the Torlesse range. Prices are pretty keen with the Torlesse at around $15, and the Omihi at around $25.

Arts and crafts feature in the tasting room, with clothing, paintings of local landscapes, pottery and rock art available for sale.

Notable wines

Torlesse Riesling and Chardonnay, Omihi (Medium) Riesling, Chardonnay, Gewürztraminer, Pinot Noir. Also look out for Cassis, a blackcurrant liqueur at $25 a bottle.

Food

N/A

Vineyard dog

Chloe — Newfoundland.

Glenmark Estate

169 Mackenzies Road
Waipara
03 314 6828   Email: jsjmcc@xtra.co.nz
Open by appointment only

John McCaskey was one of the original local growers — he planted his first grapes in 1981 on his 'Weka Plains' property. By 1986 he had converted a hay barn near the Waipara township to become the area's first winery and joint processing venture. All grapes are estate grown from 20-year-old vines. Varieties grown are pinot gris, merlot, malbec, and a couple of outsiders — briedecker and siebel.

Food
N/A

7

The Old Glenmark Vicarage

161 Church Road
Waipara
03 3146 775   021 040 8826   www.glenmarkvicarage.co.nz
Tastings by appointment

The Vicarage's boutique vineyard was planted in 1999 with pinot noir, chardonnay and riesling. Winemaking is done by the local Waipara Springs winery.

Notable wines

Just three — Wicked Vicar Chardonnay, Vicar's Mistress Pinot Noir, Divine Daughter Riesling.

Accommodation

The Old Glenmark Vicarage offers a choice of accommodation in either the private self-contained Vicarage Barn or in a room with ensuite in the 1907 Vicarage Homestay. The Vicarage is a prime example of late nineteenth century architecture, set among 100-year-old trees in established grounds. Tariff: the Vicarage Barn: $130 single, $165 couple, $35 each additional person (sleeps up to five persons). The Vicarage Homestay B&B: $180 single, $200 couple.

Making it a long weekend? Then maybe add . . .

Sherwood Estate

113 Church Road
Waipara
03 314 6962 www.sherwood.co.nz
Open October–May Monday–Friday 9.00 am–5.00 pm

Add this one to your list if you're not doing a weekend. Dayne and Jill Sherwood have four vineyards in Waipara, and another four in Marlborough. They are one of the region's largest producers with output in excess of 65,000 cases per year. They specialise in sauvignon blanc, pinot noir, chardonnay and riesling. Under the Sherwood umbrella there are three labels. At the top of the range is Clearwater — exclusively their own Waipara grapes (around $30). Next step down, but still great value, is Sherwood Estate with grapes sourced from Waipara, Marlborough and contract growers (around $20). Finally the Stratum range comes in at entry level (around $18).

Notable wines

Clearwater Sauvignon Blanc, Clearwater Chardonnay, any of the Rieslings.

Food

N/A

Waipara Springs

409 Omihi Road
Waipara
03 314 6777 www.waiparasprings.co.nz
Cellar and café open seven days 11.00 am–5.00 pm

Waipara Springs is jointly owned by the Moore and Grant families. Bruce and Jill Moore have lived on the property for many years, and together planted the first vines at Waipara Springs in the early 1980s. The vineyard of 26 hectares (164 acres) is planted with riesling, sauvignon blanc, chardonnay, gewürztraminer, pinot noir and merlot with the wines made in two different styles: fresh fruit-driven wines under the Waipara Springs label (around $20), and structurally driven wines of the Premo label (around $30).

Notable wines

Standard label: Barrique Chardonnay Riesling and Merlot. Premo range: Riesling, Sauvignon Blanc and Pinot Noir.

Food

Wine bar and café. Relax into rustic indoor/outdoor dining with great service among trellis and umbrellas. Wines are by the glass or bottle and the extensive menu has brunch items, a kids' menu, cheese platters and daily specials, plus a very serious dessert menu.

10

Daniel Schuster Wines

192 Reeces Road
Omihi
Waipara Valley
03 314 5901   www.danielschusterwines.com
Open daily 10.00 am–5.00 pm

Prague-born Danny Schuster is one of our wine industry's true characters. He has over 30 years' experience in winemaking, both here and overseas, and has authored several books on wine and grape growing. Since 1986, Daniel Schuster Wines has been a small producer (10,000 cases per annum). Danny is a great believer in the wines reflecting the character of the 'terroir' — the soil and microclimate. He also uses biodynamic viticulture, which results in extremely clean, flavoured wines with pronounced minerality, reminiscent of European wine characters.

Pinot noir has done particularly well and he also produces chardonnay and riesling.

The cellar door tasting room has spectacular views overlooking their Omihi Hills Vineyard with the inland Kaikoura Ranges in the far distance.

Notable Wines

Petrie Vineyard Chardonnay, Omihi Hills Vineyard Selection Pinot Noir.

Food

N/A but very good C4 brand espresso coffee available.

Vineyard dogs

Rosie, Gordon — setter puppies.

Places to eat

There is not much to offer in this area for dinner, but there are quite a few lunch options, especially at the wineries Pegasus Bay, Waipara Springs and Mud House.

Nor'Wester Café

95 Main North Road
Amberley
03 3149411 www.norwestercafe.co.nz
Open seven days for brunch, lunch and dinner

This is Amberley's multi-award winning restaurant, recommended for its good food and attentive service. The extensive wine list has a special local Waipara section. Entrées are around $16 and mains around $27, with local wine matching suggestions. Sides of salads and vegetables are around $6. Game features on the menu — duck breast, venison and lamb rack, also salmon, corn-fed chicken, beef fillet and a vegetarian option. They even provide a menu glossary for people (like me) who don't know the difference between haloumi and hollandaise.

Karma Café (Thai)

Main North Road (just down the road from the Nor'Wester)
Amberley
03 314 7181
Open Tuesday–Sunday 5.00 pm–late

Reasonably priced standard Thai food with a good wine list.

Brew Moon Café and Microbrewery

Main Highway
Amberley
03 314 8030
Open Wednesday–Sunday 10.30 am–8.00 pm

Café-style food, beer tastings and microbrewery tours available. A tasting selection of beers and ales is available for about $9.

The Blue Rooster Café and Bar

90 Victoria Street
Rangiora
03 313 3493   www.bluerooster.co.nz
Open Monday 8.00 am–5.00 pm, Tuesday–Sunday 8.00 am–late

A little bit away from Waipara, but worth the travel as this is a renowned Rangiora restaurant with excellent food. Entrées are about $17, mains around $30. Food and wine matches are suggested.

Things to do

Waipara Valley Farmers' Market

Every Saturday November 1–April 30 (rain, hail or shine) 9.00 am–12 noon at the Pegasus Bay Winery

On offer is seasonal produce — asparagus, strawberries, salad greens, flowers and plants, free-range Caiuga duck eggs and hen eggs. Deli items include olive oils, speciality meats, bread, sweet treats, ice cream, honey, lavender-infused sugar, homebaking, preserves and condiments, and Texel lamb meat.

Mount Cass Walkway

Just up the road from Mount Cass Wines

A reasonable fitness level is required. Recover from quads-burn and shortness of breath, while enjoying panoramic views of the Waipara Valley and Omihi Hills and Kaikoura Ranges. There is a 20-minute walk to the summit, or the option of a two-hour return hike. Well worth the effort. Take a camera.

Colmonell Clydesdales

03 3149001 027 2276 120

Now for something completely different — wine tours by horse power. Ian McMillan runs a team of three obedient Clydesdales hitched to a covered wagon, available for hire for winery tours and other occasions. The wagon leaves from the Waipara Hotel car park at 11.00 am, returning at 5.30 pm. A four-winery tour costs $40 per person. Bookings are essential. BBQ lunch at the pub is available for an extra $12.

Weka Pass Railway Excursions

03 9622 999 www.wekapassrailway.co.nz

Excursion trains run every first and third Sunday of each month, every Sunday in January and most Public Holidays

Run totally by member volunteers, the Weka Pass Railway is a historic rural railway using both vintage steam and diesel-electric locomotives on 12.8 kilometres of scenic line through the limestone country of Weka Pass. Trains are usually hauled by a 1909-built A Class steam locomotive number 428, the only one of its type still operational. Fares: adults $18, children $10. Family ticket (two adults and two children) $50.

How to get there: turn off at the State Highway One and State Highway Seven junction and follow the signposts through the village of Waipara on Glenmark Drive to find Glenmark Station on the north side of Waipara Village.

Hanmer Springs Thermal Pools and Spa

03 315 7128 0800 442 663 www.hanmersprings.co.nz

For at least 125 years, Hanmer Springs has been a renowned thermal spa and one of New Zealand's top tourist attractions. As well as a variety of hot pools there is massage and beauty therapy available. The Garden House licensed café serves light lunches and à la carte evening dining.

Mt. Lyford Alpine Resort

www.mtlyford.co.nz
Open June–October, full day pass from $15 primary age to $50 for adults

This boutique ski area, halfway between Kaikoura and Hanmer, caters for beginner to advanced skiers, and features one T-bar, one poma, two platters, one 180 metre fixed grip and one advanced rope tow. Café and day lodge onsite. Rental log chalets are available (phone Sharon Dixon 03 315 6432).

Places to stay

There is not a lot of choice really, compared to other wine regions, but here are a few that I could track down. Bear in mind that a massive new development, Waipara Wine Village and Day Spa, is planned for completion in 2009. This will feature a high-end hotel and conference facility, restaurants, bars, microbrewery, and an interactive wine tasting facility. Timeshare type hotel suites and villas are also planned.

The Old Glenmark Vicarage

See page 308.

Dunnolly Cottage

157 Church Road
Waipara
03 314 6940 www.vineyardcottage-dunnolly.com

Luxury bedrooms, separate parlour and library facilities are all available with breakfast provided. There is a choice of two bedrooms with shared facilities inside the homestead, or a brand new self-contained cottage with ensuite. Luxury linens and appointments. Also has a picturesque view of north-facing pinot and chardonnay vineyards. Tariff: $165 for two people.

The Dutch Station
135 Bentleys Road
Hawarden
03 314 2200   www.thedutchstation.co.nz

A tad out of the way, it is centrally located in Hawarden between Christchurch, Kaikoura and Hanmer Springs with views of the Southern Alps. Run by Dutch couple Rein Bakker and Gertruud Steltenpool, who speak Dutch, French and German. They have a B&B room with King-size bed, plus a self-contained guesthouse with two bedrooms and fully equipped kitchen. Tariff: B&B $140, guesthouse $200 (reduced rates off season).

The House of Ball
345 Mackenzies Road
Waipara
03 314 6909   Email: houseofball@xtra.co.nz

On the western side of the Waipara Valley, four kilometres from the village, The House of Ball provides traditional B&B with spectacular views. Dinner is available to match your BYO wines. Tariff: $75–$150 for two–four people.

Claremont Estate
828 Ram Paddock Road
Waipara Gorge
Amberley
03 314 7559   021 120 0323   www.claremont-estate.com

Spoil yourself rotten in this very upmarket Qualmark 5-star lodge that was nominated twice in the 2007 World Travel Awards for 'Australasia's Leading Boutique Resort'. Their in-house chef creates fab food from seasonal produce. But be prepared to pony up between $655 for one night, and $2016 for two nights — depending on the season and your accommodation choice.

Heritage Hanmer Springs

1 Conical Hill Road
Hanmer Springs
03 315 0060 0800 368 888 www.heritagehotels.co.nz

The historic lodge is restored and now part of the Heritage Hotel chain. Tariff: from $219 for the deluxe room for two–four persons, to $388 for the three-bedroom villa. However, last minute deals and specials are often available (see their website). The food and service in the grand dining room are also recommended.

Hanmer Resort Motel

7 Cheltenham Street
Hanmer Springs
03 315 7362 0800 777 666

Centrally located, with two-storey studio units. Tariff: $90 per queen- or twin-bed unit.

Canterbury

Canterbury's wine history goes quite a way back — to 1840, when French immigrants brought the first vines to Akaroa on the long sea voyage all the way from France to Banks Peninsula. However, commercial winemaking didn't get going until 1973, when Lincoln University trials were begun to assess the best grape varieties to suit the local climate and soils. Prague-born winemaker Danny Schuster (see Waipara region) was enlisted at the time to help with research and education.

Nowadays, most of the vineyards in Canterbury are located in the broad, alluvial Waipara Valley region. However, the flat plains near Christchurch also have a sprinkling of established producers. The dry, cool climate conditions of the Canterbury region favour chardonnay, pinot gris, riesling and pinot noir.

At any time of year, Christchurch, that most charmingly English of New Zealand's cities, offers visitors a wide choice of restaurants, cafés, accommodation, art galleries, gardens and historic buildings — not to mention punting down the Avon River.

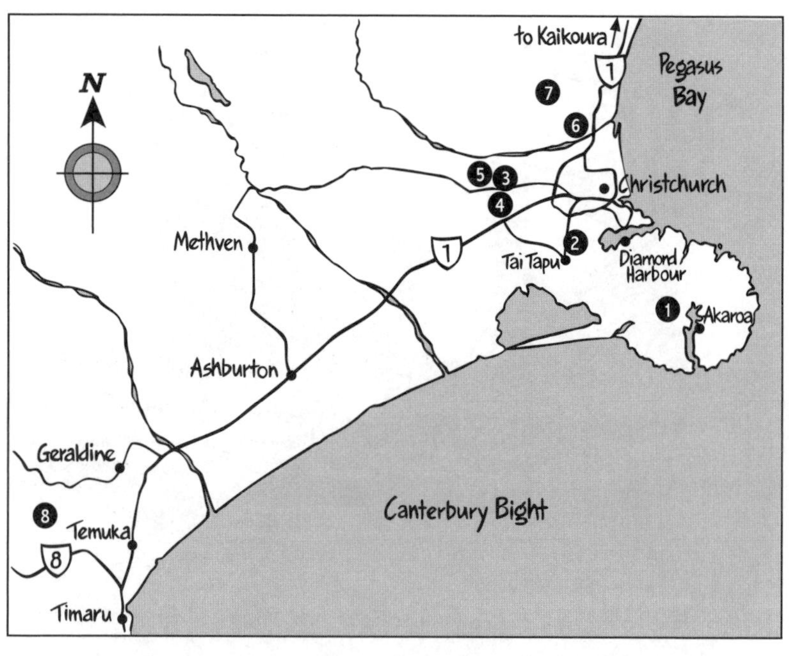

to Kaikoura
1
Pegasus Bay
N
7
6
5
3
4
Christchurch
2
Methven
1
Tai Tapu
Diamond Harbour
1
Akaroa
Ashburton
Geraldine
8
Temuka
8
Timaru
Canterbury Bight

Christchurch weekend — Saturday

Off we go. French Farm, our first destination, is a tad out on its own, on Banks Peninsula. The French settlement of Akaroa in 1840 left a legacy of French flavour, with street names in French, as well as other Gallic influences. Many descendants of the original French families are still living there. The picturesque harbour offers secluded safe beaches, sailing and cruising, historic walks, garden rambles and seal and penguin colonies.

French Farm Winery

French Farm Valley Road (take State Highway 75 toward Akaroa, after you pass through Little River you will go over a hill, turn right when you reach the bottom of the hill, the Barry's Bay Cheese factory will be to your left, follow the signposts to French Farm)
Akaroa
03 304 5784 www.frenchfarm.co.nz
Open seven days 10.00 a.m–4.00 pm. for lunch and wine tastings

Sited overlooking the Akaroa Harbour, French Farm is an hour's drive from Christchurch. In 1989, eight hectares (20 acres) of vineyards were established to grow sauvignon blanc, chardonnay, pinot gris, pinot noir and merlot. The winery is a stunning French Provincial-style ochre building set among white roses and lavender, overlooking the harbour.

Notable wines

Sauvignon Blanc ($22).

Food

The French Farm restaurant is open seven days from 10.00 am–4.00 pm for lunch and wine tastings. Dinner is by arrangement. Mains are bistro-style around the $22 mark — chicken chasseur with bacon, mushrooms and tarragon in a cream sauce ($25). There is also a kids' menu at $10, including penne pasta with tomato sauce and cheese.

La Pizzeria, for more casual outdoor dining, is tucked against the hillside with terraced dining areas and a waterfall. A variety of crispy thin base pizzas are on offer alongside a selection of beers, soft drinks and French Farm wines.

Now head back towards Christchurch . . .

The Wineshed

Cossars Road
Tai Tapu
03 329 6940 www.thewineshed.co.nz
Open for lunch Monday–Sunday from 11.00 am, evening dining Friday and Saturday (these hours are from December–February and subject to change)

Owned and operated by the delightfully named Lolly Fairweather, and her husband John, The Wineshed is just 15 minutes from central Christchurch. The restaurant and winery are fittingly in French Provincial-style, with spacious rooms and high vaulted ceilings, surrounded by a pebbled limestone courtyard and waist-high purple lavender bushes. Lolly's daughter, international chef Julie Sokolsky, heads the kitchen, which specialises in Californian-inspired, French Provincial cuisine. Son Jeremy runs the front of house operations.

The wine list includes their own sauvignon blanc, chardonnay and rosé. The restaurant seats up to 120 punters. Private functions are available on request.

3

Melton Estate Vineyard

Johnson Road (off Weedons Ross Road)
West Melton
03 347 4968 www.meltonestate.co.nz
Open Friday–Sunday 10.00 am–4.00 pm for wine tastings and cellar door wine sales (otherwise by appointment)

Philip and Tracey Caunter own what was previously the Sherwood Winery. Melton Estate is a small boutique producer with a café and function venue onsite. It is surrounded by a sheltered garden and a large lawn area. The estate grows sauvignon blanc, riesling, chardonnay and pinot noir.

Food

The café is open all year for lunch Friday–Sunday 10.00 a.m–4.00 pm, and open for evening dining during the summer months. Platters are from $5 per person and lunch mains around $18, such as asparagus tart (seasonal) — freshly steamed asparagus on a puff pastry base with an orange Hollandaise sauce, served with salad greens.

Tresillian Estate

45 Johnson Road
West Melton
03 347 4103 www.tresillian.co.nz
Open for tastings Saturday and Sunday 11.00 am–5.00 pm or by appointment

Tresillian Estate is a luxury B&B vineyard in West Melton, close to Christchurch city. Heather Anderson and Graeme Lindsay have eight hectares (20 acres) planted in pinot gris, pinot noir and riesling. They also make a sauvignon blanc from Marlborough fruit and have a Banks Peninsula vineyard, plus Canterbury suppliers. The tasting room is a former tiny one-room sleepout (4 m x 2.5 m), but the upside is that the owners offer all tastings.

Food

N/A

Accommodation

The main house is a handsome building inspired by the Prairie House concept of iconic American architect Frank Lloyd Wright. All the guest rooms face north, and open to the wide veranda with views over the vineyard. Pre-dinner drinks with your hosts are included. Breakfast is in your suite or in the dining room and evening meals are by arrangement.

Tariff: a luxury Super King / Twin room is $275 per night and two Queen rooms cost $175 per room, per night. (Single party bookings only).

Vineyard dog

Grousie (aka. Famous Grouse) — fox terrier/tennis ball retriever cross.

Vineyard cat

Gris.

Sandihurst

1320 West Coast Road
West Melton
03 347 8269 www.sandihurstwines.co.nz
Open seven days 11.00 am–5.00 pm

With 12 hectares (30 acres) of vines planted in chardonnay, riesling, pinot gris, gewürztraminer and pinot noir in the late 1980s, Sandihurst is one of the oldest vineyards in the area. New owners Hennie and Celia Bosman have taken over the reins from the late John Brough, and — as he would have approved — gone on to develop the winery and produce some very successful wines. In a unique recycling effort, in consultation with Lincoln University, crushed glass is used as groundcover under the vines, to reflect heat and retain moisture.

Notable wines

Halbtrocken Riesling ($25), Spätelese (sweet) Riesling ($25), Pinot Noir ($38).

Food

Picnic hampers available.

Langdale Vineyard Restaurant
161 Langdales Road
West Melton
03 342 6266 www.langdalerestaurant.com
Open summer Wednesday–Sunday 11.00 am–4.00 pm, evenings by arrangement, open winter Thursday–Sunday 11.00 am–4.00 pm, evenings by arrangement

Langdale Vineyard Restaurant is a country restaurant set in rose and lavender gardens, overlooking vineyards on Langdales Road about 20 minutes from Christchurch. They make wines specifically for the restaurant: pinot gris, riesling, rosé, pinot noir, and a blended red — Enigma.

Food

The restaurant has a reasonably priced and extensive menu. An example of a brunch treat: breakfast pie — bacon, sausages, tomatoes and egg all in a tasty pie shell ($17) and a main: tagine of lamb and shallots with mango and raisin couscous and broad bean puree ($28). On the children's menu: crumbed chicken, potato wedges and salad ($7).

St Helena Wine Estate

Coutts Island Road
Belfast
03 323 8202 Email: sthelena@xtra.co.nz
Open Monday–Friday 10.00 am–4.00 pm

Former spud farmers Robin and Norman Mundy turned to grape growing back in 1978, establishing Canterbury's oldest commercial winery. They pioneered pinot noir growing in New Zealand, and won a Gold medal back in 1982. St Helena has expanded from the original 20-hectare (50 acre) operation and now sources fruit from Marlborough's Wairau Valley, with production at around 100,000 cases a year. Winemaker is Alan McCorkindale, who has his own

Waipara-based label.

Notable wines

Gewürztraminer ($20), Single Vineyard Pinot Gris ($24), Riesling ($20).

Food

N/A

Tram Road Vineyard

1490 Tram Road
Swannanoa
03 312 6061 www.tramroadvineyard.co.nz
Open Saturday, Sunday and Public Holidays from10.00 am onwards

Owners Janine and Digby Briggs have lived on the vineyard for the past nine years. What started as an enjoyable lifestyle has developed into a passion for their wines. They produce sauvignon blanc, riesling, chardonnay and pinot noir mainly from the home vineyard, but also use a few grapes from Canterbury contract growers.

Notable wines

Tram Road Riesling.

Food

From late 2008 they plan to open an Italian-style restaurant and function centre on the property.

And finally — for the really motivated wine buff — here is one you might like to add to your list, about half way between Ashburton and Timaru.

Opihi Vineyard and Vineyard Café

804 Opihi Road (25 minutes from Timaru, south Canterbury, off State Highway Eight towards Lake Tekapo)
Hanging Rock
Pleasant Point
03 614 8308
Open Tuesday–Sunday 11.00 am–5.00 pm, seasonal hours apply September–May

This vineyard was established in 1991 by Colin and Brenda Lyon, after they planted a few trial vines on the slope in front of their house in Opihi, 30 kilometres inland from Timaru. The café and tasting room are in a lovely 1882 restored high-country homestead, constructed of rough-hewn limestone blocks quarried from the property. Today, while Colin and Brenda get on with the winery business, Stella Doubleday and Allan Lambie run the tasting and cellar door sales, as well as the café. Vineyard lunches are available in a peaceful rural setting, either inside or at tables under large umbrellas.

Notable wines

Riesling ($18), Pinot Gris ($22), Dessert Late Harvest Riesling ($21).

Food

The café is reasonably priced and has a varied menu. Soup of the day ($9), breads and spreads ($9), bistro-style mains (about $18). How about walnut crusted venison with sage roasted pumpkin, wilted greens and Opihi Pinot Noir-spiked sauce?

Places to eat

Apart from Christchurch's fine dining and the obvious choices at vineyard restaurants above, here are a couple of gems out in the region.

Seagars at Oxford

78 Main St
Oxford
03 312 1435
Open 8.00 am–4.00 pm

Celebrity cook Jo Seagar set up this upmarket café and also has a cooking school onsite. Expect bistro-style food plus fab 'high teas' with dainty sandwiches.

C'est la Vie Restaurant and Café

33 Rue Lavaud
Akaroa
03 304 7314
Open for dinner 6.00 pm–late, bookings essential

Chef de cuisine Karl Joachim Lau creates sumptuous French dishes for this renowned Akaroa restaurant. It has a warm and friendly ambience, and you can bring your own wine.

Things to do

There are three farmers' markets to choose from. Buy direct from the growers and farmers. Organic fruit and veggies, free range eggs, meats, flowers, artisan breads and cheeses, chutneys and jams.

Tai Tapu Farmers' Market

Saturday from 10.00 am in the barn and courtyard adjacent to The Wineshed's winery
Cossars Road
Tai Tapu

Canterbury Farmers' Market

Riccarton House
16 Kahu Road
Christchurch City
Every Saturday morning 9.00 am–12.00 noon (rain, hail or shine)

Lyttleton Farmers' Market

Lyttelton Main School grounds
Oxford Street
Lyttelton
Every Saturday 10.00 am–1.00 pm

Barrys Bay Cheese

Main Road
Barrys Bay
Akaroa
03 304 5809
Open seven days

Traditional, handcrafted cheeses. View cheesemaking every second day during the season. Tastings are available and you can buy condiments and wine to complement the cheeses.

Lavender Downs

Lawford Road
West Melton RD 6
03 347 9520 www.lavenderdowns.co.nz
Open August–end April Thursday, Friday and Saturday 10.00 am–4.30 pm, other days by appointment

Virginia McNaughton and her late husband, Dennis Matthews, established Lavender Downs, which now features over 60 varieties of lavender along with other ornamental plants in a garden setting. The small gift shop offers a range of lavender products including plants, soaps, candles, chocolates, pure essential oil, books, dried lavender, body care products and other gifts.

Airborne Honey

Factory shop
41 Pennington Street
Leeston
03 324 3569 www.airborne.co.nz

Producers of many honey products including monofloral honeys, comb honey, creamed honeys and beeswax.

Balloon Adventures

Unit 6, 31 Stevens Street (opposite AMI Stadium)
Christchurch City
03 381 4600 www.ballooning.co.nz

Up Up and Away Ltd have operated for 15 years and own five of the largest and most advanced balloons in New Zealand, with an overall capacity for up to 75 passengers at a time. Allow around five hours total, with an early start and an hour's actual flying time. See rural Canterbury from the air, and finish your flight with a celebratory glass of chilled Champagne after landing. How civilised. Prices: $290 per adult, $250 per child (aged 5–11 years).

Russley Golf Club
Memorial Avenue Christchurch (right next to Christchurch Airport)
03 358 4748 www.russleygolfclub.co.nz

Established in 1927, this is considered one of the best courses in the South Island. Green fees: overseas club member $65, New Zealand affiliated member $35.

Places to stay

Christchurch offers many accommodation opportunities, giving you the chance to base yourself there and venture out into the broader area. However, for a real taster there are also a few options in the vineyard regions.

Bredon Downs B&B
233 Carters Road
Amberley
North Canterbury
03 314 9356 Email: lucy.lucy@xtra.co.nz

Situated on State Highway One, just one kilometre south of the Amberley township and 48 kilometres north of Christchurch. Hosts Bob and Veronica Lucy, are ostrich breeders. In the vicinity are Tram Road Vineyard and St Helena Estate. Dinner is by arrangement, or they can book you in at the local, Nor'Wester (see the Waipara region). Tariff: double room with ensuite, $140 per night, twin-bed room with private bathroom, $120 per night, single room, $75 per night.

Wilderness House
42 Rue Grehan
Akaroa
03 304 7517 www.wildernesshouse.co.nz

There are four rooms to choose from, with Victorian furnishings and ensuites or private bathrooms. The owners have a vineyard, planted in 1995 and located barely 100 metres from where the early French settlers planted their grapes in the 1840s. Close by is French Farm Winery and restaurant. Tariff: $260.

Castle View Vineyard Retreat B&B

84 Johnson Rd
West Melton
03 3651 952   027 680 1005

The brand new luxury vineyard retreat is close to vineyards, Christchurch city and ski fields. Indulging you with gas fire, large luxury ensuite with double shower and spa bath, LCD TVs, home theatre system and heated swimming pool, this is very quiet accommodation with views to the Southern Alps. Tariff: $195–$245.

The Oaks Historic Homestead

State Highway 73
Corner of Clintons Road
Darfield
03 318 7232   027 241 3999   www.theoakshomestead.co.nz

Madeleine de Jong is your host. She speaks five languages and is a keen cook, using fresh organic local produce. The lovingly restored historic homestead is one of Canterbury's oldest. It features guest rooms with ensuite/private bathrooms, a guest dining and living room with open fires, and a traditional large homestead kitchen. Tariff: homestay $150–$275

Country Life B&B

137 High Street
Oxford
03 312 4167

Operating as a B&B since 1987, the house is 80 years old and has a spacious, warm and sunny garden. Accommodation is a self-contained apartment that sleeps up to four. Tariff: $75–$80.

Central Otago

Central Otago seems to have come out of nowhere to become one of, if not *the* hot New Zealand wine region, recognised for its sought-after, highly priced pinot noirs. The area was previously better known as a winter sports playground. But wine tourism is another drawcard in addition to the ruggedly beautiful alpine scenery, stunning mirrored lakes and outdoor adventures. Autumn in particular is a special time to visit, when the exotic tree foliage is a mass of vivid oranges, browns and yellows, contrasting with the grey, stony soils and misty landscape.

As with most overnight successes, Central Otago has been many years in the making. In fact, a Frenchman, Jean Desiré Feraud planted the first grapes in Clyde in 1864, winning a prize in an 1881 Sydney wine competition. In 1885 an Italian viticulturalist, Romeo Bragato, visited Central Otago and pronounced it 'suitable for grape growing'.

But it was not until 1976 that the first of today's crop of successful wineries was established. The late Rolfe Mills and his wife Lois planted their first vines at Rippon Vineyard in Wanaka. Then in 1981 Alan Brady started Gibbston Valley.

Despite producing only around four per cent of New Zealand's grapes, Central Otago — or plain 'Central' (as the locals call it), is our fastest growing wine region. Ten years ago the region boasted six wineries. Today there are around 93, and climbing.

Just one suggestion — base yourself outside Queenstown. If you haven't been there — imagine a bunch of chain hotels plus a slice of high-end shopping slap-dab next to a beautiful South Island lake and mountain range. Of course it's gorgeous, the tourists love it, and it also has some good restaurants and cafés. By all means land at Queenstown and maybe stay a night or two, but then it might be a good idea to get yourself a rental car and head for somewhere a bit more relaxed, for example Wanaka or Alexandra.

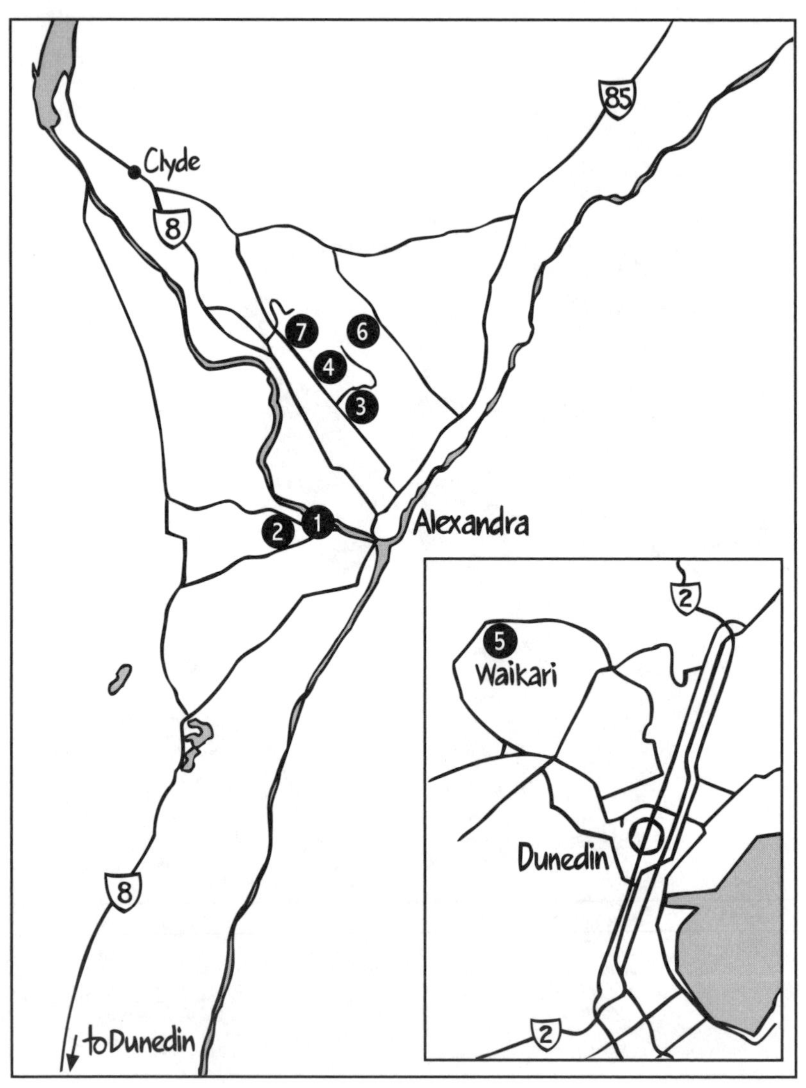

Clyde
8
85
7
6
4
3
2
1
Alexandra
5
Waikari
2
Dunedin
8
2
to Dunedin

Dry Gully

113 Earnscleugh Road
Alexandra
03 449 2030 Email: drygully@xtra.co.nz
Open seven days 10.00 am–5.30 pm

Bill and Sybilla Moffitt's 1.5-hectare (4-acre) plot grows 3000 pinot vines and produces a tiny amount of highly regarded wine. The vineyard is a former apricot orchard sitting on historic goldmining dredge tailings above the banks of the Clutha River. Their label features a drawing of the 125-year-old stone packing shed, where Bill Moffitt happily dispenses his samples to visitors.

Notable wines

Pinot Noir ($35).

Food

N/A

Black Ridge Vineyard

Conroys Road (turn into Earnscleugh Road from State Highway Eight near the Alexandra Bridge, travel four kilometres along Earnscleugh Road and turn left on to Conroy's Road, the vineyard is 700 metres on the right)
Alexandra
03 449 2059 www.blackridge.co.nz
Open seven days 10.00 am–5.00 pm

They claim to be the most southern winery in the world — six kilometres south of Alexandra and nine hectares (22 acres) of vineyard in some extremely unpromising 'soils'. The rocky ground was so hard they needed gelignite to blast out the postholes. Starting off in 1981, Verdun Burgess and Sue Edwards struggled against rocks, rabbits and searing summer temperatures to establish their winery. Nearly 28 years later they have ten wines available for sale at their two-storey stone winery facility, which has spectacular views over the Old Man Range and the Dunstan Mountains.

Notable wines

Pinot Noir ($35) Gewürztraminer ($20).

Food

Cheese boards and platters.

Winery cat

Kuce — Burmese and scourge of the rabbits (over 200 kills so far).

Judge Rock Wines

36 Hillview Road
Alexandra
03 4485059 www.judgerock.co.nz
Open in summer Friday–Sunday 11.00 am–5.00 pm, reduced hours in winter

Another small-ish producer, Judge Rock has eight hectares (20 acres) of western-facing slopes with half planted in 13,000 pinot noir vines. The oldest vines were planted in late 1998. Husband and wife Paul Jacobson and Angela Chiaroni had their first vintage in 2002. Paul is a local boy, who did a degree in civil engineering and always swore he'd never resort to horticulture. Yeah right. Angela comes from an old Otago family who emigrated from northern Italy in the 1890s.

Notable wines

Judge Rock label Pinot Noir ($30), Venus Pinot Noir ($25).

Food

N/A

And if you've extra time consider . . .

William Hill Winery

Graveyard Gully Road
Alexandra
03 448 5111 www.williamhill.co.nz
Open Monday–Friday 10.00 am–4.00 pm

Marketed overseas as Shaky Bridge Wines, William Hill has a range of white wines and pinot noir. Starting off as a small producer, they now crush nearly 300 tonnes of grapes per vintage. William and Gillian Grant are the owners, and winemaking is by their son David — helped by Californian winemaker Gerry Rowland.

Notable wines

William Hill Chardonnay ($23), William Hill Pinot Noir ($35). Shaky Bridge Unoaked Chardonnay ($22), Shaky Bridge Gewürztraminer, ($24), Shaky Bridge Riesling ($21), Shaky Bridge Pinot Noir ($36).

Food

Shaky Bridge Café — named after the adjoining suspension bridge.

Otherwise head off towards Dunedin to . . .

Weston Winery

25 Forrestbank Avenue
Wakari
Dunedin
467 5544
Open seven days 10.00 am–10.00 pm

Geoff Weston owns this unique Dunedin-based winery in a small brick building in the suburb of Wakari. Geoff is pioneering a new alternative to screwcap and cork closures — the Zork, a hybrid plastic closure that has a tamper-proof seal. With the backing of the *Guinness World Records*, he claims the southernmost winery in the world. Guess he'll have to arm-wrestle the guys from Black Ridge for the title.

Notable wines

Chardonnay, Pinot Noir.

Food

Platters.

Hawkdun Rise Vineyard

241 Letts Gully Road
Alexandra
03 448 7782 www.hawkdunrise.co.nz
(Sue) 027 410 4818 (John) 027 201 7230
Open seven days 11.00 am–4.00 pm

John Grant and Suzanne Bali own the tiny 1.5 hectare (4 acre) vineyard which produces solely pinot noir, at about 700 cases per annum. Busy local contract winemaker Carol Bunn makes their wine at Vinpro's facility in Cromwell.

Notable wines

Pinot Noir ($37).

Food

N/A

Accommodation

Semi-detached accommodation. Two Queen-size bedrooms complete with ensuites and verandas. Rooms overlook the vineyard and privacy is assured. Breakfast consists of fresh local fruits in season accompanied by cereals plus light dishes served at the long table. Tariff: $200 per night per couple.

Winery dog

Sam — Maltese.

Springvale Estate

Dunstan Road (opposite Orchard Gardens)
Alexandra
03 4492995 Email: springvale.estate@xtra.co.nz
Open seven days October–March 11.00 am–5.00 pm

Damian and Clare Russell are the new owners, with wines made by David Grant at CowCo (Central Otago Wine Company). Springvale Estate is a cellar door and restaurant, which also caters for wedding functions and small conferences. The cellar door and restaurant is in a unique rammed-earth building.

Notable wines

Pinot Noir, Gewürztraminer.

Food

Restaurant — hours as for cellar door.

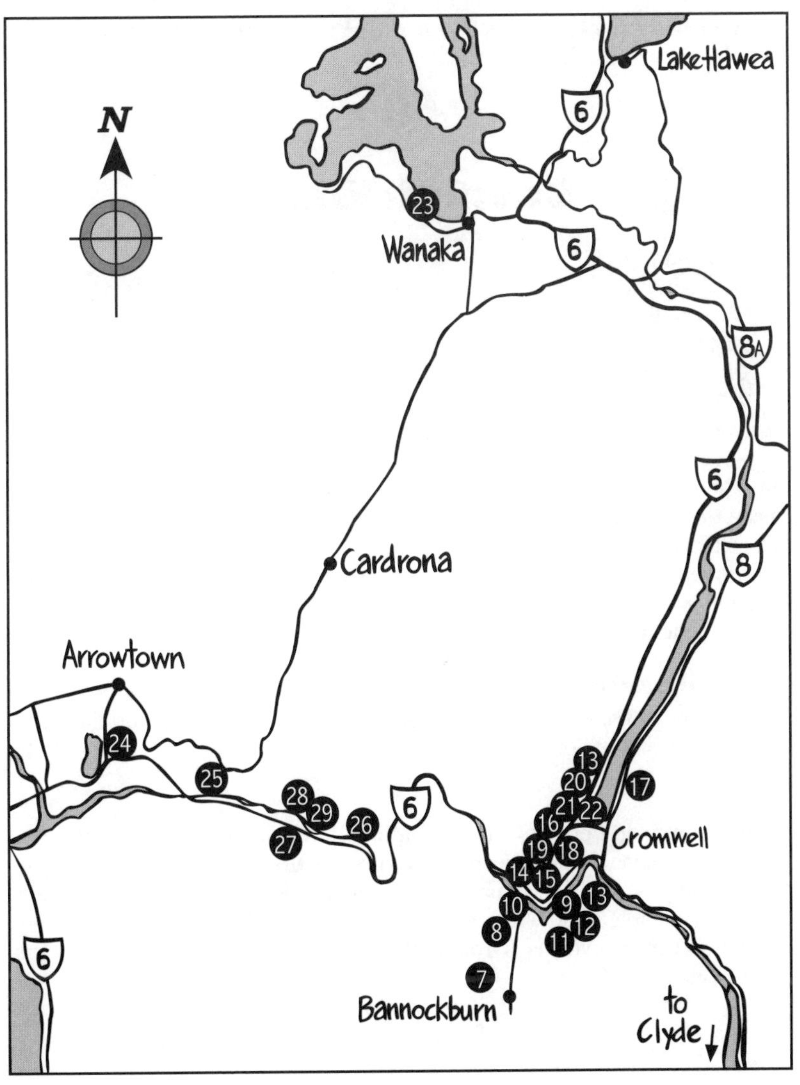
N
Lake Hawea
6
23
Wanaka
6
8A
6
8
Cardrona
Arrowtown
24
25
28
29
26
27
6
13
20
17
21
22
16
Cromwell
19
18
14
15
13
10
9
12
8
11
7
Bannockburn
to
Clyde
6

Carrick Wines

Cairnmuir Road
Bannockburn
Cromwell
03 445 3481 www.carrick.co.nz
Open seven days 11.00 am–5.00 pm

Carrick has an impressive tasting room and restaurant overlooking the Bannockburn inlet of Lake Dunstan, and in the distance is the Carrick Range. On a fine day you can eat al fresco and enjoy the superb views. Meanwhile, inside the cellar door, glass floor panels allow views of around 300 barrels in the cellars below.

Around 30 hectares (74 acres) are planted in pinot noir, chardonnay, sauvignon blanc and pinot gris. The sauvignon blanc undergoes some oak ageing before bottling.

Notable wines

Chardonnay ($32), Pinot Gris ($25), Riesling ($30), Central Otago Pinot Noir ($45), Unravelled Pinot Noir ($25).

Food

Mains, nibbles and platters. How about a rich tomato and herb ragout made with venison shank on a delicately flavoured potato mash with a sharp lemon, parsley and garlic garnish? Or pancetta-wrapped pork fillet oven roasted on warm parsnip and apple salad with red cabbage pickle and jus? Moderately priced. Restaurant: open seven days from 12.00 noon–4.00 pm, at weekends brunch is from 10.30 am–1.00 pm.

Akarua Winery

Cairnmuir Road (located seven kilometres south of Cromwell, turn left after the Bannockburn bridge and then follow the signs for approximately two kilometres)
Bannockburn
Cromwell
03 445 0897 www.akarua.com
Open Monday–Friday 10.00 am–5.00 pm, Saturday and Sunday from 11.00 am–4.00 pm

Founded by South Island businessman Sir Clifford Skeggs in 1995, 50 hectares (123 acres) were planted mainly in pinot noir. The other grapes are chardonnay and pinot gris. This is another 'location location' winery, on the slopes above Lake Dunstan. Cellar door and café await you . . .

Notable wines

Otago Chardonnay ($25), Pinot Gris ($25), Gullies Pinot Noir ($35), Cadence Pinot Noir ($40).

Food

The Lazy Dog Café is open for lunch 11.00 am–3.00 pm, dinner from 6.00 pm onward. Closed Monday and Tuesday, except summer and public holidays. The café-style menu features specialty burgers and a 240-gram fillet steak. There are also thin crust pizzas — complemented by local wines and good coffee. There's a children's menu too.

Bannock Brae Estate

Cairnmuir Road
Bannockburn
Cromwell
027 221 0695 www.bannockbrae.co.nz
Open October 1–December 24 Wednesday–Sunday 1.00 am–5.00 pm, December 26–January 31 11.00 am–5.00 pm, February 1–March 31 Wednesday–Sunday 11.00 am–5.00 pm, closed April 1–September 30, other times by appointment

Small self-described 'Mum and Dad' operation, Catherine and Crawford Brown are the owners with just 8.5 hectares (21 acres) in total, and a very small annual production of around 3000 cases. Tastings are on the terrace of the family chalet, with spectacular mountain views. Crawford was master brewer for Lion Nathan NZ, and prior to that, Speight's Brewery manager for a number of years.

Notable wines

Goldfields Riesling ($25), Barrel Selection Pinot Noir ($44), Goldfields Pinot Noir ($30).

Food

N/A

Vineyard dog

Rocky — yellow lab — official welcoming committee.

Mt Difficulty

Felton Road
Bannockburn
Cromwell
03 445 3445 www.mtdifficulty.co.nz
Cellar door open seven days 10.30 am–4.30 pm

Another high-profile winery with a popular café and tasting room, Mt Difficulty is a joint venture among four Felton Road vineyard owners, with 40 hectares (100 acres) between them. First vintage was 1998. In short order they started racking up prizes — their 2003 Pinot was judged the best international Pinot Noir in the 2007 World Pinot Noir Conference. Winery and restaurant views are suitably fab — from the slopes overlooking the Cromwell basin.

Notable wines

Mansons Farm Pinot Gris 35, Target Gully Riesling ($25), Otago sauvignon Blanc ($25), Long Gully dessert Riesling ($30). Pinot Noirs — Otago ($40), Roaring Meg ($28), Long Gully ($75), Pipeclay Terrace ($80).

Food

They have an easy to read menu — not too many choices for a change. Breads and spreads to start are $12.50, mains start at $20.50 such as seared Aoraki salmon pieces with chargrilled eggplant, capsicums, courgettes and fennel, balsamic glaze, lemon vincotto and mixed leaves. All meals come with wine match suggestions. Open seven days for lunch 12.00 noon–3.00 pm. Booking ahead is strongly advised.

Vineyard dog

Frankie — staffy-foxie-bitser. Likes chasing lights and shadows.

Olssen's Garden Vineyard

306 Felton Road (on the west side, at the end of Felton Road, some eight kilometres from Cromwell)
Bannockburn
Cromwell
03 445 1716 www.olssens.co.nz
Open seven days October–May 10.00 am–5.00 pm, June–September 11.00 am to 4.00 pm

Olssen's is owned and operated by two 'Mainlanders', husband and wife, John Olssen and Heather McPherson. Heather was brought up in Central Otago, on Mt Pisa Station and then in Cromwell itself, and John is from Dunedin, and spent many school holidays in Central.

After researching soil suitability, with the help of MAF, the Bannockburn site was purchased in 1989. Now they produce a range of 13 different wines, most of which are sold exclusively to cellar door visitors and mail order customers. In addition to the ten hectares (25 acres) of vines, thousands of trees shrubs and bulbs have been planted around the grounds — where visitors are welcome to spread a rug by the reflecting ponds, picnic, relax and enjoy the tranquillity.

Notable wines

Charcoal Joe Chardonnay ($25), Riesling ($20), Slapjack Creek Pinot Noir ($58).

Food

N/A but picnickers welcome.

13

Bald Hills

46 Cornish Point Road
Bannockburn
Cromwell
03 445 3161/027 229 0032   www.baldhills.co.nz
Open seven days 11.00 am–5.00 pm

Blair and Estelle Hunt own this small winery with an output of around 3000 cases from 11 hectares (27 acres). Their son, Ross, is general manager, and winemaking is by Grant Taylor. First harvest was in 1999.

Keen gardener Estelle has planted shrubs, perennials and around 80 rose varieties — giving guests a picturesque spots for picnicking. Tastings are hosted either by Blair or Estelle.

Notable wines

Last Light Riesling ($25), Pinot Gris ($27), Pinot Noir ($39).

Food

N/A

Vineyard dog

Bella — blue heeler/beagle cross. She meets and greets customers, and may leap into their lap if she fancies them.

Quartz Reef

Building 10
Hughes Crescent
Lake Dunstan Estate
McNulty Road (off State Highway Six on the Cromwell–Queenstown road)
Cromwell
03 445 3084 www.quartzreef.co.nz
Open summer Monday–Friday 10.00 am–3.00 pm, also some summer weekends 12.00 noon–4.00 pm, reduced hours in winter, phone ahead

The website admits that the cellar door is 'no frills' — it's located in an industrial park in Cromwell — but having said that, Quartz Reef is a much-awarded producer of sparkling wine, pinot noir and pinot gris. Injecting a strong European influence into Central Otago are owners Austrian-born Rudi Bauer and Clotilde Chauvet, whose family own the Champagne house Marc Chauvet in France. Clotilde has the distinction of having made the first bottle-fermented sparkling wine in Central Otago.

Notable wines

Pinot Gris ($29), Méthode Traditionelle ($30), Vintage Méthode Traditionelle ($39,) Central Otago Pinot Noir ($42), Bendigo Estate Pinot Noir ($150).

Food

N/A

Northburn Station

Tarras-Cromwell Highway (off State Highway Six)
Cromwell
03 445 1740 www.northburn.co.nz
Open December 2008 onward, phone ahead

Northburn Station is a 12,000-hectare (30,000-acre) high country, merino sheep station; overlooking Lake Dunstan and a few minutes' drive from Cromwell. Owners Tom and Jan Pinckney have diversified from grazing sheep to follow their passions for wine, food and hospitality. Their 23-hectare (56-acre) vineyard, established in 1999, is planted in pinot noir, riesling, pinot gris and sauvignon blanc. Jan formerly owned a restaurant and plans to open a functions site around January 2009 for catered weddings and other occasions.

Notable wines

Pinot Noir ($38), Pinot Gris ($29).

Food

Coffee and nibbles.

Accommodation

On the picturesque lakeside, is a brand new three-bedroom cottage that sleeps up to six. It has two bathrooms and a fully equipped kitchen. Self-cater or cooked breakfast can be arranged. Tariff: $180–$250 depending on number of guests.

Still in town during the week? Then . . .

Felton Road

Bannockburn
Cromwell
03 445 0885 www.feltonroad.com
Open Monday–Friday 2.00 pm–5.00 pm, preferably by appointment

Felton Road's winery is in a nouveau-rustic corrugated iron barn-style building, looking north over the vineyards. Two blocks of vineyards are at either end of Bannockburn. Felton leases local Calvert Vineyard, which is entirely planted in pinot. Launched in 1997, Felton Road has achieved prominence as another one of Central Otago's star producers. Their wines are highly rated by influential *Wine Spectator* magazine. Winemaker, Blair Walter, uses only French oak barrels and has a philosophy of minimal gravity-feed handling methods.

Notable wines

Central Otago Chardonnay ($36), Block 6 Chardonnay ($42), Riesling ($26), Dry Riesling ($26), Block 1 Dessert Riesling 750ml ($34). Pinot Noir — the lot: Felton Road ($42), Calvert Road ($47), Block 5 ($66), Block 3 ($66).

Food

N/A

Vineyard dog

Penny — border bollie — chook wrangler/herder. Highly strung (and scared of cats).

Central Otago Wine Company

102 Gair Avenue
Lake Dunstan Estate
McNulty Road
Cromwell
03 445 3100
Email: mail@cowine.co.nz
Open seven days summer Labour Weekend–Easter Weekend 10.00 am–5.00 pm, winter Monday–Friday 10.00 am–5.00 pm

They first opened the doors in November 2001 with the winery housed in a totally refurbished former Ministry of Works building in Cromwell. Known locally by the handy acronym CowCo, this facility makes wine for around a dozen small Otago producers. Winemaker Dean Shaw has the job of turning grapes into wine for such famous labels as Sam Neill's Two Paddocks, and filmmaker Roger Donaldson's Sleeping Dogs. Other labels include Mt Rosa, Nevis Bluff, Kawarau Estate and Pisa Moorings.

Notable wines

Two Paddocks Pinot Noir ($42), Nevis Bluff Pinot Gris Second Edition ($35), Pisa moorings Pinot Noir ($32), Surveyor Thompson Pinot Noir ($35), Kawarau Estate Reserve Chardonnay ($29), Kawarau Estate Reserve Pinot Noir ($40), Dry Gully Pinot Noir ($30), Mt Rosa Pinot Noir ($29), Lindis River Pinot Noir ($37).

Food

N/A

Mount Michael Wines

McNab Road (off State Highway Six, 200 metre from the turnoff into Cromwell township, and opposite the Wooing Tree vineyard)
Cromwell
03 445 1351 www.mountmichael.co.nz
Open seven days Labour Weekend–Easter, weekends 10.00 am–5.00 pm, reduced hours in winter, phone ahead

Sited on the predominately frost-free eastern slopes of tiny Mount Michael, from which the name derives, this very small producer has an output of around 2000 cases per year. A group of eight families now own the winery, and managing partner Peter Morrison has moved his family to Cromwell to keep an eye on their investment. The cellar door offers spectacular views of Cromwell, surrounding mountains and Lake Dunstan. Beloved vineyard fox terrier, Bessie, is remembered in their labels.

Notable wines

Bessie's Block Chardonnay ($27), Bessie's Block Pinot Noir ($40), Estate Selection Pinot Noir ($30)

Food

N/A

Wooing Tree

Short Cut Road
Cromwell (opposite the big fruit sculpture, intersection of State Highway Six and State Highway Eight)
03 445 4142 www.wooingtree.co.nz
Open seven days 10.00 am–5.00 pm

Wooing Tree is owned by Stephen and Thea Farquharson and Stephen's sister and brother-in-law, Jane and Geoff Bews. The label takes its name from a large pine tree, which had long been a local meeting point for lovers and the site of many a proposal to southern lasses . . . and probably many a proposition.

This is another barn-style tasting room and café — with dark brown corrugated iron roof, exposed beams and slate floors. There's also a nice kids' play area with slide and sandpit. The focus here is almost entirely on pinot noir and chardonnay, with a little pinot gris used only in their sparkling Blondie (80 per cent pinot noir/20 per cent pinot gris). They do a rosé and two pinots under their standard label and — kids would love this label — Beetle Juice (pinot noir named for the rare Cromwell chafer beetle).

Notable wines

Standard label Pinot ($37), Beetle Juice Pinot ($28), Rosé ($27).

Food

Platters and deli selection.

Vineyard dogs

Bounty and Oakley — labrador brothers. Hobbies: chasing rabbits, welcoming visitors, and eating ripe pinot noir grapes.

Rockburn

Corner of McNulty Road and Gair Avenue
Cromwell
03 445 0555 www.rockburn.co.nz
Open seven days Labour Weekend–Easter Weekend 11.00 am–5.00 pm, winter Monday–Friday 11.00 am–4.00 pm, other hours by appointment

Another high-flyer, Rockburn has done very well — their 2006 Pinot Noir picked up numerous awards. Owner is Dunedin cardiothoracic surgeon Richard Bunton. The winemaker is former microbiologist Malcolm Francis, who spent four years at Felton Road Wines as assistant winemaker. A very stylish cellar door and winery was opened in 2006, and features a back wall of Central Otago river stones and a long dark polished wooden 'waka'-shaped tasting room counter. The whole range is available for tasting.

Notable wines

Pinot Gris ($25), Parkburn Riesling ($24), Central Otago Pinot Noir ($39), Eight Barrels Pinot Noir ($70)

Food

N/A

Aurum Wines

140 State Highway Six (on the main road to Wanaka and the West Coast, just two kilometres from Cromwell township)
Cromwell
03 445 3620 www.aurumwines.co.nz
Open summer seven days 10.00 am–6.00 pm, restricted hours in winter

Aurum (Latin for gold) was established in the historic goldmining region of Cromwell by Joan and Tony Lawrence in 2002. Initially contract growers, they now make their own wines using the expertise of their son Brook and his French winemaker wife, Lucie Pouthier. They also produce olive oil from their '45th Parallel' site. Their grapes are pinot noir, pinot gris and riesling. Tastings and sales are in a lovely old, restored stone farm cottage, with views of a cottage garden and the distant Pisa Range.

Notable wines

Pinot Gris ($25), Riesling ($20), Mathilde Reserve Pinot Noir ($40).

Food

N/A

Vineyard dogs

Roy — foxy-jack russell cross. Often bails up rabbits under the tasting room floor and barks madly. Best friend — Bluey, vineyard worker's dog and rabbit-chasing partner in crime.

Pisa Range Estate

Cromwell–Wanaka Highway
Cromwell
03 445 0412 0274 409 527 www.pisarangeestate.co.nz
Open by appointment only

Nestled at the base of the snow-capped Pisa Range and adjacent to Lake Dunstan, the estate is a family-owned boutique vineyard established in 1995 by Warwick and Jenny Hawker. Warwick is a retired New Zealand diplomat and together with his wife Jenny they have served in many countries around the world. They are pioneer grape-growers of the Pisa sub-region — a warm district of the Cromwell Basin adjacent to Lake Dunstan.

Notable wines

Estate Pinot Gris ($27), Black Poplar Block Pinot Noir ($37).

Accommodation

Aoturoa Luxury Lodge and fine dining. Tariff: about $400.
See: www.aoturoa.co.nz.

Now, head to Wanaka . . .

23

Rippon Vineyard

246 Mt Aspiring Road
Wanaka
03 443 8084 www.rippon.co.nz
Open seven days December–April, 11.00 am–5.00 pm, seven days July–November 1.30 pm–5.00 pm, closed May and June unless by appointment

Rippon Vineyard is renowned for its pinot noir and, as previously noted, is the oldest existing winery in Central Otago. Neat rows of vines extend down the schist slopes of the shores of picturesque Lake Wanaka. Rippon is also certified as an organic producer. Founded by Lois and her husband, the late Rolfe Mills, the winemaker is his son Nick who earned his credentials working in French wineries in Burgundy and Alsace. Very much a family business — sister Charlie, brother David and Nick's wife Jo are also involved.

Notable wines

Gewürztraminer ($30), Jeunesse Riesling ($22), Standard Riesling ($28), Jeunesse Pinot Noir ($38), Pinot Noir ($50).

Events

The Rippon Music Festival. Held every second year over Waitangi weekend (next will be February 2010) it hosts up to 5000 fans and has a line-up of top New Zealand talent. 2008 saw Anika Moa and Shihad on the bill, in a mix of rock, reggae, hip-hop, soul, dance, metal and jazz. And if anyone has any energy left, there is the official afterparty — where revellers dance till dawn. See the festival website for details: www.ripponfestival.co.nz.

Food

N/A

Five vineyard dogs

Pipette — border collie aka 'Ratbag' — likes chasing waves on the beach, Tink — wheaten terrier — partner in crime with Pipette, April — omnivorous wheaten terrier, Flynn — schnauzer elder statesman, and Lou — matriarchal collie.

Gibbston weekend — Saturday

Amisfield Wine Company

10 Lake Hayes Road (just off the main highway from Queenstown, near Lake Hayes)
Queenstown
03 442 0556 www.amisfield.co.nz
Open seven days 10.00 am–6.00 pm

Amisfield is another 'don't miss' Central Otago experience. The winery and award-winning restaurant are housed in an impressive building constructed from oatmeal colored schist with large wooden beams, and has sweeping views over Lake Hayes. Stark geometric lines of the winery contrast nicely with the yellow tussock hills. Winemaker Geoff Sinnott has had much success with the Amisfield Pinot Noir and sparkling wines, as well as aromatic styles. Geoff trained at Adelaide's Roseworthy College and has previously made wine for Isabel Estate in Marlborough. Amisfield is a small specialist producer using only grapes sourced from their vineyard near Lake Dunstan. Their 2002 Pinot Noir took top honours at the prestigious San Francisco International Wine Competition. Prices start at $30 for the sauv blanc, up to $45 for the pinot noir. The Arcadia sparkling (non-vintage) is $25.

Notable wines

Pinot Gris, Dry Riesling, Sauvignon Blanc, Pinot Noir. My personal fave — Arcadia sparkling.

Food

As they promise 'Fresh, Simple, Local Food.' Winner of Best Winery Restaurant at the *Cuisine* Restaurant of the Year 2006 and 2007 Awards. Dining is either inside or in the courtyard under stylish black umbrellas — weather permitting. Open Tuesday–Sunday 11.30 am–8.00 pm.

Vineyard dog

Jasper — chocolate kelpie, winemaking assistant.

Chard Farm Winery

Chard Road
Kawarau Gorge
State Highway Six
Gibbston
03 442 6110   0800 843 327   www.chardfarm.co.nz
Open seven days Monday–Friday 10.00 am–5.00 pm,
Saturday–Sunday 11.00 am–5.00 pm

Approaching Chard Farm is not for the faint-hearted. The road is a narrow shingle goat track which clings desperately to the slopes of the steep gorge, which races down to the green Kawarau River. Brothers Rob and Greg Hay selected the sloping former orchard and market garden site (owned by a Richard Chard in the 1870s) for their vineyard and planted their first vines in 1987. Rob now oversees a winery, which continuously clocks up awards for its aromatics and pinot noirs.

Notable wines

Pinot Gris, Riesling. Pinot Noirs — top level: The Tiger, and The Viper ($50 each), then River Run ($36), and Finla Mor ($28).

Vineyard dog

Ozzy — blue heeler, currently on holiday in Western Australia.

Food

N/A, but picnickers welcome.

Winehouse and Kitchen

(Freefall, Rock Ferry and Van Asch Wines)
1693 StateHighway Six
Gibbston
03 442 7310 www.winehouse.co.nz
Open seven days 10.00 am–5.00 pm, children welcome (sandpit supplied)

Adjacent to the Kawarau Bungy Bridge in the Gibbston Valley, the Winehouse and Kitchen offers tastings of Freefall, Rock Ferry and Van Asch Wines, together with bistro food. A 1910 vintage timber villa homestead was moved across the valley from Glenroy Station on to the site in 2003 and now functions as both tasting room and restaurant. One of Central Otago's newest tasting facilities and wine experiences, it opened in 2005, and is located at the site of one of co-owner Henry Van Asch's other highly successful enterprises — bungy jumping.

Notable wines

Rockferry Pinot Gris ($25), Van Asch Pinot Gris ($29), Van Asch Riesling ($25), Freefall Marlborough Sauvignon Blanc ($20), Freefall Pinot Noir ($25).

Food

Hearty café-style food, plus platters with wine matches. Mains around $28.

Gibbston Valley

Kawarau Gorge
State Highway Six
Gibbston
03 442 6910 www.gvwines.co.nz
Open seven days 10.00 am–5.00 pm

Gibbston is superbly set up with an onsite winery, gift shop, restaurant and wine bar, plus the Gibbston Valley Cheesery. They also have wine caves, blasted out of solid schist, holding up to 400 barrels (about 120,000 bottles). Their restaurant offers local Benmore salmon and vine-smoked venison on its tempting menu.

Winemaker Grant Taylor earned gold medals at the Sydney International Wine Competition for his 2002 Pinot Noir. The tasting room features a wine-dispensing machine sounding like something from Wallace and Grommit, the Enomatic, which allows visitors to try the same variety of wine from different vintages (known as a vertical tasting). Too many, and it becomes a horizontal tasting.

Notable wines

Reserve Chardonnay ($32), Pinot Gris ($27), Riesling ($26). Pinot Noirs — standard label ($39), Gold River ($28), Reserve ($100). Michael Cooper gives the Reserve five stars.

Food

Restaurant: open for lunch 12.00 noon–3.00 pm.

Peregrine Wines

Kawarau Gorge Road
Gibbston
03 442 4000 www.peregrinewines.co.nz
Open seven days 10.00 am–5.00 pm

High-profile Otago winery, established in 1998 by Greg Hay — previously founder of Chard Farm with his brother Rob. The tasting room is located under a spare, curved steel roof reminiscent of the label's trademark falcon's wing, starkly contrasting with the schist rock and alpine tussock. Winemaker since 2004 is Peter Bartle. There are three tiers of wine: Saddleback (at $28), Peregrine range (Pinot at $38, aromatics at about $25) and the Wentworth Pinot ($65).

The vineyard is also used as an outdoor concert venue in summer. See their website for upcoming events.

Notable wines

Chardonnay, Gewürztraminer, Pinot Gris, Riesling, Sauvignon Blanc and Pinot Noir.

Food

N/A

29

Waitiri Creek Wines

Church Lane
State Highway Six
Gibbston Valley
03 441 3315 027 446 3946 www.waitiricreek.co.nz
Cellar door open seven days October–April, 10.00 am–5.00 pm, June–September Thursday–Monday 11.00 am–4.00 pm, closed for the month of May

Paula Ramage and Alistair Ward started planting chardonnay in 1993 on free-draining north-facing slopes of the Gibbston Valley. Then followed further expansion and planting of pinot noir and gewürztraminer. The restaurant and cellar door is a charming old renovated cream wooden chapel with graceful arched windows and a grey corrugated iron roof. Winemaker Matt Connell has worked both in New Zealand and overseas, including a stint making pinot noir at Elk Cove Vineyards in Oregon's Willamette Valley.

Notable wines

Chardonnay ($25), Harriet Rosé ($20), Pinot Noir ($35).

Food

Fresh regional bistro food is featured including lamb and venison. A kids' menu is also available. Open seven days October–April 11.00 am–3.00 pm, June–September Thursday–Monday 11.00 am–4.00 pm.

Places to eat

Obviously there is plenty of opportunity for good food at the wineries, and a wide choice in Queenstown itself, but here are a few more.

Joe's Garage Café

Searle Lane
Queenstown

Happily chaotic atmosphere with good coffee and a blackboard menu of hearty items.

Saffron

18 Buckingham Street
Arrowtown
03 442 0131   www.saffronrestaurant.co.nz
Open for lunch and dinner

A finalist in *Cuisine* Restaurant of the Year 2007, rated excellent. The menu features international fine dining cuisine with entrées around $20, mains around $40.

Fusee' Rouge Café

64B The Mall
Cromwell Mall
Cromwell
03 445 4014

Friendly staff, good coffee, great food, and a cosy log burner in winter.

Capriccio Restaurant
123 Ardmore Street
Wanaka
03 443 8579 www.capriccio.co.nz

Located above the BNZ bank and with great views of the lake and mountain. Italian food with entrées around $15, pasta $24, mains around $30.

Relishes Café and Restaurant
1/99 Ardmore St
Wanaka
03 443 9018
Open seven days, fully licensed. Breakfast/lunch 7.30 am–3.00 pm, dinner from 6.00 pm.

Provincial-style kitchen, fresh/healthy fare — fish, lamb, venison, steaks, vegetarian and pasta dishes are included as daily specials.

Things to do

Skiing

Queenstown's ski fields provide some of the most reliable skiing in New Zealand, with two local fields to choose from: Coronet Peak and The Remarkables. Wanaka's field is Treble Cone.

Queenstown Winter Festival

www.winterfestival.co.nz

Held mid-winter, June/July, the Winter Festival attracts some 60,000 people for a ten-day frenzy of concerts, balls, competitions, races, fireworks, bands, comedy, debates, food and wine. Oh . . . and a bit of skiing. See the website for details.

Aside from the local ski fields in winter, there's no end of extra adrenaline stuff if you're into that . . .

AJ Hackett original Kawarau Bridge Bungy Jump

03 442 1177   www.ajhackett.com

Throw yourself off an old rail bridge and pay for it. $160 for a jump, T-shirt and transport.

Kawarau Jet Boat

Main Town Pier
Rees Street
Queenstown
03 442 6142   www.bungy.co.nz

Pass lakeside homes to the deep turquoise waters of the Kawarau River, then on to the narrow shallow braided waters of the Shotover River. The trip also includes entry into Queenstown's Underwater Observatory. From $89 Adult.

Shotover Jet

Gorge Road
Arthurs Point
Queenstown
03 442 8570   0800 746 868   www.shotoverjet.com

The jetboat drivers are licensed to scare the hell out of punters in the Shotover River Canyons area with 360-degree spins and high-speed runs. Adults from $109, children $69.

Segway on Q

Queenstown
03 442 8687   www.segwayonq.com

This eco-friendly personal transporter of the future is all yours from $89 for two hours. Cruise the lakefront around Queenstown's most scenic locations. This trip takes you over a variety of terrains and you get to hear a few points of interest about Queenstown along the way.

The Big Picture

Corner of Sandflat and State Highway Six
Cromwell
03 445 4052   www.bigpicturewine.com

Don't miss this: just off the Cromwell turnoff. Namesake Phil Parker (yes, he is a distant cousin), and his wife Cath have set up an interactive movie-themed licensed café and wine experience. The Big Picture features an interactive virtual fly-over movie of Central's wineries, tasting of local wines, plus an Aroma Room in addition to its Mediterranean-style licensed café.

Central Otago Farmers' Market

This seasonal market starts early in November and runs every Sunday through until the last Sunday in February. Open from 9.00 am–1.00 pm. The picturesque, historic precinct of Old Cromwell Town on the shore of Lake Dunstan is the setting for the Central Otago Farmers Market. The market offers an array of fresh, regional, seasonal produce. Produce includes fresh fruit from the stone fruit orchards as well as local cheeses, pheasant, olive oil, saffron, fresh fish, whitebait, venison salami, fresh sausages, herbs and salads, fresh flowers and much more.

Have A Shot Shooting Complex

Mt Barker Road (opposite Wanaka Airport)
03 443 6656   0800 428 327 468
www.haveashot.co.nz

You have a choice of clay pigeon shooting, '22' rifle range, mini-golf or archery. For just $29 you can receive a pack of 24 12-gauge cartridges plus the use of an under-and-over shotgun, and get to legally shoot the living daylights out of flying orange clay targets, which look like XXOS carrot slices. Eat your heart out, PlayStation. The 22 rifles are also good fun but not as loud. Archery is for wimps.

Puzzling World

(Heading back to Queenstown about two kilometers from Lake Wanaka)
03 443 7489   www.puzzlingworld.co.nz
Open seven days from 8.30 am

One other recommended activity, just down the road from Have A Shot, and created by the remarkable Stuart Landsborough, Puzzling World is a blend of eccentricity and conundrums — from an illusion room with a tilted floor where water appears to run uphill to a 3D wooden maze, a trompe l'oeil depiction of a Roman lavatory, and a room full of famous faces that follow you wherever you move.

Events

Clyde Wine and Food Harvest Festival

Held on Easter Sunday each year. Clyde's main street retains many of the characteristics and the buildings of the gold rush days of the nineteenth century. Part of the street is closed to traffic to allow visitors to mingle and sample food and wine and listen to live music. There is also a market in the historic Masonic Lodge, selling plants, produce, crafts and clothes, as well as an exhibition by the Central Otago Art Society.

Warbirds over Wanaka

www.warbirdsoverwanaka.com

This is a biennial air show held over the long Easter weekend. It features around 60 military planes in the air, from vintage First World War biplanes to Korean jet fighters. Beautiful Lake Wanaka is centre stage. On the ground, there are displays of military vehicles, battle reenactments, a country fair, and an aviation trade expo. See: website for the next scheduled festival.

Places to stay

Aside from vineyard accommodation there is plenty of choice around the region to suit budgets from mega-luxury to affordable.

Cardrona Terrace Estate Lodge

84 Morris Rd
Wanaka
03 3 443 8020   www.cardronaterrace.com

The lodge is a sustainable eco-building offering luxury B&B accommodation five-minutes from the centre of Wanaka. It is set in a boutique vineyard and garden estate specialising in pinot noir, pinot rosé and riesling. Organic food is featured on the restaurant menu. The Qualmark 5-star suites are all named after herbs. Tariff: Starts with executive honeymoon Coriander suite at $895 a night, down to the Sage and Thyme suites at $495.

Mountain Range Boutique Lodge B&B

Heritage Park
Cardrona Valley Road
Wanaka
03 443 7400 www.mountainrange.co.nz

Qualmark 4-star-plus, contemporary lodge located in four hectares (10 acres) of parkland just two kilometres from Wanaka. It is highly recommended by guides such as *Frommer's* and offers goodies including: wireless internet, hot tub, putting green, mountain bikes and a complimentary wine or beer at the end of a long day. There's a choice of six rooms or a loft. Tariff: from $270 to $315 a night depending on choice and season. Specials are available for more than two nights.

Carrick Lodge Motel

10 Barry Ave
Cromwell
03 445 4519 0800 445 495 www.carricklodge.co.nz

Luxury motel accommodation in Cromwell township, close to the golf course and Lake Dunstan. Consists of 16 ground floor, non-smoking studios and one-bedroom units. Double spa bath and wheelchair access units are available. Qualmark 4-star-plus. Tariff: $130–$165 per person.

Blanket Bay

Glenorchy
03 441 0115 www.blanketbay.com

This is all-out no-expense-spared luxury. One of New Zealand's five Qualmark 'exclusive' endorsed resort lodges, situated at the north end of Lake Wakatipu and 45 minutes from Queenstown. Be prepared to pay from about $1000–$3000 per room to be spoiled rotten. Award-wining cuisine, fine linens, complimentary evening cocktails and stunning scenery await. Activities: fly fishing, jet boating, hiking, horseback riding, heli-skiing, heli-fishing. Hell, any damn thing you want . . .

Almond Court Motel
53 Killarney Street
Alexandra
03 448 7667   0800 256 663   www.almondcourtmotel.co.nz

This complex with refurbished units is suited to families as well as business travellers. Eight units (sleeping two to six people). All units are self-contained with kitchen, TV, Sky Digital (six channels), radio, phone, central heating, King-size beds. The daily paper is delivered. Fenced-in swimming pool, BBQ area. Tariff $85–$120. Qualmark 4-star.

Alpine Motel
7 Ardmore Street
Wanaka
03 443 7950/0800 82 22 84   www.alpinemotels.co.nz

Well-maintained, mid-range motel complex with ground floor level suites with mountain views and studio units set in a garden setting. Self-catering units with full kitchens.Tariff: (depending on season) from one bed, two-person studio for around $90, to two-bedroom unit (sleeps five) around $200.

Index

Acknowledgements

The goodwill and support of many people have made this book possible. And most of them, surprisingly, are enthusiastic wine drinkers! Some were directly involved in the process of researching this book, and others encouraged me over a number of years during my erratic freelance career.

I would like to acknowledge their support, kindness and patience.

Sincere thanks to the many wine industry people who have generously shared their time, hospitality and knowledge over the years, particularly Susan and Anthony Ivicevich, James Rowan, Simon Nunns, David Hoskins, Michael Brajkovich, Tony Soljan, Nick Nobilo, Bob Campbell and Jane Skilton.

Also many thanks to Nicola Legat and Sue Lewis of Random House, Chris Slane, Tourism Auckland, Tourism New Zealand, Bill Fagan, Mike Chunn, Paul Rishworth, Mark Arbuckle, Stephen Stratford, Declan O'Donnell, Warwick Roger and Louise Brown.

Finally I would like to dedicate this book to the memory of my late mother, Mary Fagan, née Rasmussen (a pinot noir fan).